THE AGE OF STRUCTURALISM

Psychiatry and Social Psychology Series
Edith Kurzweil, Series Editor

The Age of Structuralism, Edith Kurzweil,
with a new introduction by the author

EDITH KURZWEIL

WITH A NEW INTRODUCTION BY THE AUTHOR

THE AGE OF STRUCTURALISM

From Lévi-Strauss to Foucault

TRANSACTION PUBLISHERS
New Brunswick (U.S.A.) and London (U.K.)

New material this edition copyright © 1996 by Transaction Publishers, New Brunswick, New Jersey 08903. Originally published in 1980 by Columbia University Press. An earlier draft of chapter 2 (Louis Althusser) appeared in *Marxist Perspectives* (1979) 2(2):8–23; and chapter 8 (Michel Foucault) in *Theory and Society* (1977) 7(3):395–420.

Library of Congress Catalog Number: 95-50655
ISBN: 1-56000-879-2
Printed in the United States of America

Library of Congress Cataloging-in-Publication Data

The age of structuralism : from Lévi-Strauss to Foucault / Edith Kurzweil ; with a new introduction by the author.
    p. cm. — (Psychiatry and social psychology series)
    Originally published: New York : Columbia University Press, 1980.
    Includes bibliographical references and index.
    ISBN 1-56000-879-2 (pbk. : alk. paper)
    1. Structuralism—History. 2. Philosophy, French—20th century. 3. France—Intellectual life. I. Series.
B2424.S75K87   1996
149.'96'0944—dc20   95-50655
                                                 CIP

for Ronald, Vivien, and Allen

Contents

Introduction to the Transaction Edition

When I first thought of writing this book, I knew I would be introducing unfamiliar French thinking to America. I had been fascinated by its complications, and to start with, by structural anthropology's objective of coming to understand the beginnings of all of human culture. I also did not realize how unknown these figures were over here. I had lived in Italy for eight years, had spent much time in Paris, and had returned to the United States before deciding to go to graduate school. For quite some time, I had observed that people in American universities were getting increasingly involved in narrow, disciplinary studies, and, as used to be said, began to know more and more about less and less. Why was this so different in European countries, I pondered. But it was only while talking to French academics that I came to appreciate their affinity for abstraction and came to appreciate the extent to which they had moved away from Descartes' rationalism, and from his clarity of thought and expression.

I knew that the Parisians foster a sort of intellectual establishment, as do the English, that their milieus encourage the formation of a broad stratum of *soi-disant* intellectuals, and that such an ambiance is lacking in the United States. I had read that, for instance, Sartre, Claude Lévi-Strauss, Simone de Beauvoir, and Paul Nizan had been introduced to Marxist philosophy by Alexandre Kojève, that they then had gone on to pursue different careers and yet had stayed in touch with each other. I had been at lively gatherings in Paris, where philosophers, anthropologists, literary figures, and sociologists engaged in intense intellectual discussions. Why is it, I asked myself, that American academics, for the most part, spend so much time speaking to colleagues in their own disciplines, whereas the French have so much to say to people from other fields of endeavor, and are familiar with work that may be quite remote from their own? That's an interesting point, said William Phillips to me, when I wondered aloud whether this might be a topic he would want discussed in *Partisan Review*. (He already had accepted my essay about Lévi-Strauss.)

In 1973, when I first visited Paris to begin my research, I started to speak to some of the professors I knew, in order to find out whom they considered to be the leading, prototypical figures. Existentialism had been passé for some time, and they all seemed to more or less agree that the eight individuals I planned to discuss in my chapters were representing specific ways of thinking, although some suggested I might want to replace the sociologist Alain Touraine with Raymond Boudon or Pierre Bourdieu, the philosopher Paul Ricoeur with A. J. Greimas, or the Marxist Louis Althusser with Lucien Goldmann. I ended up buying a trunkful of many of their books, which I began to make sense of after my return to the United States. And I became aware only then that their various theoretical premises were located within a discourse that included responses to existentialism and Marxism, as well as to French postwar politics, and to the cold war. That no one mentioned, for instance, Raymond Aron—except to denigrate his articles in *Le Figaro*—certainly was evidence of the overall *leftisant* climate among the Parisians.

II

During these years, as is customary among academics, in the corridors of universities and at social get-togethers, I would be asked "what are you working on now?" More than once, when I said "Foucault," a sociologist would inquire, "how do you spell this?" When I said "Lacan," a psychoanalyst would ask me to explain what he stands for "in three sentences." And I frequently would be informed that the overall topic itself "is not sociology." Soon, my pat answer was that, like Karl Mannheim, I was interested in the sociology of knowledge, in why people think what they think. In fact, my personal background—which includes having lived in Austria, Belgium, and Italy and, therefore, knowing intimately these countries' languages—had led me to keep wondering why the citizens of these nations as well were judging similar phenomena in different ways. Since I had gone to school in Vienna, Brussels, and New York, I was privy to much of the background to some of the answers. But I had thought that when approaching philosophical and scholarly issues, especially when it came to interpretations of past masters, such as Hegel, Kant, Marx, and Freud, and of history, there might be more homogeneity, that intellectual thought would be able to float freely across national frontiers, and that even if the workers of the world were unable to unite, intellectuals would *ipso facto* overcome all provincialism.

I was wrong. How very wrong was proven to me by the eventual applications and misapplications of some of my French protagonists' ideas in American academe. Misapprehensions derived, primarily, from one or more of the following assumptions:

1. French structuralism deals with notions of mental structures, as these are thought to have originated in individuals' minds—in response to their culture—and then have been passed down over the ages. In America, we think of more or less institutionalized structures, of the family, schools, and so forth. In other words, we deal with social structures, and with individual psyches.
2. Lévi-Strauss's "structural anthropology," which is based on his observations of kinship structures of Brazilian tribes, started to be debated, and frequently refuted, in relation to existing (mostly "American") theories. As is customary, every anthropologist was eager to defend the veracity of theoretical extrapolation from his/her own field work and training.
3. American anthropologists, just like other American social scientists, tend to stick close to their empirical data, and thus, with rare exceptions, found it rather easy to dismiss theories based on mental rather than observable structures.
4. Structural anthropology, insofar as it relies heavily on unconscious structures, appealed to the French psychoanalyst

Jacques Lacan. Ever since the late 1940s, he had battled the internationally dominating "American psychoanalysis"—that is, psychoanalytic theories based on Freud's "structural theory," namely, the heuristic division of the personality into id, ego, and superego. Therefore, a theory such as Lévi-Strauss's, which not only apprehended the individual's unconscious in terms of the relationship between Saussurean linguistic structures, but was said to allow a way into an individuals' past, offered a new means to understand Freud—a "French Freud."

5. Already during the 1950s, Roland Barthes had addressed questions of writing, such as misreading when the impact of the space between words in a text is neglected, along with the silences, with readers' comprehension and selective reading, with the arbitrariness in writers' sequencing of words, clauses, and unexpressed thought within their narratives, and much more. In other words, both the writers' and readers' unconscious were meant to be included in Barthes' analyses, and in his criticism of literature.

6. Louis Althusser had been a practicing communist ever since the end of World War II, and had evolved into the party's theorist. Since it had become evident that all children pick up their parents' habits and that even the most dedicated communists are impotent to overcome their own (bourgeois) upbringing, Althusser hypothesized that the Lacanian Freud might be able to do so. In that case, the unconscious of individuals would be revolutionized along with their society. Marxism finally would triumph.

7. Michel Foucault, who had been Althusser's student but had left the Communist party in 1952, turned his philosophical interests to the rethinking of history. His dialectical methods, which focused more on the habits of thought that pervade the thinking in specific periods and which, in turn, spur them on to perceive personal and social events in distinctive ways, and to pass these on, for a time attempted to reach the innermost depth of human history in his *Archaeology of Knowledge*—to uncover the earliest mechanism that produced human thinking, along with the resulting unconscious belief structures.

III

Since each of the five individuals, in one or more ways, relied on the theories of the others, their Parisian peers soon referred to them as "the structuralists." In 1966, they created a journal, *Les Cahiers pour l'Analyse,* where they intended to explore all avenues that might lead to the original structures of all culture. But when, in the spring of 1968, the totally unexpected uprisings by students and workers threatened every existing structure, each of these thinkers, in one way or another, gradually distanced himself from "structuralism." Soon, Lévi-Strauss went back to study the origins of myths; Lacan to explore his psychoanalytic patients' unconscious thought associations; Barthes returned to focus on epigrammatic, literary observations; while Althusser's Marxism was said to become ever more "scientific," and Jacques Derrida's "poststructuralism" and Foucault's "historicism" were moving to the fore.

The other three major intellectuals I featured in *The Age of Structuralism* did not go along with the structuralist premises. Henri Lefebvre, a so-called humanist Marxist was set against Althusser's scientific pretensions, as well as against Lévi-Strauss's understanding of Marx as one of the cornerstones of his anthropology. (Lévi-Strauss, in *Tristes Tropiques* [1955], stated that Freud had convinced him of the centrality of unconscious motivation, Marx of the fact that utopian dreams unite all of humanity, and geology had led him to assume that history leaves its unerasable traces and relentlessly keeps going on.) "Yes, the structures exist," Lefebvre told me when I asked him what he thought of structuralism, "but they mostly remain veiled, and only occasionally do we get a glimpse, when this veil lifts."

Lefebvre taught philosophy and sociology. But his sociology, even when inspired by empirical research, did not stay close to his practical findings. Instead—whether about architecture, cities, or everyday life—he always ended up proving that one or more of Marx's predictions soon would be borne out. Alain Touraine, on the other hand, though championing socialist causes—whether supporting the students during the events of 1968, providing aid to Allende's Chile, or arguing about the eventual efficacy of social movements—had his feet in empirical, social reality.

Paul Ricoeur's hermeneutic philosophy did not champion left-wing causes, and this made him an outsider to many of the debates. So did his underlying religious and moral assumptions, which he also superimposed on his comprehension of Freudian concepts. Mostly, Ricoeur responded to the structuralists' concerns by focusing on linguistics. However, he primarily incorporated notions of metaphor and symbolism into his semantic theories, and linked these to Husserl's and Heidegger's views of being-in-the-world.

As I mentioned above, in my book I included Lefebvre, Touraine, and Ricoeur to demonstrate that not all Parisian intellectuals had succumbed to structuralist ideas. Still, except for Ricoeur, they all had some affinity to Marxist ideals. However, when I came upon the Parisian scene, the heyday of the early structuralism already was over, even though few of these works had come out in English. While writing, I frequently translated one passage or another in order to quote it, only to receive the printed translation of the work shortly thereafter.

In any event, much of structuralism, deconstruction, and poststructuralism reached American universities almost simultaneously. For the timing of translations was haphazard, depending more on personal interests of academics and on the whim of publishers than on the viability of a specific subject. Of course, in the 1970s both structuralist and deconstructionist theories were part of an ongoing interdisciplinary discussion among Parisian intellectuals. They were refutations of each others' points—which frequently were assumed rather than spelled out—and also took for granted the thinking of French classical thinkers, from the philosophers to Descartes, and, among others, of Sartre, Merleau-Ponty, and Camus.

American academics were bound to have trouble in following these extraordinarily convoluted, complex, and often internal discussions, which were being introduced into more and more academic enclaves. I had set out to provide an entrée to them. To keep the confusion to a minimum, I limited my book to the arguments surrounding structuralism alone. Thus,

I conceived *The Age of Structuralism* as a sort of primer for professors and students who would not have the time or the inclination to sort out the specific background and assumptions of each of these thinkers, or to immerse themselves and follow the development of the concepts in each of the many books they had written. I also kept holding on to my original idea of following the evolving debates among them all.

In the 1980s, these debates, increasingly, were being presented. But this happened, for the most part, by academics who had become fascinated by one or another French star and started to champion his ideas. Literary critics in, for instance, Yale French studies, and in philosophy and English at Cornell University, began to introduce Lévi-Strauss and Lacan—who soon made his debut at Johns Hopkins as well. Lefebvre became known to Marxist scholars in Toronto and at Amherst College. And so on. Soon, Departments of English, of Philosophy, and of Comparative Literature began to invite, among others, Jacques Derrida to decipher his deconstructionist philosophy; Julia Kristeva to explain her semiotics; Jean Baudrillard to present his postmodern flights. Ricoeur taught regularly at the University of Chicago; Bourdieu at the University of California at San Diego; and Michel Foucault at Berkeley.

My book was published at a time when these ideas were incomprehensible to the majority of scholars exposed to them. Naturally, there was some resistance. I had been sympathetic to the thrust of structuralist ideas and yet skeptical of the eventual success of the enterprise. Consequently, professors who were championing one or another structuralist within their own disciplines did not take to anything but wholehearted acceptance. Those among their colleagues who did not want to be bothered with "convoluted French imports" were dubious. Many sociologists, at first, thought structuralism was not scientific enough. But after a while, *The Age of Structuralism* received more and more reviews, and these were increasingly favorable. Before long, more and more colleagues would ask me whether I could advise them on how to "instrumentalize," for instance, Foucault's insights into mental illness, or into criminality. My responses, invariably, included explanations of his structures of thought and how these, in turn, were said to influence the way specific knowledge had been constructed and then had taken hold. And I cautioned against applying these ideas, directly to, for instance, structures of hospitals, psychiatric clinics, prisons, or other institutions. So, as interest in the different structuralists' ideas was sparked in all sorts of diverse places, many professors assigned the book in order to introduce their students to the French intellectual milieu.

As we know, Lacan ended up having much influence among American humanist academics and little among psychoanalysts. His practices remained peripheral among them, but for theoretical and institutional reasons. However, comments and extrapolations of his ideas, and attacks on these by his early women disciples, resonated to the concerns of American academic feminists. (See my book, *Freudians and Feminists* [1995]). Yet some of their basically nonpsychoanalytic interpretations often proved unworkable, though finding appeal in our university settings long after having been disavowed by their originators—who, increasingly, were becoming therapists and writers. This does not mean that their provocative lines of inquiry may not inspire liberating practices: Lacanian concepts now are inserted, piecemeal, into the practices of variously oriented psychoanalysts. But these are not being continued as a separate endeavor.

Foucault's reexamination of the histories of madness, psychiatry, medicine, and crime, and their location within emerging power structures, continue to inspire new associations, especially among historians, some of whom have rethought their entire discipline. Sociologists, and researchers in all sorts of fields, have reexamined the basic premises of their specialties. While Foucault was alive there was nearly no knowledge of his own sexual practices outside Paris, although he was in the process of writing his *History of Sexuality*. When he died, in 1984, I happened to be teaching a seminar on "French Structuralism" at the Johann-Wolfgang-Goethe University in Frankfurt. Peripherally, I mentioned that he had been gay. None of my students had heard about that, and some seriously questioned my statement. Since then, Foucault's sexual preferences (including sado-masochism) have become central to extrapolations of his theories, and have been widely discussed in a plethora of books and at scholarly conferences. But this is due to current concerns in American culture.

The other figures I featured in *The Age of Structuralism* have become part of the intellectual history of their time, and/ or are discussed along with others in their own disciplines. All in all, these French theories continue to be relevant, even though they were unable to uncover the origins of humankind— which in one way or another each of the early structuralists had promised to do. Without a grounding in their thought, students cannot understand extrapolations from them. Therefore, this book has provided an outline of the basic premises of structuralism for the past fifteen years—which, in turn, is necessary for anyone wanting to make sense of the debates that have come to be summarized as "postmodern." For the seeds of relativism, of value neutral ideals, of the rejection of everything that is part of modernism, and so on, are intrinsic to the structuralist method. Subsequently, these allowed and encouraged the plethora of free associations to, and among, written and oral texts, and which cross disciplinary boundaries. Many academics now lump these ideas under the general rubric of "theory." In fact, *The Age of Structuralism* has served as a manual for both proponents and opponents of these enterprises. Now it is being reprinted, because both professors and students who expect to understand any of these more recent (or in any way connected) theories—extensions of semiotics, poststructuralism, deconstruction, postmodernism, post-postmodernism, and whatever else may follow—will need to grapple with structuralism in order to grasp the ideas and premises of the French giants upon whose shoulders they, too, expect to stand.

Edith Kurzweil

Garden City, New York
January 1996

Preface

The idea of this book came to me when I suddenly realized after I had written about Lévi-Strauss for *Partisan Review* that an intellectual movement could be fashionable without being understood. I myself at that point did not know how much I still had to learn to make sense of its various forms. But I was struck by the diverse reactions to Lévi-Strauss' notions—reactions which could only partly be attributed to the fact that he is French, but which had to do with the appeal and respect accorded Parisian intellectuals. This is not to say that all the Parisian talk of structuralism was any freer of simplifications than existentialism—its predecessor—had been. Nor that the educated French understand it much better than their American counterparts.

Still, structuralism did have an impact on the French intellectual community, and did address all other philosophical systems—hermeneutics, Marxism, phenomenology, existentialism, rationalism, etc. Thus I included chapters on the most representative structuralists (in anthropology, Marxism, psychoanalysis, literature, and history) as well as on their opponents (in Marxism, hermeneutics, and sociology), so that this book about structuralism also puts structuralism in its intellectual and political milieu. For just as existentialists, under the aegis of Sartre, used intellectual positions for political ends—however ethically and honestly—so structuralists, I believe, have often avoided difficult political choices by searching for unconscious structures. This is not to denigrate structuralist aims, or to deny the extraordinary abilities of such figures as Claude Lévi-Strauss, Michel Foucault, or Roland Barthes. On the contrary, their painstaking efforts to find common roots and meaning uniting all of humanity held out intellectual and political promises everyone would applaud. In-

evitably, fame brought its customary side effects—followers, derivative theories, interviews, attributions, money, inducements,
popularizations. And when the unconscious structures remained
hidden while, in 1968, economic and political structures temporarily broke down, structuralists had to rethink their various
theories.

Hence it is important to remember, when reading the
thoughts of the various figures in this book, that they always
talked to a larger audience as well as to theoretical issues. Sometimes they had to rethink complex ideas in front of microphones
and television cameras, mixing serious thought with quick re-
partee, with political expediency, and with a position they had to
defend. For politics and tradition, even when not explicit, are in
the air that French intellectuals breathe. Even Christian doctrine
usually is pointed toward the kind of issues Camus had focused
on in the 1940s—issues about dealing with Nazi exterminators,
the death penalty, Algerian independence, and questions of honesty and ultimate truth. Such major philosophical issues are addressed by both Marxists and conservatives, and sometimes in
terms of the structuralist debates. These debates are alive in
France; and they lose in their translation to our culture. The familiarity of discussing social phenomena itself in linguistic terms
would, when talking, for instance, about metaphor, favor the
French metaphor. But this is due to the fact that the French are
rhetorical magicians, and that the French language allows for the
subtleties which only our literary structuralists address.

When I started to write this book, few people in America
had heard of structuralism. By now, however, structuralism has
spread beyond anthropology, is taught in most of the more
"elite" departments of literature; and many sociologists want to
know more about some of the "structuralists." In fact, at a recent
conference at Boston University on "The State of Literary Criticism," participants were in pro-structuralist and anti-structuralist
camps: their vehement arguments appeared to replace the former
conflict between Marxists and their opponents. Thus my critical
though appreciative and primarily sociological stance might well
offend the devotees of structuralism and/or of post-structuralism;
and they may accuse me of simplifying. But I intended to give an
overview of French structuralism, to make the subject accessible

to the general reader; and I wrote for the expert or the student who is familiar with the ideas and style of one or more of the theorists, and who might want to know more about the milieu. So the chapters do not have to be read consecutively, although it would help to begin with the introduction and the chapter on Lévi-Strauss. (The selected bibliography at the end of each chapter might be used for further reading.)

The writing of this book went through a number of revisions, as more books began to be available in English, and as the major figures I chose to include altered their systems, and refuted those of others. At various stages of the writing, Kay Agena, Lewis Coser, Elizabeth Dalton, Morris Dickstein, Eugene Goodheart, Alvin Gouldner, George Justus Lawler, Barbara Rosecrance, and René Wellek read one or more chapters and made valuable comments. But, obviously, I alone am responsible for the final product. William Phillips critically read a number of drafts, encouraging me alternately to quit and to carry on. I am particularly grateful to two anonymous publisher's readers who made me realize that not all criticism is useful, when, in the course of two weeks, one said I had underplayed Foucault's Marxism, and the other that I had turned him into a full-blown Marxist. But this is just one of the many polemics of structuralism I hoped to convey.

I particularly want to thank my friends in France, the protagonists whom I interviewed, and John Moore, my editor at Columbia University Press, and Karen Davidson, who supervised much of the typing. I also want to thank the Rockefeller Foundation for a stay at the Villa Serbelloni in 1977—the only chance I had to work without the usual obligations and distractions. I am dedicating the book to my children because, at times, they received less attention than "the book."

Edith Kurzweil

New York City
January 1980

The Age of Structuralism
Lévi-Strauss to Foucault

Introduction

"French social thought of the desperate years," says H. Stuart Hughes, "began with history and ended with anthropology." To be more exact, it changed rather than ended in 1955 with the publication of *Tristes Tropiques,* Lévi-Strauss' autobiographical anthropology. The book not only made him famous but paved the way for his *Structural Anthropology* (1958) and for the acceptance of structuralism—the systematic attempt to uncover deep universal mental structures as these manifest themselves in kinship and larger social structures, in literature, philosophy and mathematics, and in the unconscious psychological patterns that motivate human behavior.[1] Since then, both the theory and methodology of structuralism have taken on a variety of forms: some make partial use of Lévi-Strauss' method; others bypass him; and still others directly apply specific components of phonetic theory. But because Lévi-Strauss was first to adapt Saussurean linguistics to the social sciences, I am assessing the other structuralisms in relation to his ideas. And I am focusing, particularly in my conclusion, on his understanding of Freud, Marx, and Saussure and on the intellectual differences structuralist analyses generated.

Since this overview presents structuralism from no single disciplinary perspective, I chose figures belonging to different disciplines. Thus not all of the eight thinkers to whom the chapters are devoted are (or were) structuralists; but each one represents specific biases, approaches, and theories of reference; they differ in content as well as in tone; and I wanted to convey these different tones as well as some of the "difficult" language. Barthes' playful and frequently outrageous flippancy, for instance, cannot go unreported. Lefebvre's idealism and irony cannot be described in the same language as Foucault's madhouses and leprosariums;

and the mythologies of Lacan's "unconscious texts" must be seen in contrast to the culture-bound myths of Lévi-Strauss' natives. Boudon, for example, distinguishes between methodological structuralism and the philosophical structuralism of the human sciences, though Lévi-Strauss uses them both. And he adds:

> the confusion seems geographically limited: a Harris or a Chomsky, as structuralist as Lévi-Strauss on the methodological level, draw no particular philosophical conclusion from their scientific works.[2]

In Paris, the structuralist age is nearly over. Nevertheless, structuralist assumptions continue to permeate French thinking, providing a basis for post-structuralism. Until recently, American social scientists (except anthropologists) have not paid much attention to French structuralist thought, although it is taught, increasingly, in departments of literature. But more and more of our intellectuals who at first dismissed structuralism as peripheral, useless, or abstruse now want to know about it. In any event, it has already become part of intellectual history.

Since World War II, French thought has gone through several phases. During the Resistance and immediately after the liberation, Marxism preoccupied the thinking of French intellectuals. Then, in a climate of growing disillusionment with the Soviet Union and communism, Sartre's existentialist humanism promised to allow for individual fulfillment in modern society. But when Sartre, especially between 1952 and 1956, professed his humanism while continuing to support the Communists (ignoring repression in the Soviet Union), his theories became suspect. Thus it was possible for structuralism and the new theories of linguistics and semiotics to gain impetus. But it cannot be said that there has been a clean-cut succession; all these philosophies have to some extent existed side by side and have affected each other. In fact, the influence of Marxism has persisted in many explicit as well as obscure forms, so that although existentialism and structuralism are based on very different assumptions about the nature of man and society, many of the Marxist attitudes toward economic justice and social change appear in the theories of various existentialists, structuralists and semiologists—though those who profess these theories often view themselves as non-

Marxist or anti-Communist. At the same time, it will be noted that traces, or influences, of existentialism and/or Marxism continue to be found in the works of such diverse figures as Barthes, Foucault, Lacan, Lévi-Strauss, and others.

Although structuralism itself was apolitical, it did have broad political implications—implications that were not immediately apparent and tended to get lost in the ramifications and discussions of structuralism itself. In addition to its impact on a number of intellectual disciplines, structuralism, in the beginning, supplied the French Left with a pseudopolitical theory that did not negate their Socialist leanings, but removed them from the direct involvement with Marxism.

Essentially, the French Left in the mid-1950s was experiencing the agonies and conflicts that American Marxists had endured in the 1930s and 1940s. By the fifties, radical French intellectuals could no longer avoid recognizing the grim reality of Russian communism which dramatized the failure of the Marxist experiment. In France, however, this shift away from alignment with Soviet Marxism involved more than an ideological split; it upset long-standing political alliances as well. Unlike their American counterparts, French Communists had always operated from a broad political base and had had strong union support. The popularity of the Left concealed what were, in fact, serious differences among the Communists, Socialists, and the Radicals and blurred the distinctions among them. Then, with the intensification of the cold war and the growing disillusionment with Soviet communism, the semblance of ideological unity which had aligned intellectuals, labor groups, and parliamentary deputies began to break down.

While this fairly widespread split with Soviet Marxism was occurring, radical French intellectuals were becoming increasingly disenchanted with existentialism. Actually, the bond among the existentialists had always been tenuous. The high priests of existentialism had disagreed from the beginning. For example, Sartre states about himself and Merleau-Ponty:

> Too individualist to ever pool our research, we became reciprocal while remaining separate. Alone, each of us was too easily persuaded of having understood the idea of phenomenology. Together we were, for each other, the incarnation of

> its ambiguity. Each of us viewed the work being done by the other as an unexpected, and sometimes hostile, deviation from his own. Husserl became our bond and our division, at one and the same time.[3]

In fact, Sartre continues, the strongest bond among the existentialists had been their common hatred of the Nazis. When this essentially political *raison d'état* dissolved, the fragility of the ideological tie among the existentialists became apparent. It is not surprising, of course, that existentialism—a philosophy which places a high value on individual ends—would prove a shaky basis for ideological cohesion. In any event, by the mid-fifties the time was ripe for a new movement to supersede existentialism—which had been too subjective and too bound up with individual freedom to carry the weight of the social burdens that had been placed upon it. Existentialism could no longer promise to overcome the political and ideological uncertainties created by the need to break with Soviet communism.

The advent of structuralism, for its followers at least, seemed to supply an honorable intellectual escape from confronting the limitations of both Marxism and existentialism. One of the effects of its broad philosophical affirmation—that ultimately all social reality would be seen as the interplay of the as yet unconscious common mental structures[4]—was to divert French intellectuals from the political problems and theories that had occupied the Marxists and, to some extent, the existentialists. Those who drifted into the structuralist debates found a means to deradicalize themselves without abandoning their humanist convictions. The very complexities of structuralist methods obscured the fact that structuralism would become the new conservatism of the Left.

This political bias was not apparent when Lévi-Strauss began to elaborate the methodology that was to explain consciousness by life, as Marx had done, and that was simultaneously to help unravel the Freudian collective unconscious with the help of semiology—the science that studies the life of signs within society, emphasizing their arbitrariness and postulating a relationship between their *signified* and *signifying* properties. Elaborations from linguistic theories (e.g., Jakobson, Hjelmslev, Martinet) were added to Saussurean theory and became the basis of structuralist methods. When successful, techniques for uncovering the general laws of language and their relations to all other areas of human activity were ultimately to uncover a human universality. Thus the method itself remained part of the structuralist project and therefore was intrinsic to the emergence of these hypothetical mental structures. And because the inclusive nature of structuralism inspired attention, specific thinkers constructed their own complete structuralist systems and countersystems; they all influenced French social and political life.

I should mention at the start that though French intellectuals are loosely perceived as a community, many of them would deny that they comprise a community at all. They would point to their differences, their ideological and political disagreements, and their differing epistemologies. Nevertheless, they have at least as much in common as those we loosely call the New York intellectual establishment. Many of the French group went to the École Normale Supérieure; they were all trained in philosophy and share a scholar's familiarity with the works of Descartes, Kant, Hegel, Husserl, and Kierkegaard. And all were influenced by the *Annales*[5] school (founded by Marc Bloch and Lucien Fèbvre in 1929) and by Fernand Braudel's *La Méditerranée*[6]—sources of a conception of history as the study of multiple temporalities extending over a day, a week, a year, and up to the *longue durée* that can encompass a number of centuries. Because all French intellectuals have been steeped in the humanities and history, their ranks are not fragmented according to specific disciplines in the way that American academics often are. And since most of them studied in Paris, they know each other—or at least know of each other. They are generalists by tradition and by disposition; their specializations are always thought of as enriching a common pool of knowledge rather than as developing new areas of study.

In the survey which follows, I will examine the ideas of some of the leading figures within this "community"—Claude Lévi-Strauss' structuralism, Louis Althusser's scientific Marxism, Henri Lefebvre's idealist Marxism, Paul Ricoeur's phenomenology, Alain Touraine's historicist sociology, Jacques Lacan's psychoanalysis, Roland Barthes' literary criticism, and Michel Foucault's social history. Since their ideas (on many levels) were sometimes responses to each other, and to events, I have arranged the chapters roughly according to when these men attracted public attention. But throughout I will focus on the discussions and on the broader context of the structuralist enterprise.

Although Lefebvre, Ricoeur, and Touraine never were structuralists, I have included these opponents of structuralist thought as representing the main intellectual movements contending with structuralism. As such, they round out the structuralist age. Some might argue that Serge Moscovici's studies of psychoanalysis and of human nature, or Edgar Morin's work on popular culture are as important as Touraine's contributions; or that Bourdieu and Boudon, as more effective and direct critics of structuralism, ought to replace Touraine. Others might maintain that Jacques Derrida, whose *semiotics* (the general philosophical theory of signs and symbols that deals with their function in both artificially constructed and natural languages) replaced *semiology* (the science that shows what constitutes signs and what laws govern them), ought to have been included; or that A.-J. Greimas' structuralist concern with semantics, narrative structure, and the enunciation-spectacle is as important as Barthes' *semiology*. Still others might object because Lucien Goldmann's genetic structuralism does not receive much attention. But the reasons for my final choice and my emphases should become evident as we proceed. Basically, this book is an overview of the structuralist era for readers who may be familiar with the thoughts of one or more of the figures, but who have not paid much attention to the surrounding debates; it is to introduce the "missing links" of the structuralism which peaked in the late 1960s—notions of history, psychoanalysis, psychology, and ideology will be addressed along the way.

For each of the figures I have selected, the focus and field of concern, the particular mix of humanism and science, is different. Lévi-Strauss, Ricoeur, Lefebvre, and Althusser are all philosophers; but Lévi-Strauss is also an anthropologist, Ricoeur a theologian, Lefebvre a sociologist, and Althusser a "scientific Marxist." Touraine's sociology is informed by literature and history; whereas Barthes, a very special type of literary critic, frequently refers to his own sociology and to his regard for Marx. Both Lacan's rereading of Freud and Foucault's treatment of deviance span literature, psychoanalysis, history, and philosophy. Unlike Anglo-Saxon empiricists, French intellectuals are interdisciplinary and assume that their audience, too, is conversant with philosophy, literature, and history.

As early as 1933, N. S. Trubetzkoy had noted that structuralist pursuits characterized by a systematic universalism were common in chemistry, biology, psychology, and economics, as well as in linguistic studies; but Lévi-Strauss conceived the methodology which would allow him to apply structuralism to anthropology only in the late 1940s. By systematically unraveling the meaning of tribal myths (in North and South America) through an examination of linguistic oppositions and transformations in spoken language, he sought to explain how transformations occurred in culture and in the individual apprehension of social reality.

Ricoeur also focused on oppositions in language, especially on the dual aspects of metaphor and metonymy, when he first addressed Lévi-Strauss' theories in the early 1960s. But Ricoeur is not concerned with language or with metaphoric thought in itself. Instead, he attempts to explain why myths were constructed in the first place, to find out what supernatural phenomena they try to explain, or how they expect to bridge the gap between an individual's being and God. This religious concern sets him apart from all the other figures in this book.

Lefebvre, in particular, attacks Ricoeur's dialectic between man and God because, he says, it transposes all thought into Ricoeur's hermeneutics. It also invalidates Lefebvre's own Marxist beliefs. But Lefebvre's Marxist "translations" of structural linguistics, when postulating commodities (material goods) as complex Saussurean *signs* that are opposed to commodity/messages (advertising to consumers) as *signifiers,* were dismissed as vulgar and inapplicable by other Marxists. In any event, Lefebvre abandoned these linguistic preoccupations after his brief concern with them around 1963, when his focus shifted to the sociology of urbanization and of space. These latter theories are more representative of his unwavering utopian Marxism and are said, in part, to have inspired the student revolts of 1968. But Lefebvre's lack of a program, as well as his reliance on theories of the spontaneous withering away of all bourgeois structures, have been attacked by Althusser in the name of scientific Marxism.

Althusser dismisses Marx's "humanistic" early works, which Lefebvre upholds as intrinsic to Marx—everything written up to and including the *1844 Manuscripts*—and considers *The German Ideology* as a work of transition. Instead, he glorifies the "mature" Marx who, according to Althusser, dealt with political economy alone. At the same time, Althusser admires Lenin's ideas concerning the takeover of the state: he wants to expand on what Lenin tried to do by theoretically anticipating the practical problems of impending revolution. In order to do away with even the traces of bourgeois habits of thinking, Althusser, in 1962, wondered how, after a socialist revolution, these habits could be eliminated. This concern led him to examine Lacan's interpretations of Freud with the hope that he would discover a way to reeducate both parents and infants in a post-bourgeois society. The new *discourse of the unconscious* which Althusser attributed to Marx, Freud, and Nietzsche was to help implement a successful revolution. Lefebvre, however, perceived Marx, Freud, and Nietzsche as intellectual forerunners in the inevitable succession of thought before the revolution; and Ricoeur attempted to mediate between these *protagonists of suspicion* to incorporate them into his hermeneutic system.

Lacan is less concerned with social revolution than he is with revolutionizing the interpretation of the unconscious. To Lacan the unconscious is a text to be unraveled, a text which is rooted in language: "It is that part of concrete discourse, . . . that is not at the disposal of the subject in re-establishing the continuity of his conscious discourse." [7] But, continues Lacan, this "censored chapter" of individual history can be rediscovered—in hysterical symptoms, in childhood memories, and in traditions—by unraveling the structure of language. Thus, Lacan focuses on transpositions of meaning and sounds and on symbolism in the psychoanalytic situation, incorporating the methods of structuralist linguistics into psychoanalysis. His lectures at the École Normale Supérieure and on television can be credited with having popularized psychoanalysis in France since the 1960s—after its influence had declined in the United States.

Foucault's lectures are equally popular, but his focus is on the hidden connections among social institutions, ideas, customs, and power relations—particularly on transformations of the social context since the seventeenth century. He attempts to uncover the societies' codes of knowledge which are said to be in a continual process of transformation. Foucault pays special attention to the way that shifts in the definition of normalcy and deviancy alter the structure of society. Whether he writes on madness, illness, crime, or sexuality, he always shows, with the help of neo-structuralist oppositions and transformations, that those in power have hidden codes or agendas which exist behind the scientific codes of knowledge. And these codes, Foucault argues, obscure repression in modern bourgeois societies. Foucault's bold and often brilliant insights have earned him a central place in the era dominated by the structuralists although, since 1968, he has denied being a structuralist.

Barthes, too, has been daring in his attacks on established beliefs, particularly in the realm of literary criticism. Originally, Barthes viewed structuralism as an *activity;* he attempted to adopt structuralist methodology in his semiology without trying to justify its theoretical precepts. Although he has now abandoned this approach for a highly personal and, as he calls it, "erotic" brand of criticism, structuralist residues remain.

The only central figure in my book who seems to have remained almost unaffected by the linguistic aspect of structuralism is Touraine; his emphasis is on social movements, changes in social structure, and on the historical conditions that lead individuals to start revolutions. Nevertheless, Touraine's empirical sociology incorporates the same philosophical questions that all the other figures address. His assessment of the 1968 strikes is not unlike Lefebvre's or Lacan's; but Touraine is concerned primarily with the nature of social action and only peripherally addresses structuralist thought.

Today, some twenty-five years after its emergence, structuralism, which was to "discover an underlying coherence that could not be revealed from a simple description of facts which have somehow been flattened and scattered without order,"[8] appears to have been superseded. As we will see in the following chapters, Althusser, Foucault, and Barthes reneged on their structuralisms. By 1971, Lévi-Strauss had dismissed most of his neo-disciples, although they cannot entirely disown him without seriously undermining their own credibility. He himself returned to his earlier interests, to philosophy and to a more narrow concern with kinship structures and myth. Yet, even if structuralism in its original formulations has to a great extent been questioned—or relegated to the realm of utopias—its complex methodology continues to inspire. It has inscribed itself on a number of disciplines. Barthes' literary criticism, Ricoeur's hermeneutics, Foucault's analyses of power and deviance, Derrida's grammatology, and Lacan's psychoanalysis—all bear traces of the original "grand theory." Structuralism has left its mark on the intellectual tradition and continues to influence scholars—particularly in the fields of semiotics and linguistics in France and within certain disciplines in America.

In any overview such as this, one must necessarily simplify. But French intellectuals are not as disposed as we are to separate their scientific contributions from their personal histories, so it is more acceptable for memories of childhood experiences or for the systematic free association to texts to become part of theoretical observations. A critical approach to their work consequently risks violating an inherent and unique complexity rarely found, for example, in English, German, or American thinkers. Nevertheless, I hope to explain structuralist discourse without reducing its theoretical validity or its personalistic flavor for the sake of a facile clarity. Because structuralism is thought to have a conservative bias, I shall point to its political implications (those who embrace structuralist theories do not always declare themselves as political—or even as structuralist). Finally, I hope to provide a perspective on the structuralist debate that will bridge the traditional boundaries of academic disciplines.

Structuralism as originally conceived by Lévi-Strauss is dead: the universal mental structures have not emerged, albeit no one any longer searches for them. But without this structuralist antecedent, Julia Kristeva, for example, might not have argued for the revolutionary potential of the semiotic that is said to confront the symbolic dialectic of meaning and structure; Derrida might not have proposed his *grammatology* as the "science" of the written sign.[9] And Deleuze and Guattari might not have invented their *Anti-Oedipus*[10] without the pervasive influence, in Paris, of the Lacanian Oedipal drama—discovered when the child enters our symbolic and linguistic universe. Thus, the failure of Parisian structuralism itself has prepared the ground for the various "post-structuralisms."

Notes

1. This definition of Parisian structuralism leaves out Chomsky's "structuralist" approach to grammar, which postulates that there are universal (deep and generative) structures in individuals that attune them to the proper use of their own native languages. It does not address Piaget's structuralism, said to be a method rather than a doctrine (connected to no other methods), which maintains that structure and genesis are interdependent, that there is no structure apart from construction. See Jean Piaget, *Structuralism* (New York: Harper Torchbooks, 1970), pp. 140–43. For an "accessible" discussion of this subject, see Noam Chomsky, *Language and Responsibility* (New York: Pantheon, 1979). (Based on conversations with Mitsou Ronat.) In addition, for the moment, I am using the term as it is used by observers rather than by the protagonists.

2. For a detailed discussion of the various structuralisms, see Raymond Boudon, *A quoi sert la notion de structure?* (Paris: Gallimard, 1968), p. 219.

3. Jean-Paul Sartre, *Situations* (New York: George Braziller, 1965), p. 231.

4. Lévi-Strauss' ultimate concern with "the unconscious nature of collective phenomena" is to discover principles of thought formation that are universally valid, operative in both tribal and industrial societies. Later structuralists broke away from this theory. Their positions are treated in the chapters that follow.

5. *Annales* is also the name of the journal published by this group.

6. Fernand Braudel, *The Mediterranean* (New York: Harper & Row, 1966).

7. Jacques Lacan, *Écrits, A Selection* (New York: Norton, 1977) p. 49.

8. Jean-Marie Domenach, "Le requiem structuraliste," *Esprit* (November 1973) no. 3, p. 695.

9. Terence Hawkes, *Structuralism and Semiotics* (Berkeley: University of California Press, 1977), p. 145.

10. Gilles Deleuze and Felix Guattari, *L'Anti-Oedipe* (Paris: Éditions de Minuit, 1972). Translated by Robert Hurley, Mark Seem, and Helen R. Lane as *Anti-Oedipus: Capitalism and Schizophrenia* (New York: Viking Press, 1977).

I. Claude Lévi-Strauss

The Father of Structuralism

Claude Lévi-Strauss—son of an artist and grandson of a rabbi—was born in Belgium in 1908. He says that he remembers little before 1914, when he moved with his parents to Versailles. He appears to have been a lonely child, given to introspection, to thinking, and to reading. In fact, he tells us that he spent much time walking by himself and speculating about nature as he collected odds and ends—the stones, pebbles, and plants he calls *bricolage* [1]—he intended for the fabrication of "mosaics." These activities, he believes, aroused his serious interest in geology and later influenced his theories of structuralism. But he was not to become a student of science until much later. For a while he studied law at the University of Paris. He passed his *Agrégation de philosophie* in 1932, and began to work as a teacher in a *lycée*. When, in 1934, he was offered a professorship of anthropology at the University of Sao Paolo, he could not refuse it. For this post would give him the opportunity to take occasional trips to the interior of Brazil. There he studied a number of primitive tribes who were to provide him with the ideas he developed later on. In 1939 he returned to France to serve in the army but left for New York after the fall of Paris. Here he taught at the New School for Social Research and, as a result of his friendship with Roman Jakobson, became interested in structural linguistics. [2] He even contributed "Structural Analysis in Linguistics and Anthropology" to the *Journal of the Circle of New York* in 1945.

When the New School failed to grant him tenure at the end of the war, he returned to Paris. He did not write *Tristes Tropiques,* however, until 1955, so that this book is more of an intellectual reconstruction than a travelog or a field report. A curious combination of selective memory, empirical field research, and scientific deduction, *Tristes Tropiques* unexpectedly became a best-seller. Still, had it not appeared in the mid-1950s, it might not have received such instant acclaim.[3] This ethnographic auto-biography that mixes remembrances and interpretations, obser-vation and speculation, fact and free association, helped to bol-ster and legitimate both Lévi-Strauss' kinship theory, such as *Les structures élémentaires de la parenté* (1949), and his logic of myth (*Structural Study of Myth*, 1955). These scholarly works, in turn, conferred a certain amount of scientific status upon the speculative notions which provided the background for the ex-plorations in *The Savage Mind* (1962) and in the four volumes of *Mythologiques* (1964–71). In any case, the earlier works earned him a prestigious chair at the Collège de France, where he then proceeded to expand his theoretical inquiries to incorporate the myths of North and South American Indians.

II

In examining these theories, the following must be kept in mind. First, Lévi-Strauss' attempt to systematize myths—that is, the telling of all myths in every version in relation to its culture—is an ongoing task which is never complete. The basic premise of Lévi-Strauss' approach is contrary to most American systems theories, which tend to deal with observable data and to ignore unconscious structures of mind. Second, the French use of the term "scientific" is not linked to empirical proof in the same way as its American equivalent is. Third, French writers traditionally have brought personal experiences to their interpretations of his-tory. Together, these intellectual habits have generated a highly allusive form of discourse which allows for many divergent in-terpretations of Lévi-Strauss' original theories.

Lévi-Strauss, as we will see, frequently transforms specula-tive ideas into facts and past reflections into current assumptions. He justifies the mixing of personal experience with intellectual in-terpretation by claiming geology, psychoanalysis, and Marxism for his "three mistresses." For example, because Lévi-Strauss the boy had noted how plants grow in different soils, or how resi-dues of different epochs merge within the complex involutions of rocks, Lévi-Strauss the anthropologist speculated that all perceptions are permeated with past experiences, and "continue to exist in the living diversity of a moment . . . commingling space and time."[4] If we too can accept the notion that "unlike the history of the historians, history as the geologist and the psychoanalyst sees it is intended to body forth in time—rather in the manner of a *tableau vivant*—certain fundamental properties of the physical and psychical universe,"[5] then we can agree with Lévi-Strauss that history, when recollected, becomes part of the present. This ahistorical (or synchronic) perspective was, of course, unpalatable to the Marxists, especially because Lévi-Strauss thought that "Marxism proceeds in the same way as geology and psychoanalysis. . . . All three show that understanding consists in the reduction of one type of reality to another; that true reality is never the most obvious of realities . . . because the problem is always due to the relation . . . between reason and sense-perception."[6]

Lévi-Strauss also had a fourth mistress, music, whose influence is evident in *The Raw and the Cooked*. Although he appears to have later deemphasized this influence, he did incorporate the three-dimensional quality of music in his method, by insisting that the many versions of tribal myths could be read like a musical score. *The Raw and the Cooked* and the "Finale" of *L'homme nu* (Michel Panoff calls this a Wagnerian invocation)[7] are organized around musical themes.

Once introduced to structural linguistics by Jakobson, Lévi-Strauss began to look at Saussure's study of language as a self-sufficient system that postulates a dynamic relationship between the components of every linguistic sign, that is between language system (*langue*) and individual speech (*parole*), and between sound image (*signifier*) and concept (*signified*). Upon this basic dualism, Lévi-Strauss superimposed Jakobson's model of phonemic analysis, which, in structural linguistics, attempts to prove that the structure of any language always follows a certain binary path of parallel constructions.

By empirically studying language impairment and loss among aphasics, Jakobson had found a "horizontal-vertical" polarity in linguistic performance, thereby providing support for Saussure's insight concerning the syntagmatic and associative planes of linguistics. Two major types of disorders emerged ("similarity disorder" and "contiguity disorder") that seem strikingly related to the rhetorical figures of metaphor and metonymy. Metaphor, based on a proposed similarity between a literal subject and its metaphorical substitute is "associative" in character and exploits "vertical" relations in language, whereas metonymy, based on proposed contiguous or "sequential" association, exploits "horizontal" relations in language. According to Jakobson, the polarities between the horizontal and vertical aspects of language underpin the two-fold process of *selection* and *combination* of constituent elements of language. Hence messages are constructed by a combination of a horizontal (diachronic) movement that combines words and a vertical (synchronic) one that selects particular words from the available language.[8]

Lévi-Strauss likened Jakobson's discovery in structural linguistics to a revelation and predicted that it would revolutionize not only linguistics but anthropology and all the social sciences as well.

> First, structural linguistics shifts from the study of *conscious* linguistic phenomena to the study of their *unconscious* infrastructure; second, it does not treat *terms* as independent entities, taking instead as its basis of analysis the *relations* between terms; third, it introduces the concept of *system*— "modern phonemics does not merely proclaim that phonemes are always part of a system; it *shows* concrete phonemic systems and elucidates their structures"; finally, structural linguistics aims at discovering *general laws,* either by induction "or . . . by logical deduction, which would give them an absolute character."[9]

Lévi-Strauss began by incorporating Jakobson's studies of phonemic systems into the study of kinship structures,[10] but he cautioned that the phonemic method cannot simply be transposed to anthropological analysis. Instead, it must be refined to allow for the fact that, in anthropology, the laws discovered by a microsociological analysis (i.e., the terms of address used to designate kinship relation) would be invalid on a macro-level (use of these same terms in different tribes). In kinship systems, for instance, there are profound differences between the *system of terminologies* and the system of attitudes, or between systems of nomenclature and those of social organization. Nevertheless, in Lévi-Strauss' view all these systems are alike in that they are all symbolic. Thus, according to Lévi-Strauss, neither phenomena nor kinship systems can ever be explained through direct empirical observation alone; but, as in linguistics, they must be examined as sets of symbolic relationships. On the macro-level, these symbolic relationships exist between languages and cultures; and in tribal societies they are said to converge in the telling of myths.

Because Lévi-Strauss was intrigued by the way that languages as well as myths of different cultures resembled each other and appeared to be structured in a similar fashion, he attempted to show that they actually are constituted in the same way.[11] At the same time, he had to account for the fact that events belonging to the distant past are told and retold in the present and therefore seem to move back and forth in time. He also had to distinguish *la langue* and *la parole* by the different time dimension of each (synchronic and diachronic).[12] To account for the shifts in time, he added a third dimension—a dimension which required another unit of analysis. He called this new analytical tool the "gross constituent unit," defining it as a meaningful combination of two or more words in a sentence.[13] This constituent unit, which can be a sentence or a part of a sentence, is probably the most controversial component of his theory, because it allegedly overcomes limitations of time to mediate between the past, the present, and the future. Jakobson had postulated binary oppositions between consonants and vowels and between contradictory relationships (e.g., the emotive versus the conative dimension of the speech event) as the basis of his own structural linguistics. Thus, in order to "overcome the inability to connect two kinds of relationships," Lévi-Strauss assumes that in myth, just as in language, contradictory relationships can be perceived as identical as long as they are self-contradictory in a similar way.[14] When applying this method to social phenomena, Lévi-Strauss could not search in the customary manner for the "true" version of a myth; he had instead to analyze every existing version of every myth. First, he had to break down each myth into short sentences and to catalog them; each of these short sentences (constituent units) could produce a functional meaning only when it was combined with other such units into "bundles of relations" that would account for the two-dimensional time-referent, revertible and nonrevertible time, and would constitute the primary elements of most myths. He then proceeded to unravel a myth as if it were an orchestra score, to read it in three-dimensional fashion, so that, for instance, a series of "constituent units" such as 1,2,4,7,8,2,3,4,6,8,1,4,5,7,8, might be analyzed according to the scheme:

```
1 2   4     7 8
  2 3 4   6   8
1     4 5   7 8
```

Aware of the difficulty even the most sophisticated reader would have with this method, Lévi-Strauss demonstrated its use with an illustration of the Oedipus myth. Following the diagram, a horizontal reading of the constituent units, he explained, would serve to structure the telling of the myth; the vertical columns, each of which contains a common feature, would reveal the myth's meaning. In the Oedipus myth, the common feature of the first column turns out to be the "overrating of blood relationships"; the common feature of the second column (an inversion of the first) is "the underrating of blood relationships," while the third column refers to monsters, and the fourth reveals that all the names in the myth have a common meaning—namely, "difficulties in walking straight and standing upright." [15] The fourth column is also said to explain the first one "which has to do with the autochthonous origin of man," that is, with his self-creation as opposed to the origin of man born from man and woman. [16] In order to record the many versions of every myth, Lévi-Strauss proposed to organize two-dimensional charts in three-dimensional order, so that it would be possible to read diagonally (see illustration). He thought that after all known myths were charted in this fashion, a structural law of myth would emerge and an orderly analysis would ensue from the existing chaos.

As long as Lévi-Strauss discussed only straight inversions, transformations and oppositions, everything seemed relatively simple. But he set out to show how the transition from nature to culture was paralleled by changing customs; for example, food was no longer eaten raw but cooked, and eating utensils replaced fingers. This, however, was only the beginning. The theory began to seem hopelessly abstruse when, for instance, Lévi-Strauss explained that

> carrion-eating animals are like prey animals (they eat animal food) but are also like foodplant producers (they do not kill what they eat). Ravens are to gardens as beasts of prey are to herbivorous animals. But it is also clear that herbivorous animals may be called first to act as mediators on the assumption that they are like collectors and gatherers (plant-food eaters), while they can be used as animal food though they are not themselves hunters.[17]

Such transformations and oppositions, though part of the method, seemed to obfuscate the fact that the unconscious structures remained hidden. All the examples that opposed the raw and the cooked, fire and ashes, honey and table manners (they were to explain changes in tribal life) only pretended to explain the common ingredients of myths, or to reveal their constituent units. It is difficult to agree, for instance, that because two Bororo myths reveal the advent of culture as dependent upon the massacre of a community, the transition from "nature" to "culture" always corresponds, in native thought, to the transition from the "continuous" to the "discontinuous."

But Lévi-Strauss always stressed that analysis of a myth goes beyond the analysis of its terminology or contents; he focused on discovering the relations which unite all mythologies. These relations became the ultimate objects of his structural analysis. According to Lévi-Strauss, the meaningful and unifying structures of mythology surface through the analysis of myths in the way that unconscious thought emerges into consciousness through psychoanalysis. Hence, the unveiling of the structures becomes a kind of cultural psychoanalysis. At the same time, Lévi-Strauss continually asserted that by discovering the structural "laws" of myth, he would ultimately transform fairy tales into science.

Thus, the success of the structuralist enterprise promised to allow for the apotheosis, on a primitive, unconscious level, of everyone's childhood fantasies.

But we already noted these flaws in the reference myth (no. 1) in *The Raw and the Cooked,* which described the adventures of an incestuous hero who steals birds' nests, and which is, at the same time, part of a group of 187 myths explaining the origin of cooking, the connection of cooking to thought, to neighboring tribes, and to the rest of the universe; and when Lévi-Strauss explained the jaguar's closed jaws in myth no. 7 by its reverse, the wide-open jaws in myth no. 55; and when he contrasted the helpfulness of the vultures in myth no. 1 to their "pretended" helpfulness in myth no. 55.

III

Lévi-Strauss' reading of Freud leans toward the philosophical rather than the clinical. The Oedipus complex, which, as we know, occupies a central position in Freudian theory, emerges as one of Lévi-Strauss' universal structures; and he relied on it to supply at least partial credence to the argument for structuralism. Lévi-Strauss also adapted others of Freud's ideas—defense mechanisms, repression, reaction formation, substitution, and blocking—in order to explain transformations of structures from logical to irrational and from conscious to unconscious thought. But where Freud asked his patients to free-associate in order to uncover traumatic events in their individual pasts, Lévi-Strauss listened to natives retell the traumatic memories of their tribe in well-known myths. The myths, for instance, tell of a boy who fell in love with his sister. The sister, in order to escape the advances of her brother, took refuge in the sky and became the moon; he, in turn, became the sun so that he could pursue her, but—alas— catch her only briefly during an eclipse.

Insofar as this myth of the origin of the sun and moon, and other native myths, exchange one type of reality for another, they resemble dreams. But whereas Freud used the symbolic systems of dreams to reconstruct individual history, the structuralist's ambition is to decipher the symbolic systems of myth in order to reconstruct cultural history. To justify this aim, Lévi-Strauss used Freud's fleeting allusion to the "two traumas"—personal and universal myth. In *The Future of an Illusion* Freud states that "a human child cannot successfully complete its development to the civilized stage without passing through a phase of neurosis [the individual's neurotic myth] . . . which is later overcome spontaneously [or through psychoanalysis]. . . . In just the same way, one might assume, humanity as a whole, in its development through the ages, fell into states analogous to the neuroses. . . . precipitating processes resembling repression. The residue of these repressionlike processes, which took place in antiquity, has long clung on to civilization. . . . Religion would thus be the universal obsessional neurosis of humanity."[18] Lévi-Strauss, for example, used the myth about the transformation of the sister and brother into the moon and the sun in order to show the dialectic process of transformation between the two in relation to the incest taboo.

Lévi-Strauss was also inspired by the Freudian psychoanalyst Jacques Lacan, who, in turn, acknowledged how various notions of structural anthropology had enriched his psychoanalysis. The common concern of the two men with unconscious structures —the former with tribal myth and the latter with individual thought—led a few of their followers to cooperate for a brief period. They attempted by using computers to establish the connection between the "constituent units" of myth and the "constituent units" of analysands' dreams. Inevitably, the task failed. Had it succeeded, the emergence of Lévi-Strauss' structures would have proven the scientific claims of structuralism; and the use of computer technology would have furnished it with scientific credentials. As it turned out, Lévi-Strauss' interpretation of Freud seems more literary than scientific. (This argument will be pursued in relation to Lacan, in chapter 5.)

IV

Sartre was one of the first to attack Lévi-Strauss. To Sartre, who denied the existence of an unconscious, Lévi-Strauss' unconscious mental structures were unthinkable. He also considered

Lévi-Strauss' complex method of free association as a methodological tautology which demonstrated the truth of an idea simply by showing its connection to other ideas. Finally, and not least, Sartre attacked from a Marxist position. A thorough student of Marx, he had concluded that history functions simultaneously on several levels, that

> the "forces of production" were progressively developed with the inner contradiction of private ownership and socialization: [that] the "relations of production" engendered the contradictions of the class struggle; but [that] underlying the whole drama of human history was the increasing alienation of human powers that dialectically prepared the ground for emancipation, for a humanization of man, in which nature was to be transfigured in a higher symbiosis of man and nature.[19]

Thus Sartre was bound to dismiss Lévi-Strauss' rather simplistic interpretation of Marx and the meaning of history, as well as Lévi-Strauss' neglect of individual existence.

Admittedly, Lévi-Strauss was only seventeen when he first read Marx. His special brand of Marxism appears to be related to fundamental notions of exchange and production, and to the way in which culture emerges from nature.[20] But his specific application of the dialectic ignores some of Marx's central concepts. Like Marx, Lévi-Strauss assumes that economic production arises from human needs; but whereas Marx argued that culture is conditioned by the economic structure of society, Lévi-Strauss adds the notion that culture emerges from universal unconscious structures.

Lévi-Strauss seems to be more concerned with Marx's ideas of cultural transformation than with questions of causality.

> According to dialectical materialism it should always be able to proceed by transformation, from economic or social structure to the structure of law, art, or religion. . . . [and] these transformations were dialectic, and in some cases Marx went to great lengths to discover the crucial transformations which at first sight seemed to defy analysis.[21]

Although Lévi-Strauss' dialectic "springs directly from the customs and the philosophy of the group . . . [from] whom the indi-

vidual learns his lesson . . . [from] his belief in guardian spirits
. . ." and from the fact that "society as a whole teaches its
members that their only hope of salvation, within the established
social order, lies in an absurd and despairing attempt to get free
from that order,"[22] he never touches on Marx's conclusions
about the polarization of the classes, the inevitability of revolution, or the withering away of the state. Of course, some of these
omissions result from the difficulty of applying Marxism to
primitive cultures that are pre-industrial and therefore pre-class
in our sense. Lévi-Strauss later attempted to surmount this problem when he began to differentiate between primitive ("cold")
and industrial ("hot") societies. Nevertheless, his neo-
Durkheimian vision of personal freedom—based on tribal organizations in which the means of production are communally
owned—sidestepped Marx's ideas of false consciousness as well
as of class consciousness.

But the disagreement between Lévi-Strauss and Sartre not
only revolved around ideology; it also centered on fundamental
epistemological differences. Early in his career Lévi-Strauss had
dismissed phenomenology and existentialism as opposite to true
thought in their illusions of subjectivity.[23] He was also the first
anthropologist who dared question the intellectual superiority of
philosophy. Having himself been trained in philosophy and in
law, Lévi-Strauss was well-equipped to challenge seriously the
claims of existentialism.

Aside from the rhetoric of their arguments, Lévi-Strauss and
Sartre differ in their approach to history. Lévi-Strauss interprets
the oral traditions of primitive societies in an ahistorical fashion.
For him, history is reconstituted each time a myth is retold or the
past is recollected. History, rather than being a series of "objective" events tied to a specific era, exists within an interplay of
mental structures that takes place at a specific "moment." By
having the past become part of the present, Lévi-Strauss' theory
discounts traditional theories of progress or evolution. Leach explains Lévi-Strauss' system well, when he suggests that data
stored in human memories can be compared to a very complicated computer that sorts out information according to an "ad-
justable program."[24]

Whereas Kant, for example, approaches experience in terms

of basic *Anschauungen* (kinds of intuition about space, time, and causation) which do not extend to what is behind the phenomena, Lévi-Strauss assumes an as yet unknown structural order which "directs" all social variables.[25] It is an unconscious order, similar to Durkheim's collective unconscious, which appears to be—at least until its final unveiling—some sort of planned disorder. Durkheim, however, postulated "two beings in man: an individual being which has its foundation in the organism, . . . and a social being which represents . . . society.[26] Lévi-Strauss extends this notion to include humanity—on the level of deep, unveiled structures.

Sartre, for whom consciousness is linked to personal action, neither recognizes Lévi-Strauss' type of order nor the destiny it implies. He objected to Lévi-Strauss' approach to the study of man on existential grounds. In Sartre's view, structuralism is remote from human existence and even denies its fundamental condition—that is, freedom. Consequently, structuralism presents a distorted and even morally suspect concept of this existence. Sartre considers the structuralist approach to be guilty of transforming men into static, timeless objects, related to things in the world and to other men in purely formal, objective and timeless ways. For Sartre, "the world is outside . . . neither language nor culture are in the individual . . . but the individual exists in his culture and in his language, which means within a special set of conditions."[27] Sartre maintains that each person discovers consciousness of self and things in praxis, so that it [consciousness] "is no more than an apprehension of reality"[28]—which implies, of course, outer reality, not inner structure. Sartre's dialectic is between men and their surroundings and the processes through which men consciously act in relation to these surroundings. Lévi-Strauss' dialectic is between men as social beings and men as the unconscious bearers of a universal order (derived from as yet undiscovered structures). Existentialist "surface" opposes structuralist "depth."

Sartre was only one of Lévi-Strauss' critics. Lefebvre attacked structural anthropology for confusing the search for unconscious structures of myth with certain invariable natural laws which govern humanity; and he accused him of avoiding politics. Lévi-Strauss had not engaged in any of the controversies that

divided the French during the Algerian war; he had been occupied by the search for the structures that would prove the validity of his method. This circumstance led Lefebvre to denigrate
structuralism as politically effete, a "fetichism of knowledge,
baptised 'epistemology,' which sacrifices the division of labor on
the intellectual level, and which protects the division of knowledge under a mantle of encyclopaedism." [29]

Still, the nonpolitical nature of structuralism had appealed to
more conservative thinkers such as Ricoeur, whose hermeneutics
were increasingly linked to structural linguistics. Ricoeur, however, attacks Lévi-Strauss' linguistic base. He objected to a
linguistic "system which is not established at the level of the
speaker's consciousness but at a lower level . . . and to the consequences from this epistemological model which directly affect
the presuppositions of existentialism," [30] because they called his
own hermeneutics (his philosophy of will, of personal choice over
good and evil) into question. According to Ricoeur, Lévi-
Strauss' theory only "considers the closed system of discrete
[linguistic] units which compose a language; [this] no longer suf-
fices when one approaches discourse in act," for it leaves out
questions of morals and ethics. [31]

V

Though Lévi-Strauss' claims to science were never really established, his theory of the elusive, unconscious structures did lead
to the creation of various new subjects of inquiry such as the
relationships between the structures of all signs in language, their
function within messages, and their rapport with other sign systems, such as music, gestures, body language. Nevertheless, these
inquiries, though addressing many different problems, might be
said to be vulnerable to accusations of being based on "faith" or
"metaphysics." Still, if we accept the notions that sociologists
hold about knowledge and science, [32] then we can argue, with
some reservations, that between 1956 and 1968 (among French
intellectuals) Lévi-Strauss' structuralism served functions roughly
similar to those performed by Parsons' structural-functionalism in the 1940s and 1950s in America (among social scien-

tists). Parsons, who then based his theories on certain similarities in the work of Alfred Marshall, Pareto, Durkheim, and Max Weber, had by 1951 constructed a system which was to account for all social reality. The thinking of both Lévi-Strauss and Parsons had aroused enough interest to serve as stimuli for wide-ranging discussion. It is in the all-encompassing range of their aims that the two men are comparable. There are other likenesses: both became prominent during a period of relative political conservatism; and both inspired a flurry of academic activity. Their underlying assumptions, however, are in the one instance so typically French and in the other so typically American, that it may be useful to point to the differences between them.

Both Lévi-Strauss and Parsons focus on universal patterns of oppositions to explain social reality. The Parsonian actor must come to terms with one of the five universal dilemmas: affectivity versus affective neutrality, specificity versus diffuseness, universalism versus particularism, quality versus performance, self-orientation versus collective orientation. Lévi-Strauss' dilemmas, on the other hand, take place in the realm of myth and language; their resolution arises through the interplay of universal and generally unconscious mental structures. In other words, whereas Parsons' system is ultimately bound to decisions by individual actors (actors confined to social reality), Lévi-Strauss' system is not. Furthermore, Lévi-Strauss focuses on language, a symbolic system, in contrast to Parsons, whose system rests on analytic realism. Parsonian theories of motivation and emotional "need-dispositions," which are said to influence and modify social systems, are far removed from Lévi-Strauss' synchronic and diachronic analyses of tribal myths.

Lévi-Strauss and Parsons also differ in their interpretation of Freud. As stated earlier, Lévi-Strauss leans on the work of Jacques Lacan, especially on his notion of the *imaginary,* whereas Parsons "adapts psychoanalytic concepts and analyses of motivation to the technical needs of sociological theory, in terms of problems stated in sociological terms."[33] Parsons attempted to observe unconscious phenomena through behavior, so his apprehension of Freud tends to focus on the later Freud, who tried to test his empirical observations scientifically. In addition, Parsons suggests that social equilibrium is maintained with the aid of many social institutions, while Lévi-Strauss argues that social cohesion depends primarily on the strength of a common mythology.

Both Parsons and Lévi-Strauss pay homage to Durkheim and emphasize his theories of social solidarity, although the former leans on the organic solidarity of industrial societies and the latter on the mechanical solidarity of tribal societies. According to Lévi-Strauss, an individual is automatically and directly bound to his entire society, with its more or less organized totality of beliefs and sentiments.[34] For him, tribal myths emanate from a reality which is *sui generis*. Rituals that are to bring rain, fertility, or other desired goods—which we dismiss as irrational or magical thinking—become to Lévi-Strauss social facts of the same order as cooking or hunting.

VI

As we know, structuralist theories—either in Lévi-Strauss' original context or in their "deviant" forms—have few immediate political consequences. Lévi-Strauss does not deal with political conditions, because for him human behavior is preordained by unconscious forces beyond human control. The issue of human equality is symbolically solved before it is ever raised, so that structuralism's most radical components (the unconscious structures), insofar as they are beyond the reach of politics, are also its most conservative elements. Yet the implications of some of the more popularized versions and misinterpretations of structuralism are thought to bolster democracy and egalitarianism more effectively than constitutional guarantees. According to these notions, structuralism adds weight to cherished principles of human equality. It does away with disturbing differences between "savage" and "civilized" societies, between developed countries and the Third World to reveal the common human denominator in the inequities of race, class, wealth, and state of social advance; it thus implicitly dismisses invidious racial theories like those by Herrnstein or Jensen as the politicalization of appearance rather than reality.

VII

Lévi-Strauss' structuralism promised not only a new theory of nature and culture, but political and ideological unity as well. Its fusion of radical thought with political conservatism appealed to liberal reformists and to Marxist "minimalists," to all those who did not want to take "hard" political positions. Nevertheless, the social and economic upheaval that occurred in France during May and June of 1968 brought hard political realities to the forefront and quickly shunted structuralism to the sidelines. Unquestionably, the events of this brief period played a large role in prompting Lévi-Strauss to return to his earlier concern with philosophy and kinship structures.

But in the final pages of *L'homme nu*, after disposing of all the "pseudo-structuralists," he again reaffirms a belief in his own theory, suggesting that we apply "real" structural techniques to all of culture. He proposes what might be called a "superstructuralist" work-hypothesis for structuralism itself, which leads him to locate the four "major families"—mathematics, natural languages (these subsume the sciences), music, and myths—on opposite poles of two intersecting axes. This first appears to be a systematic procedure but soon turns out to be a convoluted exercise of transpositions, transformations, and oppositions along and between the "scientific" axis (mathematics and language) and the "sensual" one (music and myth). And when, for the sake of his argument and for symmetry, he states that "myth had to die for its form to depart like the soul leaving the body, in order to demand from music a means of reincarnation,"[35] or when he talks of the meetings of molecules of sound or image and those of sense as a "sort of copulation,"[36] then it is clear that he has soared into metaphysics—or bad poetry. Nevertheless, the scientific posturing, with oppositions, axes, and four-cornered analyses, is oddly reminiscent of the Parsonian four-cornered framework. Lévi-Strauss has apparently incorporated the network of "mini-structuralisms" into a "macro-structuralism."

Lévi-Strauss never seemed to realize that his questions were generally more scientific than his answers. For he sidesteps the whole question of science and myth when he talks about the ultimate and fundamental opposition of structuralism as represented in Hamlet's dilemma, which he finds to be at the bottom of everything. He says that Hamlet has no choice between being and nonbeing: he is eternally caught and forced to swing between ever-new contradictions until he dies. Thus life and death, Lévi-Strauss concludes, are both the fundamental and the ultimate opposition of structuralism. This is, of course, pure metaphysics. Inevitably, Lévi-Strauss was attacked for this conclusion to his *Mythologies*—a conclusion that appeared to belie the scientific pretensions. For this final structuralist message seemed to carry religious overtones. Clearly, Lévi-Strauss had come a long way. Perhaps not only the challenges to his theory, but his own disillusionments as well, made him retreat to a more narrow anthropology.

But even if structuralism as a "grand theory" failed, one cannot deny the impetus it gave to the French intellectual community. Nor can one question its author's genius and his intellectual versatility. Though his structuralism's complex dialectic at times seemed to rely too much upon Lévi-Strauss' free association of ideas, its failure as an all-inclusive theory should neither obscure its influence in other fields, particularly in anthropology, nor diminish Lévi-Strauss' stature. Nor can we forget that this theoretical invention did accommodate underlying political ends, insofar as the shifting focus from existentialism to structuralism (with all the diversionary discussions) was part of the intellectual climate that produced a more realistic appraisal of the Communist reality and of Marxism. Hence, Lévi-Strauss unconsciously supplied the French Left with an honorable means of reevaluating both Marxism and existentialism. Inevitably, his grand theory was bound to collapse.

Notes

1. In *Tristes Tropiques* (1955), p. 57, for example, Lévi-Strauss states that he "had been making a collection of exotica since early childhood. Later on (p. 59), he recalls his "search, on a limestone plateau in Languedoc, for the line of contact between two geological strata."

2. Leach, *Claude Lévi-Strauss*, p. 23: "The influence of Jakobson's style of phonemic analysis on the work of Lévi-Strauss has been very marked. . . . Noam Chomsky specifi-

cally recognizes the fundamental importance of Jakobson's main theory of distinctive features and phonetic universals, which is all that matters as far as Lévi-Strauss is concerned." Lévi-Strauss himself repeatedly acknowledges Jakobson's influence on his own work; for example, in his preface to Jakobson's *Six Lectures on Sound and Meaning.*

3. See my own argument in the introduction.

4. Lévi-Strauss, *Tristes Tropiques,* (New York: Atheneum, 1968), p. 60.

5. *Ibid.,* pp. 60–61.

6. *Ibid.,* p. 61.

7. Michel Panoff, "Lévi-Strauss tel qu'en lui-même. . . ." *Esprit* (November 1973), no. 3, p. 705.

8. Hawkes, *Structuralism and Semiotics,* pp. 77–78.

9. Lévi-Strauss, *Structural Anthropology* p. 33.

10. *Ibid.,* p. 34.

11. This point is repeated throughout. See especially *Structural Anthropology* (pp. 32 and 39).

12. Lévi-Strauss, "Language and Kinship," *Structural Anthropology,* p. 32.

13. Lévi-Strauss, "The Structural Study of Myth," *Structural Anthropology,* pp. 208–9.

14. *Ibid.,* p. 208.

15. *Ibid.,* p. 211.

16. *Ibid.,* pp. 209–14.

17. *Ibid.,* p. 221.

18. Freud, *The Future of an Illusion,* p. 70. In this context, we might also recall that Freud himself, and later on Roheim and Kardiner, related psychoanalysis and tribal mythology. Their findings of similarities, however, were not expanded into such a wide-ranging theory, although they would have agreed with Lévi-Strauss that the natives' myths "confuse" reality.

19. Mark Poster, p. 70.

20. This is implied in *Tristes Tropiques,* pp. 60–63, and again in the discussion with Sartre in the last chapter of *The Savage Mind,* "History and Dialectic," pp. 245–69.

21. *Lévi-Strauss, Structural Anthropology,* pp. 329–30.

22. Lévi-Strauss, *Tristes Tropiques,* p. 42.

23. *Ibid.,* p. 62.

24. Leach, "Claude Lévi-Strauss—Anthropologist and Philosopher," p. 25.

25. "Kant, Immanuel," *Encyclopedia of the Social Sciences,* p. 349.

26. Durkheim, *Elementary Forms of Religious Life,* p. 29.

27. Verstraeten, "Lévi-Strauss ou la tentation du neant," p. 81.

28. Pouillon, "Analyse dialectique," p. 64.

29. Henri Lefebvre, "Claude Lévi-Strauss et le nouvel éléatisme," in *Au delà du structuralisme,* (Paris: Anthropos, 1971), p. 11.

30. Reagan and Stewart, eds., *The Philosophy of Paul Ricoeur* (Boston: Beacon Press, 1978), p. 90.

31. *Ibid.*, p. 118.

32. Robert K. Merton, *The Sociology of Science* (Chicago: University of Chicago Press, 1973; see especially "Science and the Social Order" (1938), pp. 254–66, where Merton points out that "scientific truth is a product of cultures." By now this is taken for granted.

33. Talcott Parsons, "Psychoanalysis and Social Structure," in *Essays in Sociological Theory* (New York: Free Press, 1949) p. 364.

34. Émile Durkheim, *The Division of Labor in Society* (New York: Free Press, 1933).

35. Lévi-Strauss, *L'homme nu*, p. 583.

36. *Ibid.*, p. 586.

Bibliography

Abel, Lionel. "Sartre vs. Lévi-Strauss." *Commonweal* (1966), 84(17):364–68.

Aron, Raymond. *German Sociology*. London: Heinemann, 1957.

Barbut, Marc. "Sur le sens du mot structure en mathématiques." *Les Temps Modernes* (November 1966), 22:792–814.

Bendow, Burton. "The Instinct for Order." *Nation*, December 28, 1970, pp. 692–94.

Boon, James A. *From Symbolism to Structuralism*. New York: Harper & Row, 1972.

Boudon, Raymond. *A quoi sert la notion de structure?* Paris: Gallimard, 1968. Translated as *The Uses of Structuralism*. London: Heinemann, 1971.

Bourdieu, Pierre. "Champ intellectual et project créateur." *Les Temps Modernes* (November 1966), 22:865–906.

———. *Le métier de sociologue*. Paris: Mouton, 1973.

Bourdieu, Pierre and Jean Claude Passeron. "Sociology and Philosophy in France Since 1945." *Social Research* (Spring 1967) 34(1):162–212.

Calogeras, Roy C. "Lévi-Strauss and Freud: Their 'Structural' Approaches to Myths." *American Imago* (Spring 1973) 30:57–79.

Chomsky, Noam. *Language and Mind*. New York: Harcourt Brace, 1968.

Clastres, Pierre. "Le clou de la croisière." *Les Temps Modernes* (1971), 27:2345–50.

Courtès, Joseph. *Lévi-Strauss et les contraintes de la pensée mythique*. France: Mame, 1973.

Cuisinier, Jean. "Formes de la parenté." *Esprit* (November 1963), no. 11.

DeGeorge, Richard and Fernande. *The Structuralists from Marx to Lévi-Strauss*. New York: Doubleday Anchor, 1972.

de Heusch, Luc. "Lévi-Strauss's structuralisme." *L'Arc*, no. 26.

Domenach, Jean-Marie. "Le requiem structuraliste." *Esprit* (March 1973), no. 3, pp. 692–703.

Durkheim, Emile. *Essays on Sociology and Philosophy*. New York: Harper Torchbooks, 1960.

—— *The Elementary Forms of the Religious Life*. New York: Free Press, 1965.

Durkheim, Émile and Marcel Mauss. *Primitive Classification*. Chicago: University of Chicago Press, 1963.

Ehrmann, Jacques. *Structuralism*. New York: Doubleday Anchor, 1966.

Freud, Sigmund. *The Future of an Illusion*. London: Liveright, 1949.

—— *Totem and Taboo*. New York: Norton, 1950.

Genet, Jean. "Un Certain Regard," review in *New Yorker*. 1968.

Godelier, Maurice. "Système, structure et contradiction dans 'le capital.' " *Les Temps Modernes* (1966), 22:829–65.

Greene, Judith. *Psycholinguistics*. Middlesex and Baltimore: Penguin, 1972.

Greimas, A.-J. "Structure et histoire." *Les Temps Modernes* (November 1966), 22:815–27.

Hawkes, Terence. *Structuralism and Semiotics*. Berkeley: University of California Press, 1977.

Hayes, E. Nelson and Tanya Hayes. *Claude Lévi-Strauss: The Anthropologist as Hero*. Cambridge: M.I.T. Press, 1970.

Jaeggi, Urs. *Ordnung und Chaos: Structuralismus als Methode und Mode*. Frankfurt: Suhrkamp, 1968.

Jakobson, Roman. *Six Lectures on Sound and Meaning*. Cambridge: M.I.T. Press, 1978.

"Kant, Immanuel." *Encyclopedia of the Social Sciences*. New York: Macmillan, 1937.

Kurzweil, Edith. "The Mythology of Structuralism." *Partisan Review*. (Fall 1975), no. 3, pp. 416–30.

Lane, Michael. *Introduction to Structuralism*. New York: Basic Books, 1970.

Lanteri-Laura, G. "History and Structure in Anthropological Knowledge." *Social Research* (Spring 1967), 34(1):113–61.

Leach, Edmund. "Lévi-Strauss in the Garden of Eden: An Examination of Some Recent Developments in the Analysis of Myth." In William A. Lessa and Evon Z. Vogt, eds., *Reader in Comparative Religion*, pp. 575–81. New York: Harper and Row, 1965.

—— "Claude Lévi-Strauss—Anthropologist and Philosopher." *New Left Review* (1965), no. 34, pp. 12–27.

Lévi-Strauss, Claude. *Tristes Tropiques*. Paris: Plon, 1955; New York: Atheneum, 1968.

—— *Anthropologie structurale*. Paris: Plon, 1958. Translated as *Structural Anthropology*. New York: Basic Books, 1963.

—— "Réflexions sur l'atome de parenté." *Anthropologie structurale*, pp. 5–30. Paris: Plon, 1958.

—— "Four Winnebago Myths." In Stanley Diamond, ed., *Culture and History*, pp. 351–62. New York: Columbia University Press, 1960.

—— *La pensée sauvage*. Paris: Plon, 1962. Translated as *The Savage Mind*. Chicago: University of Chicago Press, 1966.

—— *Le Cru et le cuit*. Paris: Plon, 1964. Mythologiques I. Translated as *The Raw and the Cooked*. New York: Harper and Row, 1968.

—— "The Bear and the Barber." In William A. Lessa and Evon Z. Vogt, eds., *Reader in Comparative Religion*, pp. 289–97. New York: Harper and Row, 1965.

—— "Vingt ans après." *Les Temps Modernes* (1967), 23:385–504.

—— *Du miel aux cendres*. Paris: Plon, 1968. Mythologique III. Translated as *From Honey to Ashes*. London: Jonathan Cape, 1973.

——*L'Origine des manières de table*. Paris: Plon, 1968. Translated as *The Origin of Table Manners*. New York: Harper and Row.

——*L'Homme nu*. Paris: Plon, 1971. Mythologique IV.

—— "Comment ils meurent." *Esprit* (April 1971), no. 4, pp. 694–706.

Lyons, John. *Noam Chomsky*. New York: Viking, 1970.

—— *New Horizons in Linguistics*. Middlesex and Baltimore: Pelican, 1970.

Macherey, Pierre. "L'analyse littéraire tombeau des structures." *Les Temps Modernes* (November 1966), 22:907–29.

Malmberg, Bertil. *Les nouvelles tendances de la linguistique*. Paris: Presses Universitaires de France, 1966.

Mannoni, O. "Terrains de mission?" *Les Temps Modernes* (1971), 27:2351–53.

Maybury-Lewis, D. Review of "Mythologiques: du miel aux cendres," by C. Lévi-Strauss. In *American Anthropologist* (February 1969), 71(1):114.

—— Review of "Le Totémism Aujourdhui," by Claude Lévy-Strauss. In *American Anthropologist*, 65:931.

Mill, J. S. *Auguste Comte and Positivism*. Ann Arbor: University of Michigan Press, 1965.

Mintz, Sidney. "Le rouge et le noir." *Les Temps Modernes* (1971), 27:2354–61.

Monod, Jean. "Oraison funèbre pour une vieille dame." *Les Temps Modernes* (1971), 27:2393–2400.

Panoff, Michel. "Il faut qu'un mythe soit ouvert ou fermé." *Esprit* (April 1971), no. 4, pp. 707–22.

Paz, Octavio. *Claude Lévi-Strauss—An Introduction*. Ithaca: Cornell University Press, 1970.

Piaget, Jean. *Le structuralisme*. Paris: Presses Universitaires de France, 1968. Translated as *Structuralism*. New York: Basic Books, 1970.

Pingaud, Bernard. "Comment on devient structuraliste" *Arc*, no. 26, pp. 2–6.

Poster, Mark. *Existential Marxism in Postwar France*. Princeton: Princeton University Press, 1975.

Pouillon, Jean. "Analyse dialectique d'une relation dialectique analytique." *Arc*, no. 26, pp. 60–65.

—— " 'Présentation': un essay de définition." *Les Temps Modernes* (November 1966), 22:2769–827.

—— "Résponse à un ventriloque." *Les Temps Modernes* (1971), pp. 27:2401–7.

Reagan, Charles E. and David Stewart, eds., *The Philosophy of Paul Ricoeur*. Boston: Beacon Press, 1978.

Rossi, Ino. *The Unconscious in Culture*. New York: Dutton, 1974.

Sapir, Edward. *Language*. New York: Harvest Books, 1921.

Sartre, Jean-Paul. *Critique de la Raison Dialectique*. Paris: Gallimard, 1960.

Sartre, Jean-Paul. *Search for a Method.* New York: Vintage Books, 1963.

Saussure, Ferdinand de. *Course in General Linguistics.* New York: McGraw-Hill, 1959.

Sontag, Susan. "The Anthropologist as Hero." In *Against Interpretation,* pp. 69–81. New York: Delta Books, 1961.

Stavenhagen, Rodolfo. "Comment décoloniser les sciences sociales appliqués." *Les Temps Modernes* (1971), 27:2362–86.

Verstraeten, P. "Lévi-Strauss ou la tentation du néant." *Les Temps Modernes* (July 1963), 19:66–109.

II. Louis Althusser
Marxism and Structuralism

Louis Althusser, born in Algeria, turned thirty in 1948, the year he received his degree in philosophy from the *Eéole Normale Superieure,* began teaching there, and joined the Communist Party. Before then, he had been in the Resistance and had been active in Catholic student and youth organizations. But his decision to join the Party has dominated both his theoretical work and his life, if only because whatever he said or wrote would be judged along party lines. Thus, his silences were as duly noted as were his statements and his "resurrection" in March 1976, when he denounced Soviet repression and Stalinism. These criticisms, although at first tucked away in an introduction to Dominique Lecourt's book on Trofim Lysenko (the Stalinist scientist who found a difference between bourgeois and communist biology) made news.[1] For by then Althusser was one of the few remaining intellectuals within the Party who still hoped to construct a non-repressive theory for a Socialist state.

Aware that Soviet communism limited individual freedom as much as fascism did, Althusser set out to examine the contradictions inherent in Marxist philosophy which might have led to totalitarian practices. But Marxist philosophy, in Paris, could accommodate both Stalinism and Marx's humanism, which had become an addendum to the popular version of existentialism. From the outset, Althusser rejected both definitions of Marxism. He began with a critique of the most prevalent humanistic French Marxisms, which locate the start of Marx's economic and political analyses in the *Economic and Philosophical Manuscripts* (1843–44, first published in 1931), and then find that passages in the *Grundrisse* (notes for *Capital* written in 1857–58, first published in 1939–40) pick up these same thoughts. Such a reading of Marx, argued Althusser, assumes that the meaning of the texts, or of the term *alienation*, for instance, are the same in both texts and "forgets" that their reading itself belongs to bourgeois philosophy. Althusser actually wanted to sever all links to non-Marxist philosophy, especially the Hegelian, and therefore rejected the philosophical premise that man is a self-creating being arising out of the dialectic between his labor and the natural world it transforms. And he rejected the "corollary" interpretation of the superstructure (thinking determined by economics) as a reflection of the productive process that would allow, as it had for Kautsky, Bernstein, and other leaders of the Second International, the passive wait for the revolution as the inevitable result of the development of capitalism. Revolution, he argued, must be prepared and organized. Briefly put, he insisted that politics and ideology had to be dealt with autonomously. So he embarked on his "lonely road" that would combine his interest in philosophy with a passion for politics through the understanding of all past and future party behavior in order to provide a viable Marxist "Praxis." [2]

Pitting himself against all reformist and revisionist practices (socialist, social-democratic, or communist), Althusser attracted followers beyond the borders of France, particularly in the Third World, where practicing revolutionaries enjoy greater possibilities in an atmosphere of anti-imperialism, anti-colonialism, and anti-Americanism. But even in Paris, where, according to Raymond Aron, Marxism was so widespread that it had been posthumously naturalized, Althusser's "rereading" promised a revival. Yet this revival not only depended upon exorcising Marx's Hegelianism and discovering the "scientific" Marx in specific, later works, but was helped, in part, by reading Marx from a structuralist perspective. Althusser's readers have to be fluent in Hegel and Kant, Nietzsche and Spinoza, Husserl and Heidegger, as well as in structural linguistics, psychoanalysis, and Marxism. Undoubtedly, many understood his political aim without following his complex arguments. Aron, who, though critical and dismissive, had found Sartre the only Communist or sympathizer he could talk to, ranked Althusser as the "second-best" imaginary Marxist.[3]

Althusser became prominent about 1965—long after Sartre and Lévi-Strauss—when his essays were collected in *For Marx*

(1965) and *Reading Capital* (1968). By then he and Roger Garaudy had become the two leading Party intellectuals. In January 1967, at a meeting of the central committee, they had a well-publicized disagreement over whose theory was to prevail officially.[4] But after 1956, when Khrushchev denounced Stalin and the cult of personality, many leftists had reexamined their allegiances and beliefs and had broken with the Party. Some tended to gravitate toward a Marxist humanism, and "Hegelian Marxism"; others looked to Althusser, who promised to prove that Marxism was a science.

George Lichtheim noted in *From Marx to Hegel*[5] that the *Times Literary Supplement* first drew attention to Althusser in December 1966, that soon afterward he was alleged to have inspired his former student Regis Debray in his theories of guerilla warfare in Bolivia, and that he was next connected to the activities of the late Che Guevara during the Cuban revolution. Lichtheim also commented on Althusser's Leninist stance (that lack of concern for individual freedom) in the face of Russian intervention in Hungary and Czechoslovakia. For Althusser did not protest against these flagrant interferences in national sovereignty; he seemed to consider them "necessary means to save socialism" from the revisionists in order to bring about the revolution. Furthermore, Althusser seemed to be acquiescing in Soviet directives when in May 1968 he failed to join the students. This made his Party ties blatant. By then, it had become clear that Althusser's theory was unequipped to deal with such practical questions as national borders, military interference, or inconsistencies between Soviet domestic and foreign policy. Had his Theory—an epistemology that was to operate above the customary level of Marxist mediation between theory and practice[6]— been viable, he could have "introduced" true socialism. But Althusser's "symptomatic" reading of Marx which is "modeled" on the Freudian analyst's reading of his patient's utterances had not yet been completed; and he had already begun to accept a number of Leninist notions which "temporarily" condone the repressive functions of the state.

What then was Althusser's theory? How did it come about that events in such distant places as Bolivia or Cuba could be related to him, and that his reinterpretations of Marx and Lenin were to have so little impact on the French events of May and June 1968? The answers to these questions not only depend upon the observer's own political bias, but have to do with the specific history of communism in France.

II

Before World War II, Marxism had little impact in France: Blanqui's Jacobinism and Prudhon's syndicalism had dominated French workers' movements, although the "young" philosophers (Georges Politzer, Henri Lefebvre, Norbert Gutermann, Georges Friedmann, Pierre Mohange, and Paul Nizan) had begun to propagate Marx's philosophy between 1929 and 1934. In 1939, another group (around *La Pensée*) had started to use "dialectical materialism." But Communist leadership in the French Resistance and in the postwar political situation predisposed French intellectuals to ignore as long as possible the repressive components of the Soviet regime. When forced to choose between supporting American policies and NATO, on the one hand, and the Communists' identification with the cause of Socialism and peace on the other hand, they were bound to identify with Russia.

In addition, Marx's works had been translated late, haphazardly, and badly. Stalinist interpretations of Marx by intellectuals were therefore not surprising. According to Mark Poster:

> Revolutionary theory was schematized into two parts: dialectical materialism, a phrase never used by Marx, and historical materialism. The dialectic emerged as a metaphysical postulate about objective, exterior reality. Materialism signified that "matter is primary," that the mind is secondary . . . since it is a reflection of matter. . . . Historical materialism meant little more than economism: the economic base determined the political and legal superstructures in unilineal, mechanical manner.[7]

This version of Marxist theory, says Poster, resulted in abstract analyses of the economy, in empty hopes for a revolution, and in (non-revolutionary) strong trade unionism under DeGaulle.

Althusser hoped to avoid all these outcomes. He had introduced *For Marx* by explaining and excusing the Communists' blindness, including his own, after World War II. At that time he still believed that the French Communist Party would detach itself from Moscow, or that the party line of the Communist International would change, if only it were presented with a viable theory to practice. He agreed with Sartre that "intellectuals had felt beleaguered and . . . had been able to salvage themselves only through action"—i.e., in party politics and ideology. Hence, they neglected Marxist philosophy. French intellectuals, unlike their German, Polish, English, or Italian peers, who were denied all meaningful activity in bourgeois society, allegedly suffered because they, too, were the beneficiaries of the successful bourgeois revolution. Hence French leftists had not needed to "seek their salvation at the side of the working class" and were unfamiliar with Marx's works, especially with his later "scientific" works.[8] And, argued Althusser, even familiarity with such theorists as Kautsky, Luxemburg, Bernstein, Della Volpe, Labriola, or Lukács, whose humanistic bent he rejected, might have made it easier for them to understand Marx's political economics.

Essentially, Althusser set out to investigate "the specific nature of the science and philosophy founded by Marx." But his concern with epistemological questions also embraced the crisis of postwar Stalinism, the repressive components of which he set out to eradicate. This meant that he did not go along with such Marxist philosophers as Adam Schaff who believed that "partyhood"—analogous to brotherhood—would overcome the conflict between the person and his party through internalization of party credos.[9] Rather, he considered himself a free-floating intellectual, part of the Parisian community, whose existentialism, phenomenology, and academicism he nonetheless disdained as unscientific, idealist, and as counterproductive to his own "correct" reading of Marx.[10] Althusser's work could not, however, escape the influence of the intellectual discourse around him. In spite of his later and frequent denials that he was a structuralist, he certainly shared preoccupations about unconscious structures with Lévi-Strauss, Foucault, and Lacan. In fact he credited the latter along with Freud for elaborating on the " 'meaning' of speaking and listening [which] reveals beneath the innocence of speech and hearing the culpable depth of a second *quite different* discourse, the discourse of the unconscious." [11] He then applied this technique to a rereading of Marx. And he explained how Marx's informed gaze, when analyzing Ricardo's or Smith's economics could on second reading articulate what at first had been left out. Althusser's literary criticism, such as *The Piccolo Teatro: Bertolazzi and Brecht,* though looking for Marxist themes as well, emphasized the existence of the "visible" and the "invisible" of this reading. [12]

By now Althusser would play down these influences but would not deny them. He also used two other theoretical concepts in his method. He derived the first concept from Bachelard, a historian of science who maintained that: in the course of the development of a science, epistemological acts and thresholds suspend the continuous accumulation of knowledge, interrupt its slow development, force it to enter a new time, cut it off from its empirical origin and original motivations, cleanse it of its imaginary complicities, and direct historical analysis away from the search for silent beginnings toward the search for a new type of rationality and its various effects. [13] In other words, Bachelard postulated scientific epochs that ostensibly could create epistemological breaks of a kind Althusser then located in Marx's works.

The second, though less prominent, concept had its roots in the method of structural linguistics—in the notion that a system of lexical relationships is part of our linguistic competence. Since a reader's competence comes from experience and knowledge, some structural linguists allow for a "super-reader" as a tool of analysis, as a technique to "reread" a text. For an informed super-reader is able "to work through and to sniff out places which can be shown as particularly significant in relation to the specified knowledge which he [the super-reader] possesses." [14] Althusser's intimate acquaintance with Marx's texts allowed him to function as a super-reader—to liberate Marxism from its customary reading. He could immerse himself in the texts and reinterpret them in relation to specific events in Marx's life so as to understand the problems of scientific Marxism through the theory itself.

Althusser complicated his reading of Marx by embracing Lacan's Freud. Because some components in Freud's writing, like those in Marx's, previously had led to humanizing, Althusser perceived parallels between Lacan's scientific psychoanalysis and his own scientific socialism. Extending the comparison on an epistemological level, Althusser postulated that Marxist theory, which contradicts itself on various levels, and which contains gaps, silences, and absences, should be reread "symptomatically." Such a rereading would uncover hidden unconscious structures by interpreting transpositions, absurdities, and errors; it would thus bring forth a different text—a text whose theoretical problematics would be recognized through the symptoms that had caused these problematics. Thus the "objective text," that is both Marx's work and his life, could be "decoded." [15] And "a study of the psychological structure of Marx's personality" and of its origins and history, for example, would cast light on the style of intervention, concept, and investigation that differentiates the early writings from the later ones, when Marx's "theoretical intelligence" had already been formed and he had learned "the way of saying what he was going to discover in the very way he must forget." [16]

Althusser had to separate scientific reality from the process by which we get to know this reality. And, since the "thought-objects" of Marxism, in the form of crises in capitalism and the impending revolution, must already be contained in the preexisting concepts and theories it expects to transform, Althusser emphasized the continuation of transformations in Marxist historical-scientific practice.

Essentially, Althusser postulates three bodies of concepts which are at work in this process—Generalities I, II, and III. The distinctions among Althusser's Generalities are described by Callinicos:

> Generality I forms the starting point, the raw material of theoretical practice, that is to say, the body of *concepts*—either scientific or ideological—upon which the process will set to work in order to transform them. Generality II is the corpus of concepts whose more or less contradictory unity constitutes the "theory" of the science in question by defining the field in which the problems of the science must necessarily be posed—in other words, the science's problematic. Generality III is the "concrete-in-thought," the knowledge that is pro-

duced by the work of Generality II on Generality I, of the concepts defined by the science's problematic on the pre-existing theories that constitute the prehistory of this stage in the science's development.[17]

The relation of this science to the real, Althusser argued, is both anchored and changed through its own development. Thus, he needed a new theory of reading, the principles of which could govern the reading and the theory contained in the text—could replace the direct relation between reader and text. Because "the precondition of a reading of Marx is a Marxist theory, . . . that is, a theory of epistemological history which is Marxism itself," Althusser recognized that reading can never be "innocent" and always, at least implicitly, depends upon a theory that determines the character of the reading.[18] Simply put, Marxist philosophy must exist in order to exist—a tautology Althusser expected to resolve on his road to true Marxist practice.

Reminding the reader that, in his *German Ideology,* Marx had dismissed philosophy as having neither a history nor a subject and that Lenin too had found philosophy useless—it lives on politics and politics are usually fatal to philosophy[19]—Althusser began to reread the different meanings of alienation in the *Manuscripts of 1844* and in *Capital.* In the course of this rereading, according to Norman Geras, he distinguished in Marx the theoretical deficiencies, the terminological ambiguities, and the ideological "survivals" of the early works from the later "scientific concepts."[20] Thus, he perceived an epistemological break in Marx that denoted the new problematic which had cut all links to bourgeois ideology; he then returned to events in Marx's life and works. This epistemological break, he argued, had occurred when Marx wrote *The German Ideology,* although it could already be detected in the *Theses on Feuerbach.* Althusser considered everything from Marx's Doctoral Dissertation to the *Manuscripts of 1844* and *The Holy Family,* the "early works"; his writings from 1845 to 1857 (first notes for *Capital,* the *Manifesto, Poverty of Philosophy, Wages, Price and Profit*), the "transitional works." Only after 1857, beginning with the *Grundrisse,* had Marx fully "matured" and dealt with his science—that is, with political economy.

III

In France, where the political power of the Communist Party, linked to a strong trade union movement, continues to "promise" a socialist society, Marxist theorists count as the intellectual avant-garde. Althusser, though extremely difficult to understand, found a ready audience because Marxist "family discussions" and quarrels have potential political implications. A rupture in Marx's system might have repercussions not only for past Marxiana, but for future political actions.

By locating a major shift in Marx about 1845 and arguing that from then on Marx was committed solely to the proletarian revolution, Althusser could repudiate the early Marx along with all reformist and humanist Marxists.[21] And this refutation itself, by discrediting the basic assumptions of figures like Sartre, Lefebvre, or Garaudy, might have had far-reaching consequences. In the process, however, he did not escape accusations that to explain Marxism through Marx's life and works might be circular. But, as he showed how Marx and Engels had "settled accounts with . . . (their) former political conscience"[22] through the epistemological break, Althusser established himself through his method. The structuralist cast of this method, of course, was attuned to the discourse around him as well as to his rereading of Marx. Sometimes he sounded like a psycho-historian: when, for example, he discussed Marx's Hegelianism as an "adolescent phase" that inspired only the *1844 Manuscripts,* which deliberately attempted to invert Hegelian idealism into Feuerbachian pseudo-materialism; or when, in the early Marx, he "proved" two stages of development (thresholds) before the total rupture. From 1840 to 1842, according to Althusser, Marx was a rationalist-humanist, close to Kant and Fichte, and conceived the essence of man as liberty and reason; whereas between 1842 and 1845, Feuerbach's humanism became predominant. At that point Marx reacted to the reality of the state, which had not transformed itself. Disillusioned, he dropped his former humanism and no longer saw philosophy and the proletariat as allies in the communist revolution; by 1845, he had given up every shred of idealism.[23] Cleansed of a Hegelianism that he "had only used once," on the eve of his rupture with his "erstwhile philosophical conscience," Marx "liquidated this disordered consciousness" in an "abreaction" that was corollary to his maturing and to the true beginning of Marxism.[24]

With the acceptance of this new interpretation, that is, the destruction of Marxist humanism, Marx's economic theories (the labor theory of value and surplus value) could be rethought, and Marxists were asked to concentrate on "scientific Marxism." Althusser's works were praised for their serious intent by those who thought that only a revolution could save society, and that such a revolution needed planning. He was attacked by the "idealist" Marxists and by anticommunists who questioned his underlying political assumptions and the viability of his increasingly Leninist stance. His use of structuralist textual analysis, however, enlarged his potential readership and heightened interest in Marx. Now Althusser instructed everyone not only to read *Capital* but to read it in proper sequence, that is, in relation to the knowledge which existed at the moment this additional knowledge (i.e., Capital) was produced. Because structuralist thought had introduced new dimensions of time, with the possibility of accounting for historical moments as simultaneously happening in the past and at any specific moment—at every present conjuncture—Althusser could re-question what the Hegelian and Marxist dialectics share. He concluded that they share just one thing: a conception of history as propelled by internal contradictions. But whereas Hegel's *Philosophy of History* is said to be reflected in a unique and eternal principle, Marx's history is not the expression of a spiritual essence; it consists instead of many distinct, interrelated, and irreducible instances—economics, politics, ideology, theory.

Althusser's Marxism integrates these "fields" by postulating that the social totality in consequence of its many inherent contradictions is subject to a "structure in dominance." To prove his point, Althusser went on to argue against the familiar notion that Marx's dialectic is an inversion of the Hegelian one insofar as it roots human thought in economic conditions: it could not have been an inversion of Hegel's dialectic, for the object of the dialectic had changed (from "a mystical-mystified-mystificatory" to a rational one); to alter the object of the dialectic would be to change its nature. It could not "cease to be Hegelian and become Marxist by a simple miraculous 'extraction'." [25] So even the brief idealist period of Marx's youth had been no more than a flirtation. By discounting Marx's early works, Althusser could state that Marx had never equated civil society with individual behavior, as had Hegel; and that he had tied all economic phenomena to concrete reality—to the mode of production within a specific society. And he could stress the notion that Marx had never conceived the state in relation to individuals, but only to the ruling class and the relations and mode of production it engenders.

"One way of summing up the difference between the Marxist and the Hegelian dialectics would be to say that the former involves the unity of opposites, and the latter the identity of opposites." [26] But this unity of opposites, according to Althusser, was overdetermined: Marx's totality, for instance, had been the economy (with its own internal contradictions), while Hegel's totality had been made up of universals, making the former "structural" and the latter "ideal." The complexity of the social totality then was said to lead to the differential development of all its autonomous parts; and, in the final analysis, economic elements would win out. Althusser then found the dialectic to be deterministic, insofar as contradictions are articulated upon each other, although the dominating structure (i.e., economic, political) would determine ensuing events. The unevenness of development would result in a conjuncture such as the one in 1917 that led to the Russian revolution. Since under a feudal system the political totality would dominate, and under capitalism the social, Althusser argued that conditions in Russia had been overdetermined by the combination of a weak Tsarist regime, uneven capitalist development, and the country's backwardness, fixed as it was at the highest state of feudalism. Thus, Russia had become the weakest link in the chain of imperialist states,[27] and this allowed Lenin to come to the fore in a revolutionary situation and to use the contradictions between the forces and the relations of production for revolutionary ends. The events of Russian history reaffirmed Althusser's belief that internal contradictions in Marx were overdetermined—in the way an individual's neurotic contradictions are internally overdetermined.

Inevitably, the left in developing countries such as Cuba or

Bolivia, where the extreme contradictions between the forces and the relations of production are the norm, found Althusser's theory appealing, as did Maria Antonietta Macciocchi when she decided to run for an Italian parliamentary seat from Naples. But Althusser's Marxist guidelines to prospective revolutionaries in the Third World remained more implicit than explicit. If Althusser was correct, they would be able to perceive revolutionary conjunctures, and the spread of communism in some parts of the world might also become the signal for revolution elsewhere. But such a reduction of theory to politics, he warned, could easily become another revisionist deviation unless each instance was severed from ideology and theoretical discussion kept scrupulously separate from, for example, electoral campaigns or cold-war rhetoric.[28]

IV

In his introduction to Maria Antonietta Macciocchi's *Letters to Louis Althusser* (1969), Althusser spelled out how Marxist philosophy might "properly" be tied to revolutionary activity. He perceived Macciocchi's wish to try out her theories during an election campaign as furthering the aims of the revolution, especially since he also saw Italy as the weak link in current capitalism, with the greatest internal contradictions. Were Macciocchi elected, he argued, her subsequent position in parliament could itself be used as a form of revolutionary vanguard. With this reliance on Lenin's practice of securing the state apparatus, he also repudiated politics as both the expression of the ideas of the masses and as a need imposed by the systematization of power. Thus he left himself even more vulnerable to accusations of Stalinism, dogmatism, and totalitarianism, accusations which he again countered by relying ever more strongly on Lenin, for whom true humanism could exist only in a socialist society, and for whom repression had been a necessary first revolutionary stage. He agreed with Lenin that ideology in its mystified form, experienced by all men in relation to the world, exists even in communist society. But there, he continued, it expresses itself as socialist humanism.

Without mentioning how communist ideology is imposed on the masses, Althusser reiterated that true humanism could never grow out of bourgeois ideology. He then split this humanism into two types: class humanism (exemplified by China, where the dictatorship of the proletariat still rules) and socialist personal humanism (exemplified by the U.S.S.R., where it has been superseded). "Class humanism contemplates its own future," argued Althusser, while humanism in Marx's works is still rooted in bourgeois thought and therefore must be erased. So he "proved" that whatever traces of it remained in Marx's "mature" works were due to "former sentiments and residues" that the mature Marx himself had criticized and defined as ideology.[29] Althusser addressed such statements to his critics—to those anthropologists who locate man in his surroundings, whether they then postulate, with Lévi-Strauss, that underlying structures dominate thought processes, or, with functionalists, that cultural changes are due to evolution, and/or come about with changing needs. For theories that assume historical continuity and/or the elimination of practices as they become dysfunctional cannot accommodate the notion of epistemological breaks without reservation.

Predictably, the attacks on humanism and anthropologism got Althusser into conflict with Sartre, who all along had minimized the importance of *Capital* and of Marx's political economy to stress the humanism of the early Marx. Antagonism between Althusser and Sartre was thus built into their work. Raymond Aron, eager to discredit Marxism in any form, found that the actual differences between the two men were "less radical than would seem, for Althusser did not know *Capital,* capitalist economy, or Soviet economy any better than Sartre."[30] *Reading Capital* was too abstract, said Aron. And, while Sartre, in *Critique de la raison dialectique* had wanted to base Marxism on the "comprehension of the historical totality, . . . Althusser had wanted to detach theory (or practice of theory) . . . in order to show the scientism of *Capital*—an impossible task for a philosopher unfamiliar with economics."[31] Aron, among others, concluded that Althusser and his friends were rethinking Marxism-Leninism in order to remain in the Party; that "engagement" in reflections could not be censored by the "guardians of the faith"; and that the theory was sufficiently abstract so that, even when condemned as revisionism, it would neither offend Moscow nor Peking.[32]

Althusser's Marxism served not only as an antidote to the idealist hopes of existentialism, but, more generally, to the search for total history in which all the differences of a society are reduced to one form, one world view, or one value system. Foucault calls this "the sovereignty of the subject and the twin figures of anthropology and humanism."[33] Actually, by 1969, Foucault, in *The Archeology of Knowledge*, had himself introduced the notion of epistemological breaks. History was "no longer the continuity of the subject, but the structural discontinuity of ruptures." Simply put, Foucault postulated historical epochs dominated by codes of knowledge that corresponded to dominant structures and that some thought allowed or even heralded Marxist practice. Dominique Lecourt argued that this was a take-off from historical materialism.[34] Foucault did not declare himself a Marxist, and he has always been an outspoken anti-Stalinist; but his preoccupation with epistemological breaks, itself, called attention to Althusser's ideas.

Within the Communist Party Roger Garaudy, until his defection, was Althusser's strongest opponent. As fellow members of the central committee, they clashed over Party aims, the work of the trade unions, and the spontaneity, well-being, and function of the masses. Garaudy's individual, who was to be a "militant of the revolution against all alienation and a poet of creation against entropy,"[35] descended in greater part from the young and "unscientific" Marx. Althusser discredited him along with the other human ideologists, as he attempted to create what I would call his "autochthonous" Marxism.

Althusser never forgot his central premise—that a successful revolution would need its viable philosophy as much as its practice. In "Philosophy as a Revolutionary Weapon" he deplored the obstacles encountered by an intellectual of petit bourgeois origin who, to become a Marxist-Leninist philosopher, had to "re-educate himself in a continuing internal and external struggle," whereas proletarians are blindly guided to revolution by their class instinct.[36] Yet, because the revolution needed its theoretical vanguard, he proselytized his philosophical practice, so that philosophers would recognize the importance of the epistemological break *within* Marx in order to change their own practice. And since Lenin had already dealt with some of these problems, he justified reliance upon Lenin, who, according to Althusser, had also resisted all Hegelianism. Had Lenin not done so, he could not have fought the betrayal of the Second International, built up the Bolshevik party, conquered state power at the head of the Russian masses, installed the dictatorship of the proletariat, and constructed socialism.

But the more Althusser idolized Lenin, the more he exposed himself to accusations of inviting and excusing those Stalinist practices he had set out to obliterate. By 1971, former disciples had become neo-Maoist and had, for the most part, turned against him. More recently, some of these disciples have been hailed as the new philosophers who, among other things, proclaim Marx's death and argue that the Gulag prison camps follow from the nature of socialism.[37] André Glucksmann had already argued in 1967 that Althusser's theory comes apart philosophically because it lacks internal consistency. Since production both "regulates the primordial divisions of the Althusserian universe, and establishes the breaks by which the theory ensures its independence vis-a-vis ideology and politics," everything is production, and all productions are accorded the same status. But, continued Glucksmann, Althusser used different types of structural analyses for his central concepts of production and of theory; and his division of Marx's concepts of production into four kinds of production (material, political, ideological, and theoretical) never achieved the unity of theory and practice between the different productions, but only within each of them.[38] Althusser is thus said to have arrived at the specific practice of theory that acted on its own subject and ended up in a knowledge. Such a conclusion, of course, destroys Althusser's project, since, contrary to Marx's central premise, theory is no longer united with practice.[39]

Many of Althusser's polemical refutations as well as his Leninist formulations were designed to explain these internal inconsistencies. He dealt at length with Lenin's philosophy, practices, and concept of the state, for if Lenin's thought was "of a piece," then Althusser's system would "hold up." Gradually, then, Lenin's philosophy, subdivided into the great philosophical theses, the philosophical practice, and the partisan philosophy, came to replace all philosophy. Since philosophy itself, according to Althusser, has no object, it ipso facto is said to be "relative to the history of scientific practices and of the sciences." Lenin read Hegel as a materialist, continued Althusser, and thus offers the beginning of a "specific form of *philosophical practice.*"[40] Althusser focused on Lenin, because Lenin had had the chance to "fill in the gaps left by Marx." Marx had not accounted for capitalist units of production or of consumption, which Lenin dealt with in his theory of imperialism. Lenin ostensibly followed Marx's intentions, argued Althusser, by implementing Marx's plans, and filling in the missing links at the head of a real revolution.[41] Thus, Lenin's "partisan practice"—his means of asserting personal and party power in the newly formed communist state—turned from a survival kit into philosophy.

Althusser "proved" these contentions by claiming that all the various new sciences grew out of former ones—there are successions as well as breaks; that the original sciences consist only of Plato's mathematics, Descartes' physics, and Marx's history; and that even the epistemological break can be explained as a continuing event that has extended through Leninism and has not yet ended.[42] Althusser's Lenin "proved" to be free of Hegelian influences if only because when he wrote *What the Friends of the People Really Are* (1894), he had not yet read Hegel but had already concluded from reading Marx that "Marxism cannot be accused of Hegelian dialectics but uses the directly opposite method."[43] In other words, Lenin had already understood Hegel through Marx, and consequently, for Althusser, Hegel could only be understood through *Capital* and through a reading that would incorporate a proletarian viewpoint.[44]

In 1969 this line of reasoning led him to admonish French Communists to follow Lenin in dealing with the de facto split of international communism, to give up their absolutist position,[45] and to remember that philosophers must know how to handle the masses in order to make history together. As he attacked idealism and humanism within the Party, he avoided all censure of Lenin and failed to differentiate between his predictions and the actual events of the revolution. Althusser ignored the charge that Leninist practice, in effect, had stopped the dialectic between the

masses and its leadership and that the dictatorship of the proletariat ended up as a dictatorship by the Party, by the Central
Committee, and by the Politburo.

Althusser only implicitly touched on the power struggles
within the Party, the purges, the repression, the exiles to Siberia,
and the totalitarian practices, when explaining Lenin's struggle
against bourgeois ideology. But even then he rationalized that
Lenin mediated between Marx, who had seen the state as "a
force of repression in the interest of the ruling classes," and the
practice that "superseded Marx's descriptive theory." [46] To explain Lenin's "unexplained" seizure of the state, Althusser argued
that Lenin had subdivided the state apparatus into two parts—
the (politico-legal) Repressive State Apparatus and the Ideological State Apparatus, since the state is said to have no meaning except as a function of its power and the surrounding class struggle.
Whereas the repressive apparatus contained government, administration, army, police, courts, and prisons and used harsh
means that ultimately included violence, the ideological apparatus consisted of educational, family, legal, political, trade union,
communications, and cultural functions, which partly belonged
to the private domain. Yet, since this distinction itself had grown
out of the bourgeois order, as part of bourgeois law, Althusser
concluded that the state itself was not only the *stake* but also the
site of the class struggle and reproduced the relations of production with the help of both the legal-political and the ideological
superstructure. If the repressive components of this Marxism-
Leninism were thought to wither away along with the state, this
idea was never spelled out. For Althusser forgot that Lenin had
had only four years; that when ill at the end of his life, he had
had doubts; and that he had seen the danger of political centralization and of a powerful party.

Althusser eventually realized that his unpacking of the old
scientist critique of philosophy was becoming another type of
positivism, and an ideology. But most of all, he became aware
that he had been silent for too long and had to expose repression
within communism. So he wrote his *Essay on Self-Criticism*
(1976). Just like previous Party dissidents such as Lefebvre,
Morin, or Garaudy, who had expressed their self-criticism in
book format, Althusser as well used this means of rethinking his

intellectual and personal position. But Althusser's formulations were even more careful than those of his predecessors and have not led to the official expulsion-cum-withdrawal from the Communist Party. He continues to extol the virtues of Marx and Lenin and attempts to criticize Soviet repression without, however, refuting his own theories. Althusser did not, as he initially intended, resolve his personal conflict between being a revolutionary activist and an academic philosopher. Yet, his attempt

> to rediscover Marxism both under the paralyzing freeze of Stalinism and under the Lenifying chaos of detente, . . . this double platform, [had] made him the founder of the Maoist left which has claimed autonomous theoretical authority against PCF politics; and it has made him the proponent of a new PCF orthodoxy particularly attractive to intellectuals who push the autonomy of theory to the point of paranoia and who let others dirty their hands with politics.[47]

More recently, Althusser invoked Gramsci to address yet another contradiction within Marxism. Alvin Gouldner seemed to be on target when he perceived this as "Althusser's effort to lay the *theoretical* basis for the French collaboration with the Italian Party, and their emerging maneuver toward Eurocommunism, while providing a theoretical storm cellar for Stalinism."[48] And after the elections in March 1978, when the union of the left (Communists and Socialists) was defeated, and Georges Marchais as the leader of the Communist Party gave his interpretation of the events in *L'Humanité* (April 28, 1978)—without open discussion—Althusser criticized this unilateral action. He interpreted the secrecy of the debates within the central committee as an indication of the distance between the party leaders and the masses; he demanded that the leaders engage in true Marxist analysis of their own political and organizational practices; and he again accused the French party of repressive practices similar to the Stalinism that he himself had not always avoided but had denounced.[49]

Thus, Althusser's right foot appears to remain in philosophy and his weightier left foot in an uncertain politics. With the Italian and French Left see-sawing at the edge of participation in government, Althusser's dilemma continues to raise in new form the questions of a Marxist evaluation of the Soviet experience and of the prospects for a non-Stalinist communism; and it strengthens those who doubt that the liberating potential of Marxist theory can ever be realized in practice. Reading Althusser reminds us that no one is ever neutral about Marx.

Notes

1. Dominique Lecourt, *Histoire réele d'une science prolétarienne* (Paris: Maspero, 1976).

2. Althusser, *For Marx*, pp. 22–25.

3. Aron, *Marxismes imaginaires*, p. 194.

4. Garaudy, *Le grand tournant du socialisme,* was the beginning of his self-criticism and of his open rift with the Party.

5. Lichtheim, *From Marx to Hegel*, p. 143.

6. Althusser, *For Marx*, p. 162.

7. Poster, *Existential Marxism in Postwar France*, p. 40.

8. Althusser, *For Marx*, pp. 24–25.

9. Adam Schaff, "What Philosophers Do," in Bontempo and Odell, eds., *The Owl of Minerva*, p. 187.

10. Althusser, *For Marx*, Introduction, pp. 21–39.

11. Althusser and Balibar, *Reading Capital*, p. 16.

12. Althusser used this run-of-the-mill play to show the dissociation between forty characters and the three main protagonists (parallel to ruling class and proletariat) and their false consciousness. Analyzing the structure of the misery of the masses through a critique of the "melodramatic consciousness," he illustrated the latent tragedy of the Milanese subproletariat and its inherent powerlessness. Whereas his neostructuralist mediations tied the social conditions on the stage to a "direct perception of this period, to the visual parallel between the 'wasteland' and the 'non-chalance of the unemployed,' " the technique itself, reaffirmed Althusser's Marxism. Bertolazzi, like Brecht, was tied to structuralist notions of time that "abolished the other time and the structure of its representation, and introduced a third dimension" (*For Marx*, pp. 129–51). In any event, *The 'Piccolo Teatro': Bertolazzi and Brecht* served as an illustration of Marxist-structuralist criticism in 1962 and as such was not a central concern to Althusser.

13. Foucault, *The Archeology of Knowledge*, p. 4.

14. Fowler, "Language and the Reader," *Style and Structure in Literature*, p. 87. (Fowler discusses Riffatere's introduction, in response to Roman Jakobson, of the "super-reader" as a "tool of analysis").

15. Callinicos, *Althusser's Marxism*, p. 35.

16. Althusser, "On the Young Marx," *For Marx*, pp. 85–86.

17. Callincos, *Althusser's Marxism*, p. 56.

18. Althusser, *For Marx*, p. 38.

19. *Ibid.*, p. 30.

20. Geras, "Althusser's Marxism," pp. 57–86.

21. Althusser reiterates this point in most of his essays, and argues in all kinds of ways that the later writings were based on economic realities and thereby refuted every notion rooted in idealism.

22. This quote from Marx's *A Contribution to the Critique of Political Economy* (1959) is frequently cited; Callinicos, for instance, leads off from it (correctly, I believe) as the basis of Althusser's thought. Callinicos, *Althusser's Marxism*, p. 10.

23. Blackburn and Jones, "Louis Althusser and the Struggle for Marxism," in Howard and Klare, eds., *The Unknown Dimension*, pp. 347–68.

24. *Ibid.*, p. 369. This is particularly well explained by Blackburn and Jones, who argue that Marx's rejection of a human essence as the theoretical foundation of philosophy includes a whole organic set of postulates in history, political economy, ethics, and in philosophy itself.

25. Althusser, *For Marx*, p. 91.

26. Callinicos, *Althusser's Marxism*, p. 44.

27. Althusser, "Contradiction and Overdetermination," *For Marx*, pp. 89–127.

28. Rancière, *La Leçon d'Althusser*, p. 65. Rancière, originally a disciple of Althusser's, gradually became more inclined toward Maoism and criticizes from this perspective.

29. Althusser, *For Marx*, pp. 223–27.

30. Aron, *Marxismes imaginaires*, p. 196.

31. *Ibid.*, p. 197.

32. *Ibid.*, p. 199.

33. Foucault, *Archeology of Knowledge*, p. 12.

34. Dominique Lecourt, "Sur l'archéologie et le savior," *Pensées* (1974), no. 152, pp. 69–87.

35. Garaudy, *Le grand tournant du socialisme*, p. 57.

36. Althusser, *Lenin and Philosphy*, pp. 93–94.

37. Bernard-Henri Lévy, *Barbarism with a Human Face* (New York: Harper and Row, 1978).

38. André Glucksmann, "A Ventriloquist Structuralism," p. 69.

39. *Ibid.*

40. Althusser, *Lenin and Philosphy*, p. 62–63.

41. *Ibid.*, p. 93.

42. *Ibid.* Also André Glucksmann, "Ventriloquist Structuralism" pp. 68–92.

43. Althusser, *Lenin and Philosophy*, p. 107.

44. *Ibid.*, p. 108.

45. *Ibid.*, p. 60.

46. *Ibid.,* p. 12.
47. Lacoste, "Les fausses oppositions de Louis Althusser," p. 21.
48. Alvin Gouldner, "Louis Althusser, Essays in Self-Criticism," a review in *Theory and Society* (1977), 4(3):449–50.
49. Althusser, Introduction, *Ce qui ne peut plus durer,* pp. 5–30.

Bibliography

Althusser, Louis. *Pour Marx.* Paris: Maspero, 1965. Translated as *For Marx.* New York: Pantheon, 1972.
—— *Lenin and Philosophy.* London: New Left Books, 1971.
—— *Politics and History.* London: New Left Book, 1972.
—— Avant-propos to Dominique Lecourt, *Histoire réele d'une science prolétarienne.* Paris: Maspero, 1976.
—— *Essay on Self-Criticism.* London: New Left Books, 1976.
—— *Ce qui ne peut plus durer dans le parti communiste.* Paris: Maspero, 1978.
Althusser, Louis and Etienne Balibar. *Lire le capital.* Paris: Maspero, 1968. Translated as *Reading Capital.* London: New Left Books, 1970.
Aron, Raymond. *Marxismes imaginaires.* Paris: Gallimard, 1970.
Atlan, Jacques. "Le plus Lacanien des livres d'Althusser." *La Quinzaine littéraire* (June 16–30, 1976), p. 20.
Blackburn, Robin and Gareth Stedman Jones. "Louis Althusser and the Struggle for Marxism." In Dick Howard and Karl E. Klare, eds., *The Unknown Dimension.* New York: Basic Books, 1972.
Bontempo, J. and S. Jack Odell, eds. *The Owl of Minerva.* New York: McGraw-Hill, 1975.
Callinicos, Alex. *Althusser's Marxism.* London: Pluto Press, 1976.
Cane, Michael. "Althusser in English." *Theoretical Practice* (January 1971).
Chatelet, François. "Une introduction à la lecture d'Althusser." *La Quinzaine littéraire* (March 15–31, 1974), pp. 19–20.
Domenach, Jean-Marie. "Un marxisme sous vide." *Esprit* (January 1974), no. 1, pp. 111–25.
Foucault, Michel. *The Archeology of Knowledge.* New York: Pantheon, 1974.
Fowler, Roger, ed. *Style and Structure in Literature.* Ithaca: Cornell University Press, 1975.
Garaudy, Roger. *Le grand tournant du socialisme.* Paris: Gallimard, 1969.
George, François. "Reading Althusser." *Telos* (Spring 1971), 6:73–98.
—— "Lire Althusser." *Les Temps Modernes* (1969), 24:1921–62.
Geras, Norman. "Althusser's Marxism: An Account and Assessment." *New Left Review* (January-February 1972), p. 57–86.
Glucksmann, André. "Un structuralisme ventriloque." *Les Temps Modernes* (1967), 22:1557–98. Also in *New Left Review* (1971), pp. 68–92.

56 Althusser: Marxism and Structuralism

Glucksmann, Miriam. *Structuralist Analysis in Contemporary Social Thought.* London: Routledge, Kegan Paul, 1974.

Howard, Dick and Karl E. Klare. *The Unknown Dimension.* New York: Basic Books, 1972.

Karsz, Saul. *Théorie et politique: Louis Althusser.* Paris: Fayard, 1974.

Kurzweil, Edith. "Louis Althusser: Between Philosophy and Politics." *Marxist Perspectives* (1979), no. 2, pp. 8–23.

Lacoste, Jean. "Les fausses oppositions de Louis Althusser." *La Quinzaine littéraire* (February 16–28, 1975), pp. 18–19.

Lichtheim, George. "A New Twist in the Dialectic." *From Marx to Hegel and Other Essays,* pp. 143–95. New York: Herder and Herder, 1971.

—— *Marxism in Modern France.* New York: Columbia University Press, 1966.

Macciocchi, Maria Antonietta. *Lettere dal'interno del P.C.I. a Louis Althusser.* Milan: Feltrinelli, 1969.

Poster, Mark. *Existential Marxism in Postwar France.* Princeton: Princeton University Press, 1975.

Rancière, Jacques. *La leçon d'Althusser.* Paris: Gallimard, 1975.

Rocquet, Claude-Henri. "Quand le matérialisme dialectique codifié par Staline devient philosophie d'État." *La Quinzaine littéraire* (July 16–31, 1976), pp. 20–21.

Veltmeyer, Henry. "Towards an Assessment of the Structuralist Interrogation of Marx: Claude Lévi-Strauss and Louis Althusser." *Science and Society* (Winter 1975), pp. 385–421.

Walton, Paul and Andrew Gamble. *From Alienation to Surplus Value.* New York: Sheed and Ward, 1972.

III. Henri Lefebvre
A Marxist Against Structuralism

Henri Lefebvre was one of the earliest and one of the most vehement critics of structuralism as formulated by both Althusser and Lévi-Strauss. For he remained faithful to Marx's vision of history and to existential notions of subjectivity, from the time he encountered the young Marx's philosophical writings—writings he first translated into French (with Norbert Guterman) in 1933.[1] He was a member of the early Marxist-Leninist group of philosophers in Paris, between 1929 and 1934.[2] Ever since then, he stated in *La somme et le reste* (1958), he had considered Marx's concepts of alienation and of "total man" as central; and he continued to insist on the Marxist idea of the union of "theory and practice."

Born in 1901, Lefebvre's life is the history of the twentieth-century Left, for it illustrates the anguish and dilemmas communism posed for intellectuals in France and everywhere else and reflects the promises and disappointments engendered by the Russian revolution, the successes and failures of Leninism, the birth of Mao's China, and the repressive party discipline of Stalinism. Yet Lefebvre is different from many other leftists insofar as he always tried to pursue his own interpretation of Marx, an interpretation which attempted to fuse the early and the late writings, as well as Marxist concepts of history, humanism, and economics, and which, above all, constantly addressed the most current political issues. Lefebvre's innate humanistic socialism allegedly remained intact, even while he was a party member, from about 1928 to 1957. Alert all along against both right and left totalitarianism, his views about the various crises of capitalism always assumed that the workers' revolution would occur. Thus he frequently "rethought" Marx, Engels, and Lenin, or supplied practical details they "forgot" in order to explain current events as he thought they might have perceived them. Helped by his extraordinary knowledge of the classics, literature, the German language, sociology, politics, and criticism, he continued to "demonstrate" the decline of capitalism through his analyses of both economic and cultural productions. By now his positions tend to be predictable, and, upon occasion, almost simplistic.

But Lefebvre's ideas were influential: they served the propagandists who refracted, projected, and interpreted Marxist doctrine; the political leaders and organizers who transformed them into instruments of mass action; and the working-class movement itself.[3] True, his visibility was diminished during his years as a party member, but even then he fought against the political dogmatists who fetishized texts by Stalin, who reduced Marxism to political economy and/or Leninist practices, and who ignored Marx's humanism and his notion of alienation.

A fervid anti-fascist, he denounced nationalism in 1937[4] and Hitler in 1938,[5] supported the Republicans during the Spanish Civil War, and later was active in the Resistance. But when, in 1958, he wrote about *Les problèmes actuels du Marxisme,* the Party tried him, as he says, not for what he had written but for insubordination, and expelled him. *La somme et le reste,* the tour de force he wrote the following year (it won the *Prix des Critiques*) is probably the best of the "revisionist" autobiographies—a history of French communism and Stalinism. Until then, Lefebvre had written a number of Marxist interpretations of philosophers—on *Nietzsche* (1939), *Descartes* (1947), *Diderot* (1949), *Pascal* (1949, 1954), *Musset* (1955), *Rabelais* (1955), *Pignon* (1956)—as well as general treatises on Marxist dialectics, communism, and philosophy. He had interpreted and updated the ideas of the young Hegelians and had commented, endlessly, on capitalism and industrialization. But his most interesting works were written after 1958, when he was free to write what he wanted and began to analyze urbanization and everyday life, to attack both capitalist and communist ideology, and to comment on the meaning of structuralism and other cultural phenomena. His *Dialectical Materialism,* originally published in 1939 as a "protest" against the increasingly dogmatic economism of the Communist Party, retained its validity even when reprinted in 1961 and when translated into English in 1968. This fact would confirm that Lefebvre was never completely subjugated by the Party.

Much has been written about French communism, about the Communist Party as the principal organizing force of the Left and its relation to the proletariat, about the "family quarrels," the alternating rifts and rapprochements with the Socialists.[6] Before his break, Lefebvre for the most part went along with the official party position and did not openly contradict its stand; so that he, too, alternately joined the Socialists in the Popular Front or disdained them. And when Hitler attacked Russia he joined the Resistance.

Yet all along, in Hegelian fashion, he consciously attempted to take in the "totality" of human existence, to catch "everything": he explicitly spanned all past and present phenomena, from Vivaldi to Schumann, from God to Satan, from Socrates to Descartes, from feudalism to modernism, from surrealism to linguistics, from language to science, from Baudelaire to Beckett. Like Lévi-Strauss, he believed in man as a total being, in his spontaneity, in his wish to raise himself to the highest degree of existence. (This centrality of the individual made scientific Marxism of the Althusserian type, Stalinism, and economism unacceptable.)[7] He frequently indicated how he himself tried to live up to this ideal man, to overcome restrictions through work in an open society. This goal led him to "existentialize" Marx by appropriating notions of subjectivity as well as by orienting theory toward action, in order to "free" the society as well as himself. He tried constantly to reconcile humanism with communism only to find that seeming solutions raised new problems. But, like Marx, he thought every crisis of capitalism was the final one, and expected that the revolution would help "overcome" the contradictions. He also thought that the application of capitalist technology to socialist ends might humanize socialist practice. However, regardless of the viability of his views, his political influence was considerable; and it is claimed that the student revolt in 1968, which spread from Nanterre to the rest of France, was not only started by his students but was directly inspired by his books and lectures. But I will get to that later.

II

Henri Lefebvre was born in Hagetmau, France and grew up in Navarrenx in the Bas Pyrrhénées, the native village he often refers to in his books. Some of his field work was done there, as he observed the changes from ruralism to urbanism every summer. Contact with this remote village and with its "unalienated" labor continued to offer him the chance to lead a more unstructured life and "allowed" him to derive his theory from observing the practices of village life. In addition, his return to Navarrenx, to his roots and to nature, seemed to serve the same ends as Barthes' sojourns near Bayonne, Lévi-Strauss' excursions in the Languedoc region, or Althusser's and Foucault's retreats to their country homes: French intellectuals, like most Frenchmen, do not simply escape to suburbia, to exurbia, or to nature. They reestablish links to ancestral homes, to personal histories.

Thus, Lévi-Strauss seems to have invented structuralism, as he tells us in *Tristes Tropiques,* by letting his mind free-associate during his customary walks in the country. And since he later looked at history, geology, etc., as "knowledge-in-action," his peers, too, have, as it were, exploited nature more systematically. Lefebvre, for example, explored *Les Pyrrhénées,* to become an ethnologist and a sort of "local patriot," when he turned the beautiful and somewhat romantic excursions through his native region into yet another Marxist practice. True, his returns to nature are more ritualistic than real. Lefebvre observed the takeover of "progress," as he noted that Navarrenx's grocers carried frozen vegetables while its farmers sold to wholesalers, or that tourism left its imprint everywhere. And in his own village household, his role was that of the patriarch rather than of the practicing revolutionary—a contradiction he claimed to have overcome through work; he did, for instance, write most of *La somme et le reste* there, during the summer of 1958.[8]

What we know about his youth comes from that work, from self-conscious flashbacks that occasionally provide the background to his intellectual history. He earned his *license* at the university in Aix-en-Provence but asserted that he did not choose philosophy, that it chose him through the person of the liberal Catholic Maurice Blondel, whom he saw "through the eyes of the beautiful female students around him." After about two years he left them all—the women he says he then loved but with none of whom he made love, and Blondel, with whom he had studied Augustine and Pascal—to go to the Sorbonne. There, summarized Alfred Schmidt,

> he worked with Leon Brunschvig, the "intellectualistic" philosopher of judgment who was an enemy of every dialectic. What made Lefebvre (by no means without conflict) turn to Marxism had little to do with university philosophy. It was the political and social upheavals of the postwar period, and more particularly personal problems, psychoanalysis, and association with the literary and artistic avant-garde, the surrealist movement. Lastly, it was the suspicion, which turned into a firm conviction, that philosophy as it had been handed down had demonstrated that it increasingly was less able to come to grips with, not to mention master, the problems posed by the historical situation of being and consciousness in society.[9]

Lefebvre became a Marxist between 1925 and 1930, at a time when, as he said, one could not easily overcome one's youthful romanticism, when Marxism sprouted on the ruins of one's youth and of one's absurd and unlimited hopes, when converts were unaware of Marx's early works and mostly found interpretations by Lenin and Stalin.[10] It appears that he had been criticizing the increasing fragmentation of society and of individuals for some time, but that he had himself withdrawn into "pure interiority" even while recognizing that subjectivity, or a focus on personal existence, was no answer. Joining the Party then, signified also a return to objectivity, to political action.

Clearly, Lefebvre was not alone in converting a personal crisis into politics. At the time, the French Communist Party, in spite of its break with the Socialists in 1921, represented a strong and quasi-legitimate force, and communism still held out the hope for an ideal socialist society—once the Communist International took over the world. Yet the Party itself tended to be increasingly concerned with its "Bolshevization," to be more and more influenced by Stalin; and party intellectuals had to think within rather dogmatic positions, within a narrow orthodoxy that did not permit independent thinking. This ideological position, of course, was reflected in the works Lefebvre wrote between 1930 and 1940, and some of them are out of print. According to Alfred Schmidt, Lefebvre nevertheless stood up to

> both modern authoritarian, irrational ideology *and* [to] attempts of Party Communists to either reduce Marx's teachings to a narrowly conceived economistic theory, or to broaden them into a positive world view ("scientific ideology") and an abstract methodology of the natural sciences.[11]

Lefebvre himself insisted that he always wanted to transcend both "narrow" dialectics and "abstract" logic, and "tried to show in coherent fashion that the dialectic does not destroy logic," but that there is a transition, since dialectical and logical contradictions are of different essences. Furthermore, he continued, only vulgar Marxists attribute this thesis to Hegel, since it was explained by Engels (badly) as the condition that "dialectical logic" is located exactly between formal logic and the most general exposition of the laws of dialectic.[12]

Obviously, Lefebvre knows how to argue his Marxism. But while a communist, he stuck to translating and quoting Marx, Hegel and Lenin; some of these books he wrote on his own; others with Norbert Guterman;[13] most of them were seized and destroyed by the Nazis. His *Dialectical Materialism* (1939), according to his 1961 foreword, allegedly indicated that the use of the concept of alienation did not have to be confined to the study of bourgeois society, but could also "uncover and criticize ideological and political alienations in socialism, particularly during the Stalinist period."[14] With revisionist hindsight, he found that even though this book "was slightly tainted with dogmatism," he had "rejected all popular economism, sociologism, and stress on non-human materiality." This made for problems within the party, problems which Lefebvre habitually solved by suggesting that Marx be "reread with fresh eyes."

III

But the rereadings that predate his break with the Party, such as *Marx et la liberté* (1947), and *Le Marxisme* (1948), differ considerably from *Problèmes actuels du Marxisme* (1958) and *La somme et le reste* (1959). If Lefebvre was aware of the shortcomings of institutionalized communism, of its repressive qualities, then why did he stay in the Party for so many years? After all, his American "equivalents," the intellectuals who began *Partisan Review* in the late 1930s, had had similar experiences and were privy to the same information. Whether it was France's geographical and emotional vicinity to Spain, French chauvinism, the arguments surrounding Marxism, fellow traveling or anti-Americanism, or even the strong popular support for the Communist Party, the verbal arguments became almost more important than the substantive issues. Even when Khrushchev denounced Stalin and the "cult of the individual,"[15] Lefebvre (among others) would have preferred to continue ignoring the Gulag and totalitarian practices. The Russian invasion of Hungary soon afterwards, however, shocked the French and finally led to the exodus of most of the remaining intellectuals from the Party. Yet by then Marxist concepts and language had become common currency among all intellectuals and among the general educated public.

Lefebvre himself went on to publish a number of works to explain Marx better: *Marx philosophe* (1964), *Metaphilosophie* (1965), *La fin de l'histoire* (1970), *La sociologie de Marx* (1966). In fact, the *Problèmes actuels du Marxisme* (1958) had already opened up the issues he enlarged on in the later works. In this work he wondered whether to discuss Marx logically, pedagogically, or historically; to recall his principles of philosophy, political economy or politics; or instead, to expose the transformations and applications of Marx in communist societies (Russia and Yugoslavia), their internal differences and tensions. Reminiscent of the early Althusser, he accused philosophers of scholasticism, doctrinairism, and excessive theorizing in their analysis of the contradictions interior to socialism—contradictions the politicians are said to hide, or only allude to.[16] Obliquely, he attacked practicing Marxists for reveling in vulgarizations:

> They contradict themselves disastrously; on the one hand they affirm with Stalin that there are no isolated phenomena in the world, that all phenomena depend on and condition each other, that the dialectic is opposed to ancient metaphysics insofar as nature is considered as a whole and its objects

and phenomena are independent; on the other hand they put the objects outside their own conscience but into the [collective] conscience. . . . This amounts to a tautology . . . and is a crime against the dialectic.[17]

This is only one of many passages calculated to ridicule the arguments surrounding the debates between Lévi-Strauss and Sartre, as well as Althusser's attempt to explain Marxism solely through the writings of Marx and Lenin. As Lefebvre's instinct for irony took over, he compared all the "naive and impatient" Marxists (mostly Althusserians) who "want absolute liberty subject to definitive rules and norms," to Stalin in 1924. For they too (like Sartre and his disciples) proclaim themselves communists, men apart, cut from different cloth, and then abandon humanism, so that nothing human remains. Yet when addressing the actual unfolding of capitalism, the fragmentation of the working class or the growth of nationalism, Lefebvre did find fault with Marx: neither he nor Lenin had predicted the innovative agrarian reforms made by the Algerian Communist Party, the specific and national character of the French and Italian parties,[18] the impact of urban growth, or the expediency of politics that maintain a *status quo*. As a member of the *Arguments* group (1958–1962), a circle that invited contributions by every type of Marxist, Lefebvre's attacks on Stalinism and his critical inquiries into historical and social conditions led him also to focus on the contradictions within the socialist state—its military and diplomatic activities, its ideologies and propaganda, its economic, social, and cultural planning.[19] Hence he touched all the untouchables, all the problems Marxist philosophy poses for "official" communism, and systematically began to criticize both capitalist and socialist states as he claimed Marx would perceive them were he alive.

Official Marxism was attacked for its ritualized application of the classical texts, its institutionalized use of words (they express little and signify much), its political directives (they have become frozen into terminology and only produce conditioned reflexes and sacrosanct epithets), for its organizational gestures, rites of celebration and ideological unity.[20] Instead of assertions and canonized methods (they reduce all phenomena to formal logic, grammar of thought or approximation), he suggested that dialectical logic alone is equipped to examine the rational use of categories of thought, their theoretical connections, and the conditions that allow reflection to be rediscovered in concrete content; thus not content but forms of thought are to be studied.[21] But one cannot separate, philosophically, forms of thought from the negative power of analysis which kills content in order to reconstitute it. This "is one of the errors of summary materialism—to have the form arise from the content as a simple reflex."[22] Marxist philosophy

> ought to concentrate on specifically philosophical concepts, on alienation and "total man," on reflection about the individual, so that . . . humanism can return to the light and return to its place at the apex of philosophy and of revolutionary critique of reality."[23]

Superficially, Lefebvre's Marx was attached to the same humanistic works as Lévi-Strauss'—to the articles in the *Rheinische Zeitung*, the *1844 Manuscripts*. But Lévi-Strauss, we recall, emphasized their language, while Lefebvre's concern was with their political impact, even as he gradually shifted his discourse to the "language of the state which has become the language of decision," and to the resulting misunderstandings. He found that the suppression of information and the affirmation of the political and ideological unity of Marxism-Leninism (with its internal and symbolic meaning) conspire to silence adherents and political enemies alike,[24] when party functionaries run the state, act like business executives, and use a "scientific vocabulary."[25] This stress on language and on rhetoric (both as capitalist propaganda and as betrayal of socialism) reflected, to some extent, the upsurge of structural linguistics as the new theoretical means of discourse; it was also intended to show that Marxism was the more viable theory. And a Marxist political system (in contrast to a linguistic one) was expected to *work*. Thus, whereas the structuralists (except for Althusser) subsumed Marxism, Lefebvre was busily demonstrating that Marxism was supreme and could integrate structuralism.

Politically, unlike Aron, Malraux, Servan-Schreiber, and others, Lefebvre did not go along with French participation in NATO (those who did believed increasingly in a European community under French hegemony), and continued to denounce

American imperialism. But French postwar political attitudes were in constant flux: many French intellectuals wanted to think of themselves as both Communists *and* liberals. Thus they chose to ignore the totalitarian practices of the Soviet regime or to acknowledge them later rather than sooner. Sartre and Merleau-Ponty, for instance, had disagreed early, when the latter first published *Humanism and Terror* in 1947 (in response to Koestler's *Darkness at Noon*), and their public disagreements had led to various qualifying stances by other left intellectuals.[26]

In his essay on *Democratic Planning* (1961), for example, Lefebvre argued for a French socialism that would avoid the Russian fiasco.[27] He believed that the French state, when regulating prices and wages, stimulating investment and inflation to push general technical development (e.g., twentieth-century oil pipelines, electrical energy, and arms take the place of nineteenth-century railroads) could gain only a short-term reprieve for capitalism: unequal development proceeds, quasi-anarchic interest groups still abound, and socialization is chaotic (the spontaneity of individuals evaporates). If Marx were around, insisted Lefebvre, he would avoid proliferation of technocrats and administrators, so that the state would "wither away"; and he would invent techniques to create an overall social network to cover every organization of information, management, national policy, and finance. But because Marxist political thought had deteriorated under the aegis of "dogmatists" and "empiricists" who tend to forget the individual and "operationalize" Marx, Lefebvre called for the restoration of a "dialectical critique of morals" that would eliminate the various brands of Marxist morals, esthetics, science, philosophy and politics which emerged along with the socialist state.[28]

He understandably looked to Yugoslavia and China for possible solutions. For a while Titoism, because of its dual authority structure in industry, allowed for economic growth with a minimum of political interference, "subtly" planning its "concrete" democracy. Yet Lefebvre was aware that Yugoslavia is a "special case" rather than a model for Third World development (its independence did not follow colonial rule, and industrialization did not depend on imported techniques and ideas which ultimately could serve as means of oppression); unlike the Russians, continued Lefebvre, the Yugoslavs could separate social needs from biological, physiological or economic ones. In 1961, however, his friends of the *Praxis* group had not yet been silenced, and their "sociological reflections" were still heeded.[29]

Lefebvre's rather brief fascination with the Chinese model had to do with the notion of the "non-antagonistic contradictions" between capitalism and socialism. He perceived an affinity between Chinese politics and his own, and supported their aim of avoiding another world war. Yet, as he deliberated about Chinese and Russian communism, their differing ideologies, and the power politics of the "historical pause," he kept returning to the question of revolution and concluded that the class struggle, though a bit deadened by the "pause," would rebound later.[30] Once again, Lefebvre's analyses were linked to current events, events he chose to apprehend through Mao Tse-tung's and Khrushchev's speeches. Now his "totalizing" dialectics mediated between East and West, China and Russia, French and world politics, socialism and capitalism, as he warned of the probability of war and of its devastating consequences. Khrushchev, he argued, "minimizes the maximum of his enemy's chances," while the Chinese ideologues "maximize the minimum of chances."[31] In trying to bring about a "spontaneous" socialism, he increasingly addressed notions of mondiality and of "the planetary" (partly in response to Paul Ricoeur and to Kostas Axelos), which were to solve questions of industrialization and world economy. After venting his pent up frustrations about Stalinism and justifying both his long membership and his rupture with the Communist Party, he attacked official socialism from the left. The appropriate watershed for his thought is around 1962, when he "returned" to philosophy, began to make urbanization the pivot of his Marxism, and started to turn against structuralism.

IV

Lefebvre's *Introduction to Modernity* (1962) seemed attuned to the methodology of Lévi-Strauss' *Structural Anthropology*. Although Lévi-Strauss' *The Raw and the Cooked* was not published until 1964, Lefebvre's use of musical themes, the subdivision into twelve "preludes" rather than "chapters" (preludes about "irony, the majestic and history," "Oedipus," "the metamorphoses of the devil," "vision," or "the new romanticism") resembled Lévi-Strauss' approach to Bororo mythology. Lefebvre introduced his discussion of modernity with these words:

> With or without majesty, sumptuous or untidy, opulent or in rags, always more brutal, more rapid, more noisily, the modern world advances. . . . It imposes itself . . . in modern painting, [and art, literature, music, science], techniques, love. . . . It has its partisans and its adversaries. But it needs no theory.[32]

According to Lefebvre, Marx's original conceptual tool had been the reflection on modernity pushed by critique; Lefebvre decided that this was to be his own tool as well. And because Marx, like Socrates, had used it in conjunction with irony (Socrates had not known where he *or* his city were going but tried to introduce social and political practice), irony became the organizing principle of this book. In typical Lefebvrian fashion,

> irony [was said to] touch sarcasm, but [to be] different from spirit. . . . Voltaire, Diderot and Stendhal had more spirit than irony. [For] irony rescues the smile more often than the laugh, never the laughter, it is weak and defends itself. This does not keep it from becoming aggressive. . . . [And] it risks the anger of giants.[33]

Implicitly, Lefebvre put himself in Socrates' place; Socrates too had been condemned because the judges had been afraid of the truth, because he had belonged to no party. And he put France in the role of Athens—unable to recognize its political dreams (socialism), because "society's midwives" are politicians, party bosses and generals.[34]

By now, Lefebvre's customarily wide philosophical range had become affected by the structuralist climate, a climate that invited "systematic" free association. He adopted the manners of structuralism without its method, as he jumped, for example, from Hegel's humor to the irony of religion (the orders enriched themselves in the name of poverty), to the cult of Stalin as political religion, and to its dissemination through terminology, vocabulary, concepts, and grammar; for words filter sentiments, bring rules, maxims, and action, and manage to destroy true communism.

Like a criminal who revisits the scene of the crime, or the analysand who "abreacts" the traumatic event, Lefebvre always returned to his pet subjects—"socialism, psychoanalysis, and existentialism, which dominated Parisian thinking in the 1960s. Because art and literature had been his passions when he was a young man (before he had become a party member, and had been expected to apply them dogmatically to revolutionary ends), structuralism's "creative horizon," he stated, appealed to him. But Lefebvre formulated his own views about language and writing and about their impact on politics and philosophy, and legitimated his free association of oppositions as Hegelian rather than structuralist. He found, for instance, that the "Faustian and demoniacal values" of Stalinism had destroyed the possibility for creative activity in all the arts; that the coming of socialism would restore love of work, of family, of the homeland; that honesty, work, and citizenship would further artistic production;[35] and that this socialism would refute pretensions of authenticity and of the power "subjectively" to verify reality. Although he suggested that his idealism would be overcome by irony, he seemed unaware that he was extolling all the bourgeois values Marx had derided.

In such a summary of Lefebvre's themes, his mythological tone is lost. For each prelude-cum-chapter in the *Introduction to Modernity* was in the form of a myth or a fable, usually with a number of morals couched in analogies or lessons. Eloquent descriptions were interspersed with clichés. Or was it ethnology? For example, he recalled on a walk in Mourenx (near Navarrenx):

> Man has always created, vitally, just like animal life. Each father produces a living child. Each artist, each epoch has created works. Wasn't your village too, in its time, a new city? It too was founded on the shores of the river Gave and since then has lived, has taken form. Precisely because you refute estheticism, it is in art that you must find the mode; in the art of living. The new city makes man afraid to create human life! . . . But one can't say that it is easy![36]

These reflections (they sound authentic in French, and melodious) announced the direction of some of Lefebvre's subsequent works, when urbanization became the key indicator of the decline of capitalism.

Inadvertently, Lefebvre's Hegelianism retained its structuralist tinge even as he attacked structuralism for its underlying conservatism—in *Le langage et la société* (1966). He began by affirming notions of structure, but questioning the emphasis on language in contemporary thought—in the social sciences, philosophy, literature, and the arts. Picking up on the earlier discussions between Sartre and Merleau-Ponty, he sided with the latter, who (already in 1949) had reproached Sartre for looking at language as a sign of thought rather than simply as a sign and who had shown how the power of the Hegelian negation could penetrate being.[37]

Saussurean theory, he affirmed, has its validity but transforms written language into positivity and, like Nietzsche's individual, infuses material things with value. Such a conception inevitably (in linguistic terms) would locate sense in the *signifié*, that is, in the *signified,* and would be contradictory to Marx, who, according to Lefebvre, in *Capital,* tried to seize the juncture of the *signifier* and the *signified* in the "real," that is, in actual relationships.[38] This dialectic, explains Rolle, which is said to function as "concrete logic" or "mediation" between form and content, allegedly adds another obscurity, and possibly another solution, if one considers mediation the most important element (irreducible to its antecedents), as an element of .formalization.[39] But this is exactly why Baudrillard, another "Hegelian" sociologist, rejects Lefebvre's conception of the dialectic: it implicitly conceives the class struggle as a conflict between the substantial and the formal, where the first term, sooner or later promises victory (that is, the revolution). Baudrillard wants to keep the opposition between form and substance, arguing that form is subordinated to substance without making it disappear entirely. Hence he attacks Lefebvre's dialectical logic as powerless and faulty, because it leaves out the *symbolic* dimension—a dimension that would not separate the end from its function.

Lefebvre, of course, opposes this line of reasoning: to him all practice, including structuralist practice, is considered as just another milestone (or step) toward the Marxist revolution. Thus he could proceed to explain structuralism as a contemporary intellectual production, as part of the superstructure, a production of bourgeois culture. And he could go on to demonstrate that the paradoxes of language had existed since the beginning of philosophy and throughout modern thought. Although rarely mentioning "reification," he kept illustrating how all thought, when written, takes on a life of its own, and how Lévi-Strauss' theory reduces all thought because it mediates between components of language that are not directly related to social reality.

Lefebvre was particularly critical of the new time dimension of structuralism, the third dimension that was said to mediate between past and present. Contrary to Marx, Saussure, and Husserl, argued Lefebvre, Jakobson, Lévi-Strauss' mentor, reduces linguistics to phonology; he does not really eliminate the differences between social and language science, diachrony and synchrony, opposition and combination. Instead, with the help of a number of successive reductions, Lefebvre finds that "thought and conscience, thus miniaturized, resemble the head 'reduced' by a Jivaro Indian more than a twentieth-century conscience."[40] From there, it was allegedly but a small step to reduce science to nomenclature and to explain cooking through phonology.[41] Hence the Bororo "neither merit the honor nor the indignities of Lévi-Strauss' analyses" and do not justify the "leaps" to historic continents and into musical orchestrations. These leaps were said to forget scientific concepts of form, function, and structure, so that

> analogous functions can be achieved with diverse forms and different structures. The same form can cover different functions. Thus, among living beings, organs of varying forms and structures (lungs, bronchie) assure respiratory function. . . . Analogous forms hide enormously differing functions and structures. . . . [Similarly] when analyzing urbanization, the *form* of an ancient city has burst through exterior proliferations (suburbs, etc., no longer have anything urban). But the *functions* of the city have not disappeared; on the contrary, numerous functions have been added . . . As to the *structures,* (living space, street, neighborhood) they are transformed before our eyes.[42]

Structures, in other words, have limits but structuralism has none. Quoting André Martinet, who refuted Jakobson by arguing that "universal binarism of phonological oppositions is but a view of the mind,"[43] Lefebvre attacked structuralism's three-dimensional fetishism (time ought to be a fourth dimension), and Barthes' notion of "white space" (why not superwhite or non-white) so central to French writers since Robbe-Grillet or Sarraute.[44] He insisted (with diagrams that were takeoffs on Lévi-Strauss') that social reality or origins cannot be explained through linguistics and accused Lévi-Strauss of neglecting symbolisms, symbolic universes, and organized symbolic systems that forget about individual and cultural imagination and imagery.

Yet Lefebvre's own three-dimensional symbolism of language (paradigmatic, symbolic, syntagmatic) which was to "improve" as well as "reject" Lévi-Strauss' structures, seemed almost as facile as his criticism of Barthes' literary structuralism. Essentially, Lefebvre denounced

> writers and artists [who] are divided and classified according to their relation to language, [who] push towards dissolution, accept discourse, [or] . . . search for an animating rhetoric. One reacts as one can against triviality of discourse that springs from these projects of total art (language, music, plastic arts), and from the (faulty) invention of new myths and symbols. . . . Briefly, this discourse is the zero degree of the word.[45] (A takeoff on Barthes.)

The recurrence of such passages reminds the reader that, in spite of his protests and his ideological isolation, Lefebvre was in touch with the rest of his intellectual community. This was clear in his long-standing feud with Lucien Goldmann about ideology and Pascal (Lefebvre perceived Pascal as the victim of Christianity, Jansenism, the bourgeoisie and the monarchy) and in his comments on Barthes (he deplored his linguistic excursions but liked his Marxian use of symbols in fashion, literature and social criticism).[46] He dismissed Foucault's "rewriting of the history of knowledge" as deliberately obscure, as holding onto illusions about the specific historical epochs while forgetting their conflicts (and thus Marx's law of unequal development). A focus on unconscious structures by Foucault, Lacan, or anyone else, main-

tained Lefebvre, ignores the truth that ultimately economic matters control thought. He means that unconscious mental
structures, insofar as they do not derive directly from the economic base, contradict Marx's notion of superstructure and
derive from subjective experience. Were these unconscious structures to exist, they would be conservative and would act as an
obstacle to the revolution.

V

Lefebvre's foremost opponent, however, was Louis Althusser,
whose "scientific" Marxism, as we have noted in the previous
chapter, itself attacked Lefebvre's Marx as idealist and unrealis-
tic. In fact, the massive and spontaneous strikes by students and
workers in May/June 1968 accentuated the rifts between "humanistic" and "scientific" Marxists. For very different reasons,
both Althusser and Lefebvre stayed off the barricades. But
whereas Althusser's silence was engendered by party discipline,
Lefebvre did not join the students because he believed that a
"revolution" without strategy was doomed. His own students,
who led this revolt, reproached him for avoiding the practice he
had preached—at the first opportunity for testing his theories.
But even though Lefebvre approved the students' actions, he
thought that they could not sustain the momentum; they had no
concrete program beyond the takeover of the state's structures.
The technocrats and bureaucrats were therefore bound to prevail.
Because of the students' belief that society's superstructures had
already eroded, that the state, civil society and politics had become dissociated in an entrenched system, "thought was separated from spontaneity"—professors thought and students
acted.[47] At least in retrospect, Lefebvre perceived this revolution
as "unhealthy," because Lenin's law of uneven development had
not been applied to all sectors of social life, to knowledge, technology, science, art, daily existence and the production of knowledge and social relations.[48] He excused his own lack of support
in *The Explosion: Marxism and the French Revolution* (1968),
explaining that the contradictions of capitalist society had not yet
reached the crisis. To him, private ownership and the social char-

acter of the means of production and their management in the interests of a class had only assumed new forms and continued to establish their power over the entire society.[49] He went on to compare students to workers (both sell their labor power); students produce knowledge rather than goods. Referring to the students' objections to the repressive use of knowledge (in its application) as a means of domination, Lefebvre was convinced that his continuing critique of politics and of ideology would unify knowledge, so that it would be put to rational use through political awareness.[50] This meant that his own writing would prepare workers and students to cooperate during future crises; it also meant that Althusserianism had to be invalidated (Lévi-Strauss had already conceded the breakdown of *his* type of structures), not only to assure a mass base for future practice, or to verify Lefebvre's own theories about everyday life, but to save France from a Russian-style state socialism.

Yet the students' fascination with Althusser, that likened the notion of an *epistemological break* with the break *they* had initiated by mounting the barricades, and that had threatened the entire state system, seemed to be reinforced by the contradictions between anti-intellectual students and professors (and/or technocratic administrators), which went beyond the customary generation gap. As students increasingly looked to *The Red Book of Chairman Mao* and equated their own actions with the closing of the universities in China in June 1966 (this had grown out of the ideological bases of China's cultural and "ongoing" revolution and out of the political decision to remain essentially agricultural), Lefebvre felt he had to show that none of the "neo-Marxist" notions had resolved the contradictions within Marxism, and that hence Althusserianism too was useless.

He found that Althusser's Stalinism evaded concrete problems by relying on structuralist tautologies that turn non-science into science. Conceding that Althusser had originally wanted to escape official Marxism with the help of structuralist ideology's links to science, linguistics and ethnology, Lefebvre accused Althusser of ignoring the resulting social stagnation under the guise of (internal) mobility, and of well-integrated and uncritical self-delusion.[51] For Althusser's theoretical revolution, maintained Lefebvre, perpetuated current administrative and political structures, cut theory off from action, encouraged suspect political tactics, and relied on circular moralizing which served the ends of the Party.[52] Althusser's pedantry, painful intellectual asceticism, lack of sensibility and sensuality, rejection of emotion, retreat from thought tied to empirical realities (for example, cities, production or space) were said to evade all reality by gazing through structuralist goggles.[53] And Althusserian economics were dismissed as theoretical discussions that avoided sociological analyses by concentrating on notions of exchange value and surplus value, notions which Lefebvre found unrelated to the formation and distribution of capital in a specific society. Briefly put, Lefebvre upheld his own Marx while attacking Althusser as "decerebrating, devertebrating and destructuring Marxism in the name of structuralism."[54]

VI

One would expect that *Everyday Life in the Modern World* (1968), one of Lefebvre's works best-known to English readers, would deal with empirical facts. Instead, this book continued where *Introduction to Modernity* left off—with philosophical ruminations about social conditions such as work and leisure, about literary works such as Joyce's *Ulysses* and Robbe-Grillet's 'new novel,' and about scholarly interests in language, music, and emotions. By looking at working-class life—mostly through literature—Lefebvre *found something extraordinary in its very ordinariness*.[55] He now focused on the notion of *festival*, linking the decline of celebration to the decline of peasant culture, to the advent of trade and of mass production, and to the transfiguration of everyday life. Festivals, he argued, cannot be replaced by art; they are linked to *style*. Even

> in the heart of poverty and (direct) oppression there was *style*; in former times *labours of skill* were produced, whereas today we have (commercialized) *products*, and exploitation has replaced violent oppression. Style gave significance to the slightest object, to actions and activities, to gestures; it was a concrete significance, not an abstraction taken piecemeal from a system of symbols.[56]

And because with the rise of the masses great styles (of cruelty, power, wisdom, civilizations) have disappeared, style and festival had to be resurrected—a resurrection that was seriously attempted in May 1968, when everyday life was to have been transformed.

In the meantime, the "art of consumption," the role of women, the need for money, the nature of working-class life, continue further to degrade style, to turn it into culture—a culture that fragments and disintegrates. Thus, Lefebvre found what we all know: everyday life is preserved in mediocrity,[57] is dominated by economic interests, and possibly, by americanization;[58] it has become "an object of consideration and is the province of organization; [and] the space-time of voluntary programmed self-regulation . . . replaces the spontaneous self-regulation of the competitive era."[59] Lefebvre's trenchant criticism, once more borrowing from structuralist language, turned especially against publicity and its very presence, through television, in every home.

> You are being looked after, cared for, told how to live better, how to dress fashionably, how to decorate your house, in short how to exist; you are totally and thoroughly programmed . . . [for] the act of consuming remains a permanent structure. The Smile Myth is out-ranked; consuming is no joke.[60]

Once more mediating among his peers, (or is it plagiarizing?) Lefebvre says that we consume signs, signs that Barthes and Lacan perceive as touching our unconscious, that reach hidden structures and form our personalities. Lefebvre extended the concept of superstructure to the Freudian unconscious and concluded that the satisfaction of some of our wants, together with the routinization and dullness of our lives (full of material comforts and consumption) leads to ambiguity (material vs. theoretical, constructive vs. destructive, affluent vs. needy). Lefebvre perceived the internal contradictions of society as the seeds that destroy everyday life, and as the basis of future society. And because our class society is full of terrorism, because its ruling class continues to exploit, organize, persuade, and punish for its own ends, Lefebvre exemplified through countless pages how history is living out Marx's predictions. He did fault Marx, however, for not predicting the details of capitalist development. But had urbanization been more advanced in his time, he argued, Marx would have recognized its significance, a significance Lefebvre now demonstrated. Marx *did* warn against the consequences of limitless expansion of trade, money, and the market. Because no one listened to him, only a total revolution—economic, political and cultural—could now save humanity. Disillusioned even with the Chinese model, Lefebvre now went so far as to suggest that the revolution might come about through *sexual revolution,* through juridical and political equality, through reforms that modify the relations between sexuality and society. (By avoiding terrorism and repression, people could make their own decisions.)

Clearly, Lefebvre's cultural speculations, which had to address the then current (urban Parisian) preoccupation with French Feudianism, fudged the revolutionary goals, goals that became reformist and that forgot the class struggle. For a change in individual consciousness, however radical its influence on industrial administration and production, cannot be likened to the overthrow of the state. Still, Lefebvre maintained that change would occur because people would rediscover the former *festival* with the help of play, art, and performances.[61] Aware of his reformism, he reminded us that the revolutionary qualities of *the festival* engender creation—first in the city and then in the entire society.

Lefebvre expanded this notion in *La pensée marxiste et la ville* (1972), where he traced every reference to the *city* in Marx and in Engels, to prove that they expected the class struggle to erupt there, insofar as the city's economic role led to the entire theory of surplus value, to the division of labor, etc.[62] Urbanization, then, was said to be central to revolution, to the *reproduction of the relations of production* and to the *production of space*— themes Lefebvre once again expanded into full-blown works.[63]

Basically, he now insisted that the extension of capitalism to the entire world did transform the forces of production as Marx had predicted and thereby created new sectors of production (and exploitation and domination), such as leisure activities, everyday life, knowledge, art, and urbanization. This double process allegedly helped to maintain and spread capitalism, so that in addition to expanding its world, capitalism continued to create more space for itself; urbanization, argues Lefebvre, is one of its extensions. And the many fragmentations of urbanism themselves were said to maintain capitalism and to impose a repressive unity through the separation of interest groups; through the consequences of speculation and of spiraling costs; through the appropriation of natural resources and of automation; and finally, through all the effects these factors have on individuals and on communities.

Convinced that urbanization is the cancer of modern life, that a Marxist research of its *space* might be the cure, Lefebvre started a journal—*Espaces et Société*—in 1970. Architects, city planners, sociologists and other urban experts were to explore problems of towns and cities—renovation, decentralization, ghettoization and commercialization—from a Marxist perspective. Lefebvre himself began with "Réflexions sur la politique de l'espace"[64] with attacks on urban sciences, urban specialists and their languages, which underneath a seeming objectivity are really concerned with spatial politics—politics that were found to be ideological, to dispose over financial, material and spatio-temporal resources. Questions and issues of policy formation were critically examined in this journal, although there was an increasing emphasis on empirical studies of development, on architectural solutions to social problems, and on social solutions through political and spatial arrangements. Lefebvre's own concern, inevitably, turned into "dialectical" quests about nature and culture, democracy and power, capitalism and socialism, production and consumption of space. Again, *La production de l'espace* (1974) enlarged these topics even further—in nearly 500 pages.

In the past, it seems, the concept of space made us think of mathematics, geometry, metaphysics, linguistics, or even knowledge, but never of social theory. Lefebvre, however, bent on proving that there exists a unity (Marx's totality) between physical, mental, and social space, recast philosophy, history, structuralism, and psychology into this new mold—and simultaneously tried to fit into it every theory about knowledge and literature. Hence, he talked of the contradictions and duality of space—its architectonic, absolute, abstract and differential components—and argued, for example, that insofar as abstract space is measured geometrically, or becomes subject to statistical and planning manipulations, it is quantified. But this quantity is said to become quality at the moment it is *consumed* as leisure (e.g., vacations use ocean, snow, or air) and to establish a class based qualitative bond. Or he discovered that

> in the area of leisure, the body takes back some of its rights, half-fictive, half-real; these rights hardly lead further than . . . to simulate natural life . . . to restitute desire and pleasure. Consumption satisfies needs; leisure and pleasure . . . get together even when falsely united in a space of representation; in consequence needs and desires oppose each other. . . . The contradictions within this dialectical unity lead to new contradictions, . . . to the reduction of mental space, of pressures and repressions, of manipulations and recuperations [and finally]. . . . of estheticism and rationalism.[65]

It would be unfair to forget Lefebvre's empirical observations, which do touch ground. His abstractions, however, relied on speculation and dealt with "intangibles," such as human values, personal well-being, political power, everyday strategy, zero population growth, and sexual freedom. It is sometimes difficult to remember Lefebvre's link to social facts, when we read:

> The space of the user is *lived*, not represented (conceived). In relation to the abstract space of architects, urbanists and planners, the space of performances that accomplish the everydayness of its users is a concrete space. That is to say subjective. Space of *subjects* and not of calculation, space of representation, has an origin: childhood with its trials, its acquisitions and lacks. The conflict between inevitably long and difficult maturation, and immaturation that leaves the initial resources and reserves intact, marks the lived space. There "privacy" affirms itself, more or less strongly, but conflictually, against the public.[66]

Unquestionably, Lefebvre's methodology "penetrated" the paradoxes of our public and private lives and traditions in order to transform them. But he never pinpointed just how he "restitutes the body through sensory-sensual space, through words, voice, smell, sound, through the non-visual, through sexualized energy . . . [and] through time;"[67] or how he found that the internal contradictions of city planning, advocacy planning, urban renewal and decentralization have been laid bare—except in his own rhetoric.

Even though Lefebvre may be correct in claiming that state and local power are at the service of a class and that politics extend to the domination of the individual's pleasure, it does not necessarily follow that individuals will assert themselves to create the ultimate revolution, a revolution that will follow the ideas of the young Marx, Engels, some of Lenin, and Fourier. At one point Lefebvre thought he could create his own *Harmony*—Fourier's ideal community—by "enlarging" the space of a spontaneous revolt in the Third World. (Such a space, he stated, might at first be political, urban, philosophical, social, theoretical, practical, intellectual, spiritual, abstract, concrete, peripheral, or central.) Because disintegration is most acute in large cities, Lefebvre was convinced that the revolution would begin on some "urban horizon," and that all the currently popular systems theories would blow up along with it.[68]

Lefebvre's strength came from the conviction that if only everything were caught in his dialectic, his theory would itself engender the revolution. (Recently he even predicted that he would bridge the ideological gap between himself and Althusser to set aside this final contradiction within Marxism.)[69] But in his strength lies his weakness. By constantly totalizing reality and philosophy, Lefebvre stretched some of his good ideas to absurdity—a fact that I have attempted to illustrate above.

Lefebvre's course was set long ago. His thirty years within the communist "church" appear to have left their mark: he was able to change his politics, his friends and his allegiances, but he could not abandon a certain amount of dogmatism. Still, his repetitious and informed arguments can be convincing when his steadfast optimism overcomes all obstacles, when he reinterprets French history, when his irony softens a trenchant social critique, or when his sparkling wit and throwaway sentences startle and beguile us. We must always keep in mind that Lefebvre is an idealist. Even though we too might like to live in the socialist society Lefebvre projects, his dialectic does not really transform social reality and space. But he can (and did) inspire young students in their first blush of Marxism to cast him, briefly, as their own

Messiah. In his enthusiasm, he resembles the young Marx, and thus he has kept Marxism alive. But his predictions of revolution have become routine.

Notes

1. Lefebvre and Guterman, Introduction, *Morceaux choisis de Karl Marx* (N.R.F.—1934); Lefebvre and Guterman, *La conscience mystifiée*, (N.R.F. 1938); Lefebvre and Guterman, *Cahiers de Lenine sur la dialectique de Hegel* (N.R.F., 1938).

2. Some of the others were, beside Lefebvre and Guterman, Georges Politzer, who soon turned his interest to psychoanalysis, Georges Friedmann, Pierre Morhange, and Paul Nizan. Until 1929 this group was not yet oriented completely toward materialist Marxism but had close contact with the surrealists, who believed that reality could be transcended.

3. Lichtheim, *Marxism in Modern France,* pp. 1–2.

4. Lefebvre, *La nationalisme contre les nations.*

5. Lefebvre, *Hitler au pouvoir.*

6. Lichtheim, *Marxism in Modern France,* provides a good overview; Ronald Tiersky, *French Communism: 1920–1972* uses a systems approach; the French figures I deal with in this book all address the subject; among political scientists, Stanley Hoffman, Mark Kesselman come to mind; see also Poster, *Existential Marxism in Postwar France.*

7. See chapter 2 on Althusser and Lefebvre's introduction to the American edition of *Dialectical Materialism.*

8. Lefebvre, *La somme et le reste,* pp. 357–58.

9. Schmidt, "Henri Lefebvre," p. 325; footnote, p. 338.

10. Lefebvre, *La somme et le reste,* p. 404.

11. Schmidt, "Henry Lefebvre," p. 329.

12. Lefebvre, *La somme et le reste,* p. 579.

13. See notes 1, 4, and 5, and bibliography up to 1957.

14. Lefebvre, *Dialectical Materialism,* Introduction, p. 17.

15. This reference is to the Twentieth Party Congress in 1956, which literally shocked the world and was to begin the "liberalization" of Russian society.

16. Lefebvre, *Les problèmes actuels du marxisme,* p. 7.

17. *Ibid.,* p. 13.

18. Lefebvre, "Marxisme et politique," *Revue Française de Science Politique* (1961), vol. 11. Also in *Au delà du structuralisme,* pp. 109–10.

19. Lefebvre, *Les problèmes actuels du marxisme,* pp. 118–19.

20. Lefebvre, "Marxisme et politique," *Au delà du structuralisme,* pp. 111–12.

21. Lefebvre, *Les problèmes actuels du marxisme,* p. 124.

22. *Ibid.*

23. *Ibid.*, p. 126.

24. Lefebvre, "Marxisme et politique," *Au delà du structuralisme*, p. 113.

25. *Ibid.*, p. 114.

26. Aron had moved right rather readily; Malraux broke with the Left over the Algerian war; Servan-Schreiber remained a Socialist—leading to a different sort of political break (see chapter 2 on Althusser).

27. Lefebvre, "La planification démocratique," *Au delà du structuralisme*, pp. 137–64.

28. *Ibid.*, pp. 121–22.

29. The nucleus of this group consists of socialist philosophers and sociologists in Yugoslavia, mostly from the University of Belgrade; at their yearly meetings they criticized both capitalism and the socialist state from a left perspective. The group was intermittently attacked by the Yugoslav government, and in recent years has been suppressed.

30. Lefebvre, "Marxisme et politique," *Au delà du structuralisme*, p. 134.

31. *Ibid.*, p. 136.

32. Lefebvre, *Introduction à la modernité*, p. 9.

33. *Ibid.*, p. 16.

34. *Ibid.*, p. 23.

35. *Ibid.*, p. 35.

36. *Ibid.*, p. 129.

37. Lefebvre, *Le langage et la société*, p. 19.

38. *Ibid.*, p. 96.

39. Pierre Rolle, "La dialectique est-elle nécessaire?" *Épistomologie Sociologique* (Paris: C.N.R.S., Centre d'études sociologiques (1972), 14 (14):127–137.

40. Lefebvre, *Le langage et la société*, pp. 193–4.

41. *Ibid.*, p. 195.

42. *Ibid.*, p. 201.

43. *Ibid.*, p. 217.

44. *Ibid.*, p. 231.

45. *Ibid.*, p. 367. Lefebvre's pleasure in playing on words is more apparent in French, as in this parody of Barthes' *écriture blanche*—the notion of the space between words (blank space). Lefebvre manages to combine appreciation with subtle ridicule and rhyming.

46. Lefebvre, *La somme et le reste*, pp. 559–73. Lefebvre, "Littérature et société," *Au delà du structuralisme*, pp. 241–459. Lefebvre, "Claude Lévi-Strauss et le nouvel éléatisme," *Au delà du structuralisme*, pp. 261–312. Also in Lefebvre, *L'homme et la société* (1966) no. 7–9, pp. 21–31, and no. 10–12, pp. 89–103. *Éléatism*, "Eleaticism," according to Webster (3d ed.), which defines the adjective "Eleatic" thusly: "relates to a school of Greek philosophers founded by Parmenides and developed by Zeno and marked by belief in the unity of being and the unreality of motion of change."

47. Lefebvre, *The Explosion: Marxism and the French Revolution*, p. 51.

48. *Ibid.*, pp. 12–13.

49. *Ibid.*, p. 130.

50. *Ibid.*, p. 154.

51. Lefebvre, "Les paradoxes d'Althusser," *Au delà du structuralisme,* p. 379.

52. *Ibid.*, p. 381.

53. *Ibid.*, p. 391.

54. *Ibid.*, p. 415.

55. Lefebvre, *Everyday Life in the Modern World,* p. 37.

56. *Ibid.*, p. 38.

57. *Ibid.*, p. 62.

58. *Ibid.*, p. 67.

59. *Ibid.*, p. 72.

60. *Ibid.*, p. 107.

61. *Ibid.*, p. 195.

62. Lefebvre, *La pensée marxiste et la ville,* p. 150.

63. Lefebvre, *La production de l'espace;* Lefebvre, *La survie du capitalisme.* The latter is, essentially, a collection of essays on the subject written between 1968 and 1973.

64. An address at the *Institut de l'urbanisme,* Paris, Jan. 13, 1970; printed in *Espaces et société,* pp. 3–13.

65. Lefebvre, *La production de l'espace,* pp. 408–9.

66. *Ibid.*, p. 418.

67. *Ibid.*, p. 419.

68. *Ibid.*, p. 432.

69. Talk on the "New Philosophers"—in particular a refutation of Bernard-Henri Lévy, André Glucksmann, and J. M. Benoist—in New York, May 1978; to be published.

Bibliography

Chalumeau, Jean-Luc. *La pensée en France: de Sartre à Foucault.* Paris: Fernand Nathan, 1974.

Ehlen, S. J. Peter, and Sigfried Rother. "Die Sinnfrage im Marxismus." *Stimmen der Zeit* (1975), no. 3, pp. 171–86.

Lefebvre, Henri. *Le nationalisme contre les nations.* Paris: Collection Problèmes, 1937.

—— *Hitler au pouvoir, Bilan de cinq années de fascisme en Allemagne.* Paris: Bureau d'Éditions, 1938.

—— *Le matérialism dialectique.* Paris: Alcan, collection Nouvelle Encyclopédie philosophique, 1939. Translated as *Dialectical Materialism,* New York: Viking, 1968.

Lefebvre, Henri. *Nietzsche.* Paris: E.S.I., collection Socialisme et culture, 1939.

—— *L'existentialisme.* Paris: Sagittaire, 1946.

—— *Critique de la vie quotidienne.* Paris: Grasset, 1947; L'Arche, 1958.

—— *Logique formelle, logique dialectique.* Paris: Sociales, 1947.

—— *Descartes.* Paris: Français réunis, collection Hier et aujourd'hui, 1947.

—— *Marx et la liberté.* Geneva: Trois Collines, 1947.

—— *Pour connaître la pensée de Marx.* Paris: Bordas, 1948.

—— *Le Marxisme.* Paris: P.U.F., collection *Que sais'je?* 1948.

—— *Pascal.* Vol. 1, Paris: Nagel, 1949. Vol. 2, Paris: Nagel, 1954.

—— *Diderot.* Paris: Français réunis, collection Hier et aujourd'hui, 1949.

—— *Contribution à l'Esthetique.* Paris: Sociales, 1953.

—— *Musset,* Paris: L'Arche, collection Grands dramaturges, 1955.

—— *Rabelais.* Paris: Français réunis, collection Hier et aujourd'hui, 1955.

—— *Pignon.* Paris: Falaise, 1956.

—— *Pour connaître la pensée de Lénine.* Paris: Bordas, 1957.

—— *Problèmes actuels du marxisme.* Paris: Presses Universitaires de France, 1958.

—— *La somme et le reste.* Paris: La Nef, 1959.

—— Fondements d'une sociologie de la quotidienneté. Paris: L'Arche, 1962.

—— *Introduction à la modernité.* Paris: Minuit, collection Arguments, 1962.

—— *Marx philosophe.* Paris: Minuit, collection Arguments, 1962.

—— *Métaphilosophie.* Paris: Minuit, collection Arguments, 1965.

—— *La proclamation de la commune.* Paris: Gallimard, 1965.

—— *Les Pyrhénées.* Lausanne: Rencontre, 1965.

—— *Le langage et la société.* Paris: Gallimard, collection Idées, 1966.

—— *La sociologie de Marx.* Paris: P.U.F., 1966. Translated as *The Sociology of Marx.* New York: Vintage, 1969.

—— *Position: contre les technocrates.* Paris: Gonthier, 1967.

—— "Sur une interprétation du marxisme." *L'homme et la société* (1967), no. 4, pp. 3–22.

—— *Le droit à la ville.* Paris: Anthropos, 1968.

—— "Forme, fonction, structure dans le capital." *L'homme et la société* (1968), no. 7, pp. 69–81.

—— "Les idéologies de la croissance." *L'homme et la société* (1968), no. 7, pp. 69–81.

—— *L'irruption: de Nanterre au sommet.* Paris: Anthropos, 1968. Translated as *The Explosion: Marxism and the French Revolution.* New York: Monthly Review Press, 1968.

—— *La vie quotidienne dans le monde moderne.* Paris: Gallimard, collection Idées, 1968. Translated as *Everyday Life in the Modern World.* New York: Harper Torchbooks, 1971.

—— *Logique formelle, logique dialectique.* Paris: Anthropos, 1969.

—— *La fin de l'histoire.* Paris: Minuit, 1970.

—— *Le manifeste différentialiste.* Paris: Gallimard collection Idées, 1970.

—— "Réflexions sur la politique de l'espace." *Espaces et sociétés* (1970), 1:3–13.

—— *Du rural à l'urbain.* Paris: Anthropos, 1970.

—— *Au delà du structuralisme.* Paris: Anthropos, 1971.

—— "Engels et l'utopie." *Espaces et sociétés* (1971), 1:3–9.

—— *L'idéologie structuraliste.* Paris: Anthropos, 1971.

—— "La ville et l'urbain." *Espaces et sociétés* (1971), 1:3–7.

—— "La commune de Paris, fête populaire." *Dialogue* (1972), 11(3):360–75.

—— *La pensée marxiste et la ville.* Paris: Casterman, "Mutation, Orientations," 1972.

—— *La survie du capitalisme.* Paris: Anthropos, 1972.

—— *Trois textes pour le théatre.* Paris: Anthropos, 1972.

—— *Espaces et politique.* Paris: Anthropos, 1973.

—— "Le mondial et le planétaire." *Espaces et sociétés* (1973), pp. 15–22.

—— *La production de l'espace.* Paris: Anthropos, 1974.

—— "What is the Historical Past?" *New Left Review* (March 1975), no. 90, pp. 27–34.

Lefebvre, Henri and Pierre Fougeyrollas. *Le jeu de Kostas Axelos.* Paris: Fata Morgana, 1973.

Lefebvre, Henri and Norbert Guterman. *Morceaux choisis de Karl Marx.* Paris: Gallimard, 1964. Originally published N.R.F., 1934.

—— *La conscience mystifiée.* Paris: N.R.F., 1938.

—— *Cahiers de Lénine sur la dialectique de Hegel.* Paris: Gallimard, 1967.

—— *Morceaux choisies de Hegel.* Paris: Gallimard, 1969.

—— *La révolution urbaine.* Paris: Gallimard, Idées, 1971.

Lewis, G. Henri. "Pascal review of v. 1." *Revue philosophique de la France et de l'étranger* (October 1951), 141:603.

Lichtheim, George. *Marxism in Modern France.* New York: Columbia University Press, 1966.

Louran, René. "Review of Henri Lefebvre's *La fin de l'histoire.*" *L'homme et la société* (1970), 18(10–12):309–12.

Lucien, Sebag. *Marxisme et structuralisme.* Paris: Payot, 1964.

Martinet, André. *Elements of General Linguistics.* London: Faber and Faber Ltd., 1960.

Menucci, V. "La molla del progresso in un revisionista: Henri Lefebvre." *Revista di filosofia neo-scolastica* (1970), 62:709–18.

Nisbet, Robert A. "Explaining the Dual Revolution." *New York Times Book Review,* May 19, 1968, p. 6.

Poster, Mark. *Existentialism in Postwar France.* Princeton: Princeton University Press, 1975.

Schmidt, Alfred. "Henri Lefebvre and Contemporary Interpretations of Marx." In Dick Howard and Karl E. Klare, eds., *The Unknown Dimension.* New York: Basic Books, 1972.

Tiersky, Ronald. *Marxism in Modern France.* New York: Columbia University Press, 1974.

Vachet, André. "De la fin de l'histoire à l'analyse différentielle: la révolution urbaine." *Dialogue* (1972), 11(3):400–19.

Hermeneutics and Structuralism

Paul Ricoeur was born in Valence in 1913. He now divides his time between the Divinity School at the University of Chicago and the University of Paris, and continues to pursue his four main interests: he is university teacher, student of the history of philosophy, member of the editorial board of the left-Catholic journal *Esprit,* and bearer of the Christian message. The latter two activities began when he studied theology with Gabriel Marcel and when, in 1932, he joined the group around Emmanuel Mounier, who had founded *Esprit.* But his concern with philosophy was sparked when as a prisoner in Germany during World War II he came upon Husserl's phenomenology—the philosophy that was eventually to provide him with the means to integrate all his interests. For he claims to have made Husserl the basis of his own thinking ever since translating Husserls' *Ideen I*[1] into French.

Sartre and Merleau-Ponty too had become acquainted with Husserl during this period, but their interpretations were radically different from Ricoeur's. They emphasized Husserl's notion of *Lebenswelt* (life-world), along with the later Husserl's and Heidegger's being-in-the-world, by stressing the primacy of thought as related to *existence* and to subject-object relations; and they enlisted phenomenology in the service of their Marxism. Ricoeur's phenomenology, however, began

> not from what is most silent in the operation of consciousness, but from its relationship to things mediated by signs as these are elaborated in a spoken culture. The first act of consciousness is meaning [(*Meinen*). . . . (And)] the act of signifying is . . . intentionality.[2]

Ricoeur, then, linked intentionality of consciousness to biblical symbolism in order to reach the deepest meaning of things-as-they-actually-are. Heidegger's appropriation from hermeneutics (associated with Hermes, the divine messenger of God) of the concept of *Vorverstaendnis* (pre-understanding)—the idea that all knowledge is relative to what is already known and therefore cannot be unprejudiced—was particularly useful in so far as Heidegger's secular revival of a biblical concept provided the example for Ricoeur's own project. (That literary scholars also apply this doctrine of pre-understanding to the reading of texts helped Ricoeur to move easily from theology to philosophy and literature.) Sartre's phenomenology, however, in its popular existentialist incarnation, was used by some to foster the primacy of their own desires and appetites, while Ricoeur's version tended to uphold Christian morals. Furthermore, especially in the 1950s, this interpretation, which in Marxist terminology would have its origin in the superstructural elements, aligned Ricoeur politically with all those who opposed Sartre's pro-communist politics, and therefore with a number of the structuralists—even though Saussurean linguistics began to interest Ricoeur only in the early 1960s. Ricoeur's political writings, "What does humanism mean?" (1956), "Faith and Culture" (1957), or "From Marxism to Contemporary Communism" (1959),[3] unlike Sartre's, were not action-oriented, but intended to influence the course of history by raising moral and ethical concerns. Hence, his colleagues on the left, such as Lefebvre, could always respect him for his sincerity, while dismissing even his most radical ideas as politically conservative.

Ricoeur taught philosophy at Strasbourg until 1956, when he accepted an appointment at the prestigious Sorbonne. Ten years later he volunteered for a professorship at the newly created and left-oriented University of Nanterre—a move his colleagues believed to have been motivated by his wish to be an active political educator. For he hoped at Nanterre to show how intervention (being-in-the-world) on three levels (technical, political, and professorial/clerical) could pave the way toward a better society; how the various philosophical concepts of ethics of conviction and of responsibility (from Plato and Aristotle to Dilthey and Weber) could be applied and turned into moral reform. But his effort was not appreciated by the radical students (many of them Lefebvre's) who believed in revolution, especially after 1969, when he had become rector. According to reports, Ricoeur had taken extremely strong positions against both conservatives and revolutionaries and by March 1970 was forced to resign. The left students had begun to refer to him publicly as the "old clown," while he "regretted that the university had allowed itself to be put on the defensive, so that it might die even before it had really been born."[4]

The entire experience appears to have come as a shock: since then, Ricoeur has devoted himself predominantly to uncover "what symbolic language conceals." His lectures at the universities of Louvain, Toronto, Yale and Princeton were, for the most part, addressed to philosophers of language, to linguists, and to professors of comparative literature, though his topics are equally interesting to educators, theologians, humanists, and political thinkers.

Ricoeur represents a frequently forgotten strain of the French tradition: an ecumenism that searches unencumbered by ecclesiastics for ethics and moral values. He always dismissed the Sartrean version of phenomenology as "covering every sort of popular presentation of appearance or appearings" and continued to fall back on his innate religion, his theological training, and his faith. As a believer, Ricoeur expects to reach people through their humanity; and, as an intellectual, he is as eager to demythologize religion and notions of good and evil as he is to point to the unscientific components of science. His search was always for the Husserlian first act of consciousness, for the basic meaning which would be the truth behind the phenomena: these would coincide, for Ricoeur, with the belief in God. This, too, accounts for the ongoing arguments with Sartre, whose nihilism Ricoeur had to disprove.

So he showed how the "sense of the negative" of which Hegel took possession reemerged in Sartre, who allegedly linked it to Husserl's concept of intentionality and thereby "carried this phenomenology of nihilating acts to the level of an ontology of nothingness."[5] Claiming to admire this tour de force, Ricoeur nevertheless "proved" that his own (and Marcel's) phenomenology used the same intellectual antecedents and yet arrived at another level of freedom, a freedom which is said to imply the possibility of giving existence, of infusing the soul, and which could never exist (as it does for Sartre) in its own nothingness.[6] For both he and Marcel allegedly never wavered from a philosophy of affirmation, an ontology of *Seinsverbundenheit,* and a belief in the mystery of being and of incarnate existence. Such a phenomenology "includes more than the repossession of consciousness, . . . includes consciousness of the body," and allows for an opening up by a liberating presence.[7] Ricoeur's accent is on "meaningful" participation. Hence he sides with Camus and Merleau-Ponty against Sartre (when they split over questions of Russian-style communism), because Camus invoked moral values, and Merleau-Ponty underlined the notion of freedom by joining the "owned body" to being-in-the-world.[8] Ricoeur praises them both for linking freedom to spontaneity and to total involvement in a situation, to a "sense of being that is said to exist," and that (by implication) cannot flourish in a controlled society. Ricoeur emphasizes the importance of freedom, whether he confronts the social determinism of large-scale bureaucracies, ideologies, the limitation of psychological studies, pacifism, colonialism, the Algerian war, or the Hungarian rebellion.

Like Hegel, and the whole idealist/critical tradition, Ricoeur integrates all thought through mediation. He forestalls his critics by looking at issues from every possible angle, thus preempting their criticism. He "thinks the thought of the *Other*," so that it is difficult to find an argument Ricoeur has not already anticipated. Even the ideas of Nietzsche, Marx, and Freud ("protagonists of suspicion who rip away masks and pose the novel problem of the lie of consciousness and consciousness as lie")[9] are mediated into his hermeneutics and become just another part of his project. Rhetoric, in its Platonic ambiguity as search for truth and ability to lie, and its location in speech as well as in linguistics, is the key to understanding individuals within their surroundings. Ricoeur always searches for underlying *consciousness,* for the *noematic* (perceived) aspect of consciousness of *something,* in a specific subjective context. This quest for truth inevitably oscillates between Ricoeur's own situation and the philosopher's aim to universalize his experience. So he must divulge his own thought, ask the questions no one else could ask, and then find the universal truth underlying this experience. According to Ricoeur, this process occurs only in communication with *Others.* Hence truth becomes intersubjective. At first Ricoeur set out to find this truth, as Husserl did, by "bracketing" things as they appear to us directly but, more recently, he has focused on language and written texts which are said to fix "every utterance or group of utterances" by writing.[10] Language, he now argues, as the basic tool of culture, contains all hermeneutics or meanings. Just as for Heidegger, "man is language": its structure and logic are intrinsic to socialization.

II

Ricoeur's overriding concern is the unity of the human person. His phenomenology of the will, which focuses on the articulations between the voluntary and involuntary moments of consciousness, is oriented by the ideal of this unity. He proposes to show how the study of their reciprocity can revitalize the classical problems of the relations between "freedom" and "nature."[11] Both his concern and his method are Husserlian.

In *Husserl: An Analysis of his Phenomenology* (1967), he traces Husserl's thought to the Leibnitzian and Kantian sense of *Erscheinung*, to Hegel's everyday experience (not to his phenomenology of the spirit), to Hume's habit of criticizing language, to Descartes' notions of doubt and of the *cogito,* and to his contemporaries—the Munich psychologists Pfaender and Geiger, to Scheler, Heidegger, Hartmann, and Jaspers.[12] He separates Husserl's idealistic interpretation and his logic from the method (a mix of phenomenological philosophy with phenomenology as an actual practice)[13] asserting the primacy of perception among intentional acts that eventually became being-in-the-world—in the later Husserl, in Heidegger, and in the other existentialists. Ricoeur says that both Heidegger and Sartre also focus on this theme, but that his own reading of Husserl puts less emphasis on existence and more on a strict problematic and on specific significations. He explicitly includes *all* of Husserl (early and late), whereas Husserl's other followers, such as Sartre and Merleau-Ponty, are said to concentrate on the later works alone, where perception took precedence over other problems and bodily experience was subsumed in consciousness (as intention and signification). Ricoeur, too, acknowledges the importance of the "owned body" (as the locus of all ambiguity) or its inherent meaning: it unites all intention, subsumes both the voluntary and the involuntary, the projected and the given, the mind and the body. But pure consciousness became associated with the dynamism of the will, he argues; thus intentionality, which was to recover and to reconstitute the subjective world of meaning, became central.[14]

Ricoeur experts point out that in this respect Ricoeur differs from Husserl, for whom consciousness was associated with reflection; his own "project" is formulated in decision and becomes associated in action with bodily motivation and then with "complete formulation and execution." Rasmussen explains that Ricoeur's "notion of project is a simple volitional task that is voluntarily initiated and voluntarily achieved."[15] But the dualism between physical and mental experience, and between voluntary and involuntary correlations and reciprocities is not so easily overcome.

Roman Leick finds Ricoeur's preoccupation with will consistent with his goal, because the unification of theoretical and practical wisdom (*Vernunft*) is said to have its locus in both human will and in the "owned body with all its ambiguities."[16] Experiences like guilt, bondage, alienation, and sin are part of Ricoeur's existentialist philosophy. His contemporaries, he argues, forget to differentiate between finitude and guilt. But he had to include the dimensions of evil in the structure of will, so that ordinary language became inadequate; and existential phenomenology did not encompass symbolic language. Without symbolism, states Ricoeur,

> guilt and evil cannot be discussed, since we have a direct language to say purpose, motive, and 'I can,' but speak of evil by means of metaphors such as estrangement, errance, burden, and bondage. These primary symbols do not occur unless they are embedded within intricate narratives of myth which tell the story of how evil began: how at the beginning of time the gods quarreled; how a primitive man was tempted, trespassed a prohibition, and became an exiled rebel.[17]

In order to get away from direct reflection alone, Ricoeur "introduced a hermeneutical dimension within the structure of reflective thought itself."[18] He goes on to explain that at first he tried to limit the definition of hermeneutics to the interpretation of symbolic language, whereas more recently, he links hermeneutics to the written texts and looks at the problem of language as such rather than, as previously, at the structures of will or at the symbolism of myth. At the time, he recalls, he responded to the fact that structuralism was beginning to replace existentialism; and he became increasingly interested in British and American philosophy of language.

Still, he had begun in *The Voluntary and the Involuntary* (1950), to describe will eidetically, that is, through extraordinarily accurate and vivid recall of images. He had then (in the following volume) empirically analyzed the will caught in guilt. But he found that he could not write the third volume, a *Poetics of the Will,* before working out conditions of freeing and reconstituting the will estranged in the "guilt of evil." *Fallible Man* and *The Symbolism of Evil,* both published in 1965, no longer represent the empirical descriptions of the captured will.[19] Ricoeur felt that this treatment was inadequate, but that he could solve the problem with the help of a hermeneutic detour through Freud.

In *The Symbolism of Evil,* extensive explorations of subjective views and conscience, of self-awareness, of interrogation and suspicion are said to have become a methodological problem. Ricoeur becomes the theologian when he enters realms of "radical vs. presuppositional beginnings," refers to symbolism along with the *revealing* power of the symbol, and talks about the search for the "first truth"[20]—a search he then rejects to interpret the various meanings of linguistic symbols—within language and speech.[21] Countless examples from the Bible and from Greek mythology meant to retrieve the intentions of every concept—of evil and of absolution—to show not only how sin and grace are inextricably interwoven, but how with the help of bracketing they can be explained rationally and separated conceptually.[22] Words may change the heart, maintains Ricoeur, and symbols give rise to thought, so thought leads to reflection and speculation, and to the three main links between the experiences of evil and of reconciliation.[23] First, because reconciliation is looked for *in spite of evil,* he finds hope in its signs, in its milieu, in its locus, and in its history, even though such hope is not logical, eschatological or systematic. Next, the existence of the *in spite of* itself allows for the emergence of good. And, finally, the contradiction of evil serves to instruct and thereby ties it all to God.[24] (Elsewhere he interprets the myth of punishment in much the same way, by enumerating difficulties and paradoxes, by "demythologizing punishment to find its rational core," and by reinterpreting it in Christian terms that "shatter the myth and reinstate its reality.") It all emanates from

> the miracle of the Logos; from Him proceeds the retrograde movement of the true . . . [and] what in the old theodicy was only the expedient of false knowledge becomes the understanding of hope [and] the necessity that we are seeking is the highest rational symbol that this understanding of hope can engender.[25]

Ricoeur attempts to fuse modern rationality and hermeneutics with morals, with the belief in God and a higher order. Through demythologizing religious symbols—from the myth of original sin, that is, of Adam and Eve, to the myths of the ancient Middle East, Israel and Greece—he reinstalls God by examining him "scientifically." He tries to justify his position by saying that Lévi-Strauss, too, recognizes that symbols are opaque, are related by means of analogy, and are subject to the diversities of language and culture. Instead of searching for inner structures, he tries to find out how symbols emerge in the thoughts of individuals and how they are interpreted. That is why he went to Freud, for whom symbols are central, and who also had tried to explain the connections between individual freedom and culture. Ricoeur's hermeneutics, however, are meant to span all systems of symbolic interpretation, including Freud's symbolism of dreams and of the unconscious.

III

The French, unlike the Americans, had neglected Freud and psychoanalysis. The Freudian analysts, in spite of their much publicized split in 1953, which brought Lacan to public attention, were a small group with relatively little impact. In this climate,

Ricoeur's *Freud and Philosophy: An Essay in Interpretation* was a particularly impressive tour de force.

At first glance, psychoanalysts may have difficulty recognizing their Freud in Ricoeur's version, for Ricoeur is less interested in clinical theory or practice than he is in Freud's metapsychology and in the similarities between dream symbols and religious symbols: both are said to ignore the opposition between distortion and revelation.[26] In ethical reflection, in the symbolism of the servile will, or, for example,

> in the archaic form of avowal, the image of a spot—the spot one removes, washes, wipes away—analogously designates stain as the sinner's situation in the dimension of the sacred. That this is a symbolic expression is amply confirmed both by the expressions and by the corresponding actions of purification.[27]

And in dreams, too, he continues, symbolism is the

> royal road to psychoanalysis . . . [it] attests that we constantly mean something other than what we say; in dreams the manifest meaning endlessly refers to hidden meaning . . . dreams express the private archeology of the dreamer, which at times coincides with that of entire peoples. . . . But even when they do not coincide, the mythical and the oneiric have in common this structure of double meaning.[28]

Poetic imagination, as well, he goes on, uses symbols. It is

> the least understood of the three . . . [with] its power of forming images. [For] in no way does poetic imagination reduce itself to the power of forming a mental picture of the unreal; the imagery of sensory origin merely serves as a vehicle and as material for the verbal power whose true dimension is given to us by the oneiric and the cosmic.[29]

Ricoeur finds these three types of symbolism to be coextensive with language itself. Because in all of them, cosmos, desire, and the *imaginary* achieve speech, Freud's method of free association seemed the best suited to Ricoeur's philosophy of language.

Ricoeur's interpretation of Freud is alien to all the Anglo-Saxon versions. Even Jacques Lacan's Freud focuses on symptoms as well as on symbols; he zeros in on his patient's spoken words, on the language between analyst and analysand, whereas Ricoeur scrutinizes Freud's texts from what he calls a dynamic Saussurean perspective. He differentiates, for example, various "multiple dualities," such as the structural duality of the sensory sign and the signification it carries, or the intentional duality of the sign and the object it designates, and then superimposes the duality of the sensory sign and the signification as a relation of meaning to meaning.[30] Thus Ricoeur's symbolism is said to multiply meanings and expressions of physical and mental dimensions, of levels and analogies, of relations between manifest and latent content that must be interpreted with the help of a "rigid" phenomenological dialectic. He explains this dialectic, by tracing symbols—from Aristotles' logic and biblical exegesis, to Cassirer's mediations; from Kant's questions about the objective validity of subjective representation to Nietzsche's *Deutung* or *Auslegung*, ending up with psychoanalysis. Thus he finds that a new "school of suspicion (coincidental with Foucault's age of man) has gradually emerged, represented by Nietzsche, Marx, and Freud."[31] These "three masters who are seemingly mutually exclusive" all doubt the primacy of the sacred, and "mediate a science of meaning that is irreducible to immediate consciousness of meaning."[32] Ricoeur understands their so-called "dispossession of consciousness," as an act of reflection and as a first gesture of reappropriation (of the incarnate), which, of course, is unacceptable to the followers of Nietzsche, Marx, and Freud. But Ricoeur once again counters every objection to his own argument and concludes that the real question is neither about hermeneutics nor about style, because the crises of language, of interpretation, and of reflection can be overcome only together.[33] When the unconscious becomes conscious, maintains Ricoeur, the rivalry of interpretations will be comprehended in the double sense of the term: it will be justified by reflection and embodied in the work. By implication, the irreligiousness of these thinkers is converted.

Ricoeur calls his dialectic with Freud his "concrete reflection," as he gradually mediates every conceivable opposition into his final debate with Freud.[34] And although he states that he does not bother with the post-Freudians, he picks up some of their criticisms, when, for instance, he comments on Ernest Nagel's well-known critique of psychoanalysis as unscientific and un-verifiable[35] and proceeds to show how psychoanalysis might be "reintegrated" into scientific psychology by using themes like adaptation, structurization, evolution, and ego psychology. Still, Ricoeur immediately shows how such reintegration would be neither operational enough for the psychologists nor acceptable to the Freudians, for whom motivation is primarily unconscious. Ricoeur himself locates motivation in the field of speech or near-speech, even though it is said to be dissociated from common language because it is deciphered through dreams, symptoms, and formulations of language.[36] As he mediates between psychoanalysis and psychology—from the reality of the experimentalists' stimuli to the reality that surfaces by the working through of fantasies, to reality testing as a feature of secondary process, to the concept of ego strength—he proves the legitimacy of psychoanalysis as a historical rather than an empirical science. It is a different science, because its investigations and motivations, according to Ricoeur, are limited to the semantics of desire.[37]

All this is said to be part of the dialectical war of hermeneutics which has three distinct moments of progressive encounters between a phenomenological and a non-phenomenological interpretation—opposition of motivation, approximation, and the Hegelian moment that restores a radicalized understanding of the symbol and the subject.[38] The discussion revolves around a "perceptualist model of language versus a world of perceived objects," and around reflection that is to rediscover the Hegelian being-there of the mind. Ricoeur credits psychoanalysis for having helped his original search to discover the unconscious through the conscious with the help of language. But instead of focusing on the relationship with the *Other*, as Lacan does, Ricoeur focuses on the intersubjectivity of expression, "since the intersubjective structure of desire is itself the profound truth of the Freudian libido theory."[39] Hence, "phenomenological reduction and Freudian analysis are homologous in that both aim at the same thing. *The reduction is like an analysis*. . . ."[40] Because this dialectic between psychoanalytic theory and phenomenology keeps them both within their boundaries, Ihde finds that "the Freudian hermeneutics of suspicion becomes the limiting means by which the transcendental illusion is to be overcome."[41] In its stead, Ricoeur constructs a "hermeneutics of belief." As might be expected, Lacan attacks such hermeneutics as reading in the succession of man's mutations, the progress of the signs according to which he constitutes his history . . . a history that casts into limbo of pure contingency what the analysts at every stage are dealing with.[42] Indeed Ricoeur's view of history and of the centrality of belief displaces sexuality as the nodal point of desire—in the Oedipal triangle, as well as in the analytic relationship. Thus Ricoeur's Freud leaves out clinical transference, which is the tool of all psychoanalysis, including Lacan's.

Freud and Philosophy concludes with an emphasis on symbols, (their overdetermination, their sublimation, and their hierarchical order) and with examples of cultural and religious symbolism. Using illustrations from Oedipus Rex—as tragedy of destiny and as legend, or as the drama of incest and parricide—Ricoeur, not unlike Freud, demonstrates the similarity of religious and psychoanalytic hermeneutics. This "concrete dialectic" then becomes "the poetic that keeps man's cultural existence from being a huge artifice."[43] The timelessness of symbols (they are the locus for repressed childhood conflicts and at the same time have existed through all of human consciousness) is said to unite the sublime (or sacred) with the concerns of everyday life.[44] Hence Ricoeur finds that psychoanalytic thought has enriched his understanding of evil: symbols no longer give rise only to thought but also to idols. Still, Ricoeur accepts Freud only on condition that Freud does not damage or destroy his own world of mysticism, spirituality, art, and religion.[45]

IV

Ricoeur's being-in-the-world took the form of participating in conferences and of publishing in many journals. Some of these contributions were collected in History and Truth, in The Conflict of Interpretations, and in Political and Social Essays. The articles within each volume do not follow in chronological order nor did their publication in English; they were instead arranged topically, centering around: critical and theological perspectives, questions of power and affirmation, hermeneutics and psychoanalysis, symbolism and violence, religion and faith, the meaning of man, politics and the state, Christian and society, and, in *The Rule of Metaphor* (1977), on rhetoric, semantic and metaphor. The range of concerns is impressive.

Ricoeur tends to find fault with sociology, for example, because it objectifies all organized social forms without properly accounting for belief.[46] Yet, in "Urbanization and Secularization," he links Weber's "disenchantment of nature" to both the dissolution of religion and to its "flowering as an original theme";[47] but where Weber would talk of the contradiction between the *is* and the *ought*, between the *Wertrational* and the *Zweckrational*, Ricoeur resorts to the need for belief—a concept sociologists do in fact objectify as ideology, as a social function, or as an attempt at rationalization.

Ricoeur's antagonism to Marx is rooted in both the latter's expectation of the class struggle and in his anti-religious bias. Ricoeur argues that because we live in a pluralistic world we must incorporate Marx's thought. In "Work and the Word," for example, he constructs a dialectic between the power of speech and industrial work. He enters Marx's arguments on the divison of labor to prove, eventually, that Marx may have been partially right, but that communism is wrong. So he reflects on a theology and a philosophy of work that would bring "the word" into Marxist praxis, tying it to alienated industrial work, and to the "socio-economic degradation of work [that] corresponds to the usurped dignity of the word which is all the more arrogant as it does not seem to realize that it too is negotiated on a market of services."[48]

Since industrial production, with its centralized control, is the real cause of all alienation, it is said to create a new civilization of work, with a new culture that makes workers part of the economy but fails to give them access to liberal careers, to artistic and literary expression. Both capitalism and communism are undemocratic and uncivilized: the one glorifies the efficient, pragmatic and impersonal technocrats, and the other, the use of ideology. Ricoeur proposes to replace ideology with theology and wants to "correct the miseries of the word . . through the virtues of work."[49] The word is to become a *corrective* for the division of labor and for political participation; it is to be used to relate *theoria* and *praxis* through education, and it ought to be employed to create literature, arts, and theology.

He again addressed this issue in his essay on "Violence and Language"—two subjects whose confrontation is said to underlie all of the problems we can pose about humanity: "Speech, discussion and rationality draw their unity of meaning . . . [in] their attempt to reduce violence, [since] when placing itself in the orbit of reason, violence already begins to negate itself."[50] Violence is related to tyranny through words (they seduce, persuade and flatter) and to poetry, politics and philosophy (they denounce tyranny). As components of language, the latter endeavors are said only to pursue rational goals. Ricoeur dismisses their calculating aspects, because calculation itself conspires with violence. But the recognition that violence can emerge through language is to be the first step to nonviolence, to rationality, and to "mythical interpellation and prophetic language."

Ricoeur's arguments appeal to our wish for peace when, for instance, he asks under what conditions the nonviolent man may be something other than a yogi (as opposed to the commissar in Koestler's sense), or how we can express the value of nonviolence (it is postulated as a reaction to long periods of intense violence) as a valuable form of resistance. Thus Ricoeur focuses on the peace resulting from the *Sermon on the Mount*, connecting it to history rather than to religion, and opposes it to the consequences of individual and mass psychology and to terror. When he ends up by focusing on the historical impact of language, this impact itself becomes a technique coupled to a spiritual system: the implications of Gandhi's language, for instance, included truth, poverty, justice, chastity, patience, intrepidity, contempt for death, and mediation.[51] Gandhi is one of Ricoeur's heroes, because, unlike other mystics, Gandhi applied Christian virtues to political ends and understood the "dialectic of prophetic nonviolence and progressivist violence . . . in the wish to make history."[52] His nonviolence turned into a force.

Ricoeur states that he aligns himself with Marx, insofar as they both perceive history as being made by the state—the seat of a concentration and transmutation of violence. For the state as the only legitimate arbiter of law and violence controls power; it also commands the allegiance of individuals by eliciting feelings of patriotism that make them go to war. Hence the state is frequently said to be immoral, since it sets man against man, thereby turning them all into murderers.[53] But Ricoeur denounces power, whether he mediates between the thoughts of Aristotle and Plato, Hegel and the gospels of Jesus Christ or St. Paul, or connects these thoughts to Machiavelli's murderous and deceptive Prince who with the strength of the lion and the cunning of the fox, institutionalized violence so that it became measurable by the law and administered by the court. In many different contexts, he describes war as having become sanctioned murder, which allows questions of individual responsibility and morality to be overlooked (for example in Nazi concentration camps or in Budapest in 1956). But ethical conduct that is to assure the survival of the state, always assumes murder: only total reconciliation of man with man could solve this problem.

Ricoeur has difficulty in reconciling his idealism to realpolitik, because he simultaneously searches for an assessment of current politics and for the evil of power (in such diverse forms as *The Prince,* the Socialist party, or Vietnam). He acknowledges that neither Plato, the prophets of Israel, nor Socrates ever solved the problem of the relation between power and evil, and that Marxism-Leninism has only succeeded in reducing political evil to economic evil. The false claim of the end of Stalinism in the Khrushchev report is given as an example of the evil of state-controlled socialism: its power cannot wither away; it can only suppress antagonisms and turn people into objects with the help of forced labor, inducements, and threats of deportation; it produces its own ideology.[54] Political participation by all the people in a liberal system, or in a neo-Yugoslav experiment, concludes Ricoeur, could remedy the current disaffection and disenfranchisement.

Marxists who claim to share his aims, argues Ricoeur, are so eager for the revolution that they simplify instead of limiting themselves to Marx's "initial sociological reduction . . . at the level where ideas are inherently reducible to ideology."[55] He suggests they forget about superstructure, that is, thought, as primarily a factor of domination. His own dialectic, Ricoeur feels, is more flexible and more complex, because it does not simply oppose theory and practice—it moves simultaneously between saying and doing, signifying and making, working and speaking. Thus alienation is implicitly ruled out.

Ricoeur's way of restoring meaning and belief to humanity suggests a mild Luther. His condemnation of both church and state power and his assertion that one must act in the world to manifest the Christian faith sound like sermons. Yet Ricoeur also offers specific advice. Because individuals are to be helped to think for themselves, he attacks B. F. Skinner's operant conditioning as mentalist psychology that subverts personal autonomy and subjugates people to the power of existing institutions.[56] Political action, he argues, must be connected to institutional reform, so that the state will be stronger, while its power and bureaucracy will be limited. Conditioning subverts the "actualization" of freedom. But noninterference would encourage the emergence of qualities in individuals; and liberal politics would bring about a functioning socialism. Hence, he suggests we foster artistic activity, leisure, mondiality, world civilization, and humanism to open up to new ideas and to promote a new man.[57] Both the unity and the differences of men and of nationalities are reaffirmed when he states, for instance, "in every civilization one can recover those values in motion which gave this civilization an option or a consent to these values . . . [that] are 'crystallized' in the fashions of life, customs and political conduct."[58] But whereas humanism becomes both the maintenance of the heritage and its critique, such a conception of culture must be refused in politics: artistic creation cannot be produced to fit either statist or clerical ideologies. (We have only to look at art in the Soviet Union to recognize that commissioned art is worthless.)

Ricoeur proposes to overcome problems of the separation of church and state power, of planetary consciousness versus nation states, national versus colonial interests, disparities between economic and social interests, revolutionary consciousness and racism, urbanization and secularization, political distortions and historical conditions, by suggesting that they be dealt with on an individual basis. But this brings him back to the contradiction inherent between preaching and lay action. So he suggests that both clericalism of the Left and the Right be abandoned in favor of a "new articulation of the spiritual and the political . . . that would stress the mondialization of problems, of solutions, and of politics itself." A multinational humanity would replace the multinational corporations. Given the increasingly narrow political and sectarian ends of international bodies, it is questionable that Ricoeur's idealism could win against ideology. Contrary to his assertions, FAO (Food and Agricultural Organization) and UNESCO officials do not always cooperate.[59] But Ricoeur correctly perceives the lack of ethical judgment and humanism in business. To hope, however, as he seemed to in 1965, that were he to talk to businessmen they might heed his words instead of the balance sheet—except on Sundays—appears somewhat naive.

V

In any event, when Ricoeur withdrew from Nanterre, his writing became less directly political, as he turned to reconceptualize structuralist language theories. He often reaffirms that language has no rigid beginning; that words, things, and mental life are universal; that they are expressed by sounds (significant) which designate concepts; and that we are born into a language. Thought (signified), in turn, expresses and reflects a reality of the mind, employing analogies, comparisons, and symbols—symbols which occur in dreams, myths, and everyday life, and which in themselves always have at least two meanings. Thus, duality is intrinsic to both structuralism and hermeneutics: the former primarily explains social existence with the help of thought, while the latter deals with thought itself. But together they are to help interpret the original biblical texts, to anticipate a liberated humanity with the help of the Gospel.

Ricoeur's interest in linguistics had begun around 1962 in connection with the dispute between Lévi-Strauss and Sartre. By 1963, in "Structure and Hermeneutics," he addressed the limitations of binary oppositions between synchrony and diachrony and proposed the symbol as a third dimension of temporality, with interpretation as a stage between abstract and concrete reflection to recover meaning.[60] Although influenced by Freud, this third dimension (the unconscious level of linguistic law) is said to be nonreflective and Kantian rather than Freudian. Ricoeur locates this symbolic dimension in differences between sound and meaning, in the arbitrariness of signs that change every time language is spoken, and in synchronic (nonhistorical and systematic) and diachronic (evolutions applied to the system) relations, thus questioning Lévi-Strauss' subordination of diachrony to synchrony. The addition of the interpretive third dimension was (also) to retain the independence and scientism of structuralism. Thus, understanding itself was to become a dialectical philosophical enterprise rather than just a simple recovery of meaning.[61] Ricoeur illustrates this point with sequential analyses from Lévi-Strauss, ranging from *Structural Anthropology* to *The Savage Mind*, as he mediates between the uses of linguistics and of anthropology, to find that structuralism works for anthropology and synchronic tribes, but not for philosophy or diachronic societies (these oppositions parallel that of tribalism versus industrialism).

Ricoeur, however, wants to join the two comprehensions by approaching symbolism from the *strategic level* of texts. He constructs an elaborate methodology to show that "the sole philosophical interest in symbolism is that of meaning, the equivocalness of being: 'Being speaks in many ways.' Symbolism's *raison d'être* is to open the multiplicity of meanings to the equivocalness of being."[62]

Connecting the problem of multiple meaning in *lexical semantics,* and in polysemy (he states that he uses S. Ullmann's terminology)[63] to Saussurean and other linguistic terms, Ricoeur arrives at *structural semantics,* which postulates three basic levels of analysis[64]—not only as practiced in applied linguistics but also in theoretical linguistics. Essentially, as he asserts, Ricoeur's domain of meaning is then the semantic field. And this field is said to be dominated by the symbol: it reveals; it is the root of double meaning; it has its grip on being; it is central. It is also related to the scale of discourse, which, in addition, is realized as dream or hymn.[65] Ricoeur states that he proceeds from the text via semantic to structural semantic, so that he can systematically explain the multiple meanings of symbolism which exist in all words and discourse. Intrinsic to the content and expressivity of language, symbolism becomes the true mystery of language that the philosopher must "ceaselessly reopen."[66] Ricoeur is concerned with this mystery (located in every word), because it can be found in the semantic richness of discourse and can be interpreted in relation to multiple symbolic meanings. Because language is always ordered in a structure and tied to an event, Ricoeur finds that "language thinks and is on the way toward speaking."[67]

Like Aristotle, he "takes the word as the basic unit of reference" and places it at "the cross-roads between rhetoric and poetic," where rhetoric as the technique of eloquence leads to theories of argumentation, elocution, and composition of discourse, and to persuasion. Poetic is contrasted to rhetoric, because it produces the purification of the passions, such as terror and pity. But the metaphor, which is said to constitute a displacement and the extension of the meaning of words whose explanation is grounded in a theory of substitution, is important to Ricoeur's overall project, his *Poetics of the Will:* for both good and evil can be found in the metaphor. Hence he argues against Jakobson or Barthes, for whom metaphor can be a poetic device or a flight of imagination; it is a structural element, he writes, which "contains *in* the word, one structure but two functions."[68] Ricoeur also links this duality to the difference between the political world of eloquence (it persuades) and the poetic world of tragedy (it invents). Rooted to opposing intentions, rhetoric and poetics nevertheless share a common nucleus. The metaphor, however, is also inserted into *lexis* (style, diction, excellencies of style, and the process of combining words into an intelligible sequence) in modes of elocution, prayer, recitation, menace, interrogation, and response. These are Ricoeur's schemata which, in turn, are constituents of elocution and thus of all communication and meaning.

Ricoeur's detailed chapters on how rhetoric has declined since Aristotle's original definition focus on the metaphor in relation to semantic of discourse, to the semantic of the word, to new rhetoric, to philosophical discourse, and to work and resemblance. He avers that he does not want to replace rhetoric by semantic and then by hermeneutic, or to refute one by the other,[69] but only to legitimate each theoretical point of view inside the limits of its own discipline, so that the various viewpoints will be systematically linked on each linguistic level (word, sentence, and discourse).[70]

Ricoeur's mediations are meant to bridge every gap—
between believers and unbelievers, between the Anglo-Saxon type
of *linguistic analysis* (it tends to be the domain of logicians, epis-
temologists and literary critics rather than of linguists) and the
French debate over the supremacy of semantics versus semiotics.[71] To achieve this end when, for instance, analyzing creativity, Ricoeur ranges from von Humboldt's language as an infinite use of finite means, to Benveniste's distinction between
semiotic entities (signs) and semantic entities (bearers of meaning), and then to Frege's *Sinn* (sense) as ideal content or objective
meaning (*Bedeutung*). All these ideas themselves, he argues, are
part of the creative process. But the boundary between the expressed and the unexpressed keeps receding, thus making this an
endless enterprise.[72] This lack of limitations is what gives discourse its power: it can indefinitely express itself at the expense
of the unexpressed. Now Ricoeur illustrates the use of the metaphor and of polysemy (the feature of words in natural language
which allows them to mean more than one thing). He distinguishes between the informative and the decorative character of
metaphor and reveals how it proceeds from negative to positive
traits; how it makes sense out of nonsense; how it transforms a
self-contradictory statement into a significant self-contradiction;
or how it violates semantic pertinence and can twist meaning.
But the creative moment of the metaphor is said to be concentrated in the grasping of resemblance, and in the invocation of
imagination. Thus, trivial metaphor is easier to treat than novel
metaphor (neither of them are decorative), even though both are
part of the "unitive process which produces a kind of assimila-
tion between remote ideas."[73] The process simultaneously "protests and yields," as it "speaks of the paradox between insight
and construction, between genius and calculus."[74]

This is Ricoeur's approach to questions of creativity, as well
as to a "philosophy of the imagination," and to innovative fiction, which recreates mood and feeling. Such an approach is said
to shatter previous structures of language and of reality, to apprehend a novel reality. Hence the strategy of metaphorical discourse neither improves communication nor insures agreement,
but both demolishes and increases our sense of reality. With the

help of the metaphor, argues Ricoeur, we can experience the metamorphosis of language and of reality.

VI

By finding meaning through linguistics, Ricoeur causes political and social issues to recede. He no longer emphasizes the ethical solution of social problems. Instead, he has turned back to semantics and philosophy. More recently, his word focuses on the displacement of its signification in relation to its codified usage; it distinguishes between a sentence with minimal signification and a semiotic for which the word is the sign in its lexical code; and it compares the notions of *écart* and *figure* in Ricoeur's *new rhetoric*. Or he interprets the notions of "productive imagination" and "iconic function" to "see how"; and he stops locating the function of the image in the imagination. For metaphor is said to "preserve and develop the creative force of language along with the *heuristic* power deployed by fiction";[75] and poetic discourse is non-referential and turned inward. Yet both fiction and poetry have more than a double sense, so that Ricoeur needs another level of doubling to allow for the redescription of fiction. He hopes to achieve such a "re-description of reality" through metaphoric rhetoric. Within this new scheme, Ricoeur singles out the verb *to be:* it is so important because *is* metaphorically includes *is not.*[76] He finds that *to be* subsumes *being* and *not being,* as well as the tension of metaphorical truth. (Implicitly, Sartre's existential *being* and *nothingness* have become part of Ricoeur's hermeneutics.) And it "recovers" God.

Barthes and Foucault in their systems of thought also address questions of life and death, especially in relation to the authorship of innovative literature. Ricoeur looks at this issue only peripherally, ending this discussion, as Lévi-Strauss does in *L'homme nu,* with the notions of *being* in Hamlet's dilemma about facing death. But Lévi-Strauss apprehends this problem through the telling of native myths, whereas for Ricoeur such myths continue to live on in religion and are thus his living metaphors. This focus would indicate that Riceour's original search for truth has simply taken another turn rather than, as some argue, that his preoccupation with linguistics is only a proof of his reluctance to reenter the world of politics. Or both might be true.

Ricoeur still hopes to secularize religious ethics and to transform evil and guilt into constructive politics. But will this "Aristotelian detour" end in *engagement?* Or in the long-promised *Poetics of the Will?* Ricoeur has been too long absent from politics to make a comeback. He is now more at home in departments of philosophy and literature outside France than he is in French universities. But the range of his thought and his steadfast concern with ethics and moral values do testify that he has never abandoned Husserl's and Heidegger's concern with being-in-the-world, or Marcel's acts of fidelity. As a believer, he continues to "put meaning into nothingness" and to secularize ecumenics. He may have succeeded in his intent by thus achieving a *rapprochement* between France's intellectuals and her still influential religious contingent, even if he should never complete the *Poetics of the Will.*

Notes

1. This work was published under the title *Idées directrices pour une phénomenologie* (Paris: Gallimard, 1950). Ricoeur also supplied an appendix dealing with Husserlian phenomenology to E. Brehier's *Histoire de la philosophie allemande,* 3d ed. (Paris: Vrien, 1954).

2. Ricoeur, *Husserl: An Analysis,* p. 6.

3. Reprinted in Stewart and Bien, eds., *Political and Social Essays.*

4. Leick, "Die Wahrheit der Existenz," p. 703.

5. Ricoeur, *Husserl: An Analysis,* p. 210.

6. *Ibid.,* p. 212.

7. David M. Rasmussen, *Mythic-Symbolic Language and Philosophical Anthropology* (The Hague: Martinus Nijhoff, 1971), p. 33.

8. Reagan and Stewart, eds. *The Philosophy of Paul Ricoeur,* p. 84.

9. Ricoeur, *The Conflict of Interpretations,* p. 99.

10. Rasmussen, *Mythic-Symbolic Language,* p. 135.

11. Reagan and Stewart, eds., *The Philosophy of Paul Ricoeur,* p. 3.

12. Ricoeur, *Husserl: An Analysis*, p. 4.

13. *Ibid.*, p. 7.

14. *Ibid.*, p. 213–14.

15. Rasmussen, *Mythic-Symbolic Language*, p. 32.

16. Leick, "Die Wahrheit," pp. 695–709.

17. Ricoeur, "From Existentialism to the Philosophy of Language," p. 90.

18. *Ibid.*

19. Leick, "Die Wahrheit," pp. 697–98.

20. Ricoeur, *The Conflict of Interpretations*, p. 287.

21. Ricoeur, Preface to the first edition, *History and Truth*, p. 5.

22. Ricoeur, *The Conflict of Interpretations*, p. 270.

23. *Ibid.*, pp. 287–88.

24. *Ibid.*, p. 314.

25. *Ibid.*

26. Ricoeur, *Freud and Philosophy*, p. 13.

27. *Ibid.*

28. *Ibid.*, p. 15.

29. *Ibid.*

30. *Ibid.*, pp. 16–17.

31. *Ibid.*, p. 32.

32. *Ibid.*, p. 34. Barthes gets new meaning by mediating between Sade, Fourier, and Loyola, a very different exercise; see chapter 7, pp. 180–82.

33. Ricoeur, *Freud and Philosophy*, p. 55.

34. *Ibid.*, p. 60.

35. *Ibid.*, pp. 345–50; see also Ernest Nagel, in Sidney Hook, ed., *Psychoanalysis, Scientific Method and Philosophy*.

36. Ricoeur, *Freud and Philosophy*, pp. 345–50.

37. *Ibid.*, pp. 367.

38. Ihde, *Hermeneutic Phenomenology:* pp. 140–41.

39. Ricoeur, *Freud and Philosophy*, p. 387.

40. *Ibid.*, p. 389.

41. Ihde, *Hermeneutic Phenomenology*, p. 150.

42. Jacques Lacan, *The Four Fundamental Concepts of Psychoanalysis* (New York: Norton, 1978) pp. 153–54.

43. Ricoeur, *Freud and Philosophy*, p. 524.

44. Gargiulo, "Modern Dialogue with Freud," pp. 295–301.

45. Sales, "Colloque sur le mythe."

46. Ricoeur, see "Notes on the History of Philosophy and the Sociology of Knowledge," pp. 57–62 and "The Socius as Neighbor," pp. 98–109, in *History and Truth*.

47. Ricoeur, *Political and Social Essays*, p. 186.

48. Ricoeur, *History and Truth*, p. 210.

49. *Ibid.*, p. 215.

50. Ricoeur, *Political and Social Essays*, p. 89.

51. Ricoeur, *History and Truth*, p. 230.

52. *Ibid.*, p. 230.

53. *Ibid.*, p. 226.

54. *Ibid.*, p. 265.

55. Ricoeur, "Notes on the History of Philosophy and the Sociology of Knowledge," *History and Truth*, p. 61.

56. Ricoeur, "B. F. Skinner's *Beyond Freedom and Dignity*," *Political and Social Essays*, pp. 46–67.

57. Ricoeur, "What Does Humanism Mean?" *Political and Social Essays*, p. 79.

58. *Ibid.*, p. 77.

59. Ricoeur, *Political and Social Essays*, "From Nation to Humanity: Task of Christians," p. 158.

60. Ricoeur repeats this theme in "Structure, Word, Event," *The Conflict of Interpretations*, pp. 83–84.

61. Ricoeur, "Structure and Hermeneutics," *The Conflict of Interpretations*, pp. 60–61.

62. *Ibid.*, p. 67.

63. Stephen Ullmann, *The Principles of Semantics* (New York: Philosophical Library, 1957).

64. This addresses A.-J. Greimas's *La sémantique structurelle* (Paris: Larousse, 1966).

65. Ricoeur, *The Conflict of Interpretations*, p. 67.

66. *Ibid.*, pp. 94–95.

67. *Ibid.*

68. Ricoeur, *La métaphore vive*, p. 18.

69. *Ibid.*, p. 31.

70. *Ibid.*, p. 12.

71. *Ibid.*, p. 88–89. This again leads into the most recent controversy between semiology and semiotics and to Derrida; see introduction and chapter 6.

72. Ricoeur, "Creativity in Language," p. 100.

73. *Ibid.*, p. 108.

74. *Ibid.*

75. Ricoeur, *The Rule of Metaphor*, p. 10.

76. *Ibid.*, p. 11.

Bibliography

Bauman, Zygmunt. *Hermeneutics and Social Science.* New York, Columbia University Press, 1978.

Brès, Y., "Paul Ricoeur: le règne des herméneutiques en un long détour' . . ." *Revue philosophique.* (1969), 94 (3–4):425–29.

Clemens, E., "Volonté d'interprétation." *Critiques.* (1970), no. 277, pp. 546–55.

Chomsky, Noam. *Language and Mind.* New York: Harcourt Brace Jovanovich, 1972.

Flew, Anthony. "Two Views of Atheism." *Inquiry* (1969), 12(4):469:73.

Gargiulo, Gerald J. "Modern Dialogue with Freud." *Psychoanalytic Review* (1971) 58(2):295–301.

Hook, Sidney, ed., *Psychoanalysis, Scientific Method, and Philosophy.* New York: New York University Press, 1959.

Ihde, Don. *Hermeneutic Phenomenology: The Philosophy of Paul Ricoeur.* Evanston; Ill: Northwestern University Press, 1971.

Lapointe, Francois H. "A Bibliography on Paul Ricoeur." *Philosophy Today* (1973), 17(2–4):176–82.

Leick, Romain, "Die Wahrheit der Existenz." *Stimmen Zeit* (1973), 191(10):695–709.

Lichtenstein, Heinz. "Concerning Ricoeur's *Freud and Philosophy.*" *Philosophy and Phenomenological Research* (1972), 32(3):412–13.

Magliola, Robert. "Parisian Structuralism Confronts Phenomenology: The Ongoing Debate." *Language and Style* (1973), 6(4):237–48.

Merton, Robert K. *Social Theory and Social Structure.* New York: Free Press, 1968.

Morgan, John Henry. "Religious Myth and Symbol." *Philosophy Today* (1974), 18(1–4):68–84.

Mudge, Lewis. "Paul Ricoeur on Biblical Interpretation." November 1978. Manuscript.

Muto, Susan. "Reading the Symbolic Text: Some Reflections on Interpretation." *Humanitas* (1972), 8:169–97.

Rasmussen, David M. *Mythic Symbolic Language in Philosophical Anthropology: A Constructive Interpretation of the Thought of Paul Ricoeur.* The Hague: Martinus Nijhoff, 1971.

Regan, Charles and David Stewart, eds., *The Philosophy of Paul Ricoeur.* Boston: Beacon Press, 1978.

Ricoeur, Paul. *Le volontaire et l'involontaire.* Paris: Aubier Éditions Montaigne, 1950. Translated as *Freedom and Nature: The Voluntary and the Involuntary.* Evanston, Ill.: Northwestern University Press, 1966.

—— *Histoire et vérité.* Paris: Éditions du Seuil, 1955. Translated as *History and Truth.* Evanston, Ill.: Northwestern University Press, 1965.

—— *L'homme fallible.* Paris: Aubier, 1960. Translated as *Fallible Man.* Chicago: Regnery, 1965.

—— "Prévision économique et choix ethique." *Esprit* (1966), 34(2):178–93.

112 Ricoeur: Hermeneutics and Structuralism

Ricoeur, Paul. *Husserl: An Analysis of His Phenomenology*. Evanston, Ill.: Northwestern University Press, 1967.

—— "La structure, le mot, l'évènement." *Esprit* (1967), no. 35, pp. 801–21; also in *Philosophy Today* (1968) 12(2–4):114–29; also in *Conflict of Interpretations*, pp. 79–96.

——*Le Conflit des interpretations: Essais d'herméneutique*. Paris: Éditions du Seuil, 1969. Translated as *The Conflict of Interpretations*. Evanston, Ill.: Northwestern University Press, 1974.

—— "Le règne des herméneutiques ou "Un long détour . . ." *Revue philosophique* (1969), 94(3–4):425–29.

—— *The Symbolism of Evil*. Boston: Beacon Press, 1969.

—— *Freud and Philosophy*. New Haven: Yale University Press, 1970. Originally delivered as the Terry Lectures at Yale.

—— "Volonté d'interprétation." *Critique* (1970), no. 277, pp. 546–55.

—— "Creativity in Language: Word, Polysemy, Metaphor." *Philosophy Today* (1973), 17(2–4):97–111.

—— "From Existentialism to the Philosophy of Language." *Philosophy Today* (1973), 17(2–4):88–96.

—— "The Hermeneutical Function of Distanciation." *Philosophy Today* (1973), 17(2–4):129–41.

—— "The Task of Hermeneutics." *Philosophy Today* (1973), 17(2–4):112–28.

—— "Science et ideologie." *Revue philosophique de Louvain* (1974), 72(14):328–56.

—— *La métaphore vive*. Paris: Éditions du Seuil, 1975. Translated as *The Rule of Metaphor*. Toronto: University of Toronto Press, 1977.

Sales, Michel. "Un colloque sur le mythe de la peine." *Archéolgie philosophique* (1969), 32(4):664–75.

Sawyer, Fay Horton. "Commentary on Freud and Philosophy." *The Annual of Psychoanalysis*, 1:216–28. New York: Quadrangle, 1973.

Stewart, David and Joseph Bien, eds. *Political and Social Essays*. Athens: Ohio University Press, 1974.

Vansina, Frans D. "La problématique épochale chez P. Ricoeur et l'existentialism." *Revue philosophique de Louvain* (1972), 70(8):587–619.

—— "Bibliographie de Paul Ricoeur (jusqu'a la fin de 1972)." *Revue philosophique de Louvain* (1974), 72(13):156–81.

Structures Without Structuralism

Alain Touraine is a socialist whose work, though bypassing the structuralist debates, is important to the issues structuralism addresses, and to French Marxism. In 1958, after a period spent studying French industrial workers, he founded the Laboratory of Industrial Sociology; as his interest shifted to the political discontent of the workers (and students) in the 1960s, he started the Center for the Study of Social Movements, just before the spontaneous revolt of students and workers in 1968.

Born in 1925, Touraine grew up during the war and was in the Resistance before attending the École Normale Supérieure, where he took his *agrégation* in history and also studied philosophy. His perspective was further broadened when, in 1952, he went to Harvard and learned everything about Parsonian systems theory and American research methods. This experience is evident in his studies of industry and in his effort to construct a global scientific system—a system that explicitly aims to avoid both the ideological, abstract, and revolutionary rhetoric of Marxism and the functionalist assumptions of consensus, rationality, and deviance. Convinced that theory had to be derived from empirical observation and preferably from survey research, Touraine began by studying the evolution of industrial work, work attitudes, and human relations within factories. At the time, other sociologists such as Serge Moscovici, Georges Friedmann, and Michel Crozier also worked on similar projects; they all received support from the French government, from OECD, and from UNESCO.[1] France (and other countries) wanted to industrialize and to modernize its industries, to become independent of American economics, while avoiding alienation and exploitation of workers. This association with government made

Marxists doubt Touraine's leftism, although he redeemed himself in May 1968 by joining the students in their revolt.

Touraine had set out to incorporate the best components of American sociology because he was impressed with its scientific cast; he wanted to avoid the pitfalls of subjective and phenomenological approaches and to include both the theory and praxis of *all* social relations—productions, organization, history, conflict, domination, systems of action, the state, collectivities, structure, and politics. He viewed these relations as Durkheimian social facts to be sorted, plotted and organized as productions—productions related to potential conflict in the Marxist sense. And his mastery of empirical data and techniques, together with his rhetorical style, always conveyed an aura of authority. Were the French to elevate the prestige of sociology to the level enjoyed by philosophy, they would select Touraine to guide them.

Since 1968 he has been the professor of social movements, the sociologist of revolution. But even though Touraine perceives sociology as the only viable social science and rejected structuralism, the structuralist formulations prevalent in his milieu at times have crept in. Thus, for instance, he proclaimed that his sociology "won't be heard" until the dominant ideology of the state and its ruling class is neutralized; that it can begin only after the death of the gods and of man; or that "sociology cannot exist until societies are no longer located in relation to an order exterior to them but seized in their historicity, in their ability to produce themselves." [2] Still, Touraine's central themes are historicity and action. The life of a society, Touraine keeps reiterating, is in its action, in its capacity to produce its own practice, in deciding its own future, its culture, and its class relations. Like Foucault, Touraine talks of a break in knowledge, but he locates this break in the mode of decision making that evolves from the prevalent type of production. Thus, he dismissed Ricoeur's metaphilosophy and the belief that social problems will be found in "meaning"; and he attacked Althusser for representing society as the reproduction of a dominant order and omitting the creative aspects of social conflict. Although he admired Lévi-Strauss, he considered his "mythological" structuralism irrational. Touraine's structures are strictly social and consist of all the knowledges and practices a sociologist can observe—practices that include structuralism, functionalism, Marxism and various psychological theories.

Touraine attempts to fuse the best components of existentialism (its preoccupation with humanism and daily living) and of American rationalism (its promise to set up the type of society that might make true human existence possible). But this remains both Touraine's problem and project: for to fuse rational and empirical sociology with idealist and logical philosophy requires a level of abstraction very few can follow. Still, he is a competent sociologist and seems to have constructed a system of social action that allows for every possible contingency. Although Touraine states that Talcott Parsons was only a minor influence in his work, some of his systems of action and of social production are reminiscent of structural-functionalism—though broader in their attempt to account for conflict.

Touraine did not foresee the events of 1968, and then did not expect the subsequent cooptation. But the failure of his sociology of action and its seeming inapplicability to praxis only spurred him on to more theorizing in an attempt to get rid of the "errors" in his not yet perfected sociological system. He came closest in his recent work, when he looked at how the actors in a society control their historicity and the production and politicization of culture itself.[3]

II

Touraine began by examining workers' motivations and attitudes. He studied decision making on various levels of management before looking at professional organizations; and he eventually focused on industrial growth and class analyses. The unique mixture of preindustrial, artisan, semi-automated, and mass production methods, which existed side by side in postwar France, provided a readymade laboratory for testing and comparing the hypotheses of American industrial sociologists whose social-psychological studies of work to maximize productivity had become fashionable. (The work of the Harvard team at the General Electric plant in Hawthorne had been interrupted by the war).[4] In addition, many American methods of industrialization and automation were introduced almost overnight and brought their own social and political consequences. Because France had been impoverished and ravaged by the war, quick economic recovery was imperative. Hence some ruthless business practices, such as early retirement of technologically untrained workers, or speedups of assembly lines were tolerated at first. But these practices generated increasing discord between the entrepreneurs and the leftist unions. To ease the tensions, both conservative and leftist forces within the government were willing to appropriate funds to study and improve management and labor relations: Touraine, for example, studied the workers at Renault; Serge Mallet investigated relations at La Companie des machines Bull, and Michel Crozier those in a government agency. Georges Friedmann and Pierre Naville collected in a number of volumes many summaries of studies on the sociology of work.[5]

Touraine's experience at Harvard prepared him to introduce American theories and methodologies on the sociology of work in France. In 1965 he produced an excellent survey, *Workers' Attitudes to Technical Change,*[6] which was used as an introductory text for industrial sociologists. What distinguished Touraine's work from that of his American counterparts was that he focused on the intricate connections between industrial relations, politics, and class structure, and showed that rapid development accelerated not only the workers' rising expectations, but also the polarization of the classes. His Marxist colleagues, of course, interpreted this trend as a sign of the impending revolution. But Touraine perceived it as a new type of stratification (linked to French historical conditions), which he intended to study.

Touraine viewed production methods as "perpetrators" or initiators of social change. Unlike other industrial sociologists who link workers' adjustment to their position in the job hierarchy (and the concommitant remuneration), he wanted to find out how the internal system of stratification makes for conflict. He learned that the coexistence of traditional and modern methods of work was divisive, because only skilled workers were allowed to make autonomous decisions; and management was left exclusively to the entrepreneur. Condemning studies that examine work satisfaction, adjustment, or alienation directly (workers *always* exist in relation to systems of authority, to organization and to immediate supervisors), he wanted to know how the attitudes a worker brings to the job affect his performance. So he conducted three types of analyses: of attitudes toward work, of the social reasons for the emergence of these attitudes, and of the relations of these two factors to each other. Later on, in *The Post-Industrial Society,* he established that a worker's relationship to his community correlates with his attitude toward the evolution of his work (alienation results from the changing connection of the worker to his job). Gradually, stated Touraine, an *occupational system of work* is transformed into a *technical system of work,* so that the organization of work becomes more important than the work itself.

As Touraine broadened his interests, he looked beyond systems of work. And from an increasingly Marxist perspective, he perceived social change as emanating from the changes in types of production. He postulated the activity of work as central to the conflicts between personal and professional relations; between tradition and modernization; between the old and the new; and he showed how these conflicts are both reflected in and transformed into the prevailing value system of a society. Unlike Parsons, who postulated a normative value system for an entire society, Touraine's value system tended to be more volatile. Yet he did not expect that this system would collapse or that there would be a Marxist revolution. In the course of his investigations, Touraine even began to lean on Berle and Means, and on Schumpeter, to show how, gradually, the entrepreneur is replaced by the professional manager when ownership of companies by stockholders requires impersonal corporate management.

Touraine urged the adoption of policies to design programs, services and aids that would convert negative or resisting attitudes toward change into positive attitudes and behavior.[7] By suggesting that national, community, and business policy makers use the insights he had gained into workers' behavior and attitudes, he not only facilitated the acceptance of change but also provided a tool to manipulate and co-opt the workers. The advice he offered to management—particularly concerning retraining, geographical moves, or early retirement (in the service of efficiency and productivity)—did not endear Touraine to his friends on the Left or in the militant trade unions. Touraine, however, saw himself primarily as a theoretician who wanted only to explain the processes of industrialization. Nevertheless, he believed that French progress depended upon the development of technology. And he hoped that his analyses would improve France's vulnerable position in the European Economic Market and in NATO as a bulwark against Soviet-style communism and Stalinism. His sociological theory of action, he often stated, was to become a practice—a reform/socialist practice—that would remain independent of both Marxist and academic sociology.

III

In *La conscience ouvrière* (1966) Touraine appeared to turn more toward the concerns of the Left. He became critical of co-optation, and analyzed and demonstrated the alienation and misery of specific industrial working conditions. He found that both the oppression of workers and the militancy of labor occur to the greatest extent in large plants. When many workers griped against the same boss, their class consciousness was raised; but this consciousness was found to intensify the repressive attitudes of the bosses, whose techniques of domination "improved" under these conditions.[8] Following Marx, Touraine "demonstrated" that class consciousness depends upon the ideology of the ruling class. But he also found that skilled and professionalized workers were less alienated than unskilled ones. Touraine's comparative study of workers in different industries (mines, chemical plants, construction sites, foundries, metal manufacturing, electrical plants, and oil refining) resembled Blauner's *Alienation and Freedom* (1964), which also examined the meaninglessness, powerlessness, and self-estrangement experienced by workers in relation to types of production methods. Blauner, however, was less concerned with ongoing technical change—from professional to technical systems of work, from craftsmanship to advanced automation—than was Touraine, who examined every technological change as a challenge to the worker's entire value system.

Touraine "substantiated" his findings with studies as diverse as Merton's *Social Structure and Anomie*, industrial inquiries at the University of Michigan, March and Simon's work on decision-making processes, Homans's theories of apprenticeship, Lazarsfeld's studies on work attitudes in *Personal Influence,* and nearly every other study on work available. Citing Moscovici's study of French miners whose work lives were affected by changes in their personal lives, Touraine both generalized and pinpointed the change in societal norms and values in relation to workers' adaptation, job satisfaction, and beliefs about liberty. He then compared the interaction of these variables in different types of industrial societies in terms of technical evolution, economic power, workers' action and representation. He allegedly proceeded first

> to consider the individual who manages the tensions created by his personal needs and the means to reduce these tensions; then he examined the social system of the enterprise—or a part of it—that is more or less integrated, where roles and expectations, elements of status, mechanisms of institutionalization, are to some extent reconciled; and finally he went to workers' consciousness, that means to the system of exigencies defined by the work itself, by the value placed on creativity and control of the worker over his production.[9]

Simply put, in *La conscience ouvrière,* Touraine successively looked at a worker as an individual, a social actor, and a historical subject in relation to the normative orientations of his work. The study revealed that there are no simple correlations, that the worker's connection to his work was full of contradictions—for example, that he was simultaneously tied to the world of craftsmanship and professional autonomy, and to the problems derived from organization and rationalization of work. So Touraine decided to limit the scope of *La conscience ouvrière* by concentrating only on the evolution of the worker's job (from execution to organization) and to leave the problem of innovation for a separate theoretical discussion.[10]

La conscience ouvrière was based on responses to questionnaires that asked workers about effects of automation, of leadership, of remuneration, of strikes, of rapport with superiors; the questionnaries covered issues of social class, strikes, workers' preference for types of enterprises, and the workers' desire to work independently or belong to a group. Touraine himself was critical of conclusions culled from attitudinal studies, yet the scope of some of the questions—on solidarity, on how the state does or should act, and on the role of unions—led to interesting answers about politics. Touraine found that workers were interested not only in economic gains, in stability, or in better conditions of work; they often wanted improvements in the state, in educational policies and in international politics. In a way, the events of 1968 could almost have been predicted from Touraine's workers' complaints.

Touraine concluded that these workers were part of consumer society and found that their consciousness was really "popular" or "people's" consciousness.[11] This consciousness allegedly was no longer formed at the workplace but in the popular heterogeneous meeting places of cities, where workers met artisans, dealers, and small entrepreneurs, that is all those who could not afford an upper-class style. In these places, the workers do not associate as a class or to revolt. Instead, they were found to be members of a community, to relate to their productions (without being a collectivity).[12] The relationship between the members of this community was said to exist as an "abstract principle," a potential for action rather than as a collective force. Touraine no longer postulated places of work as social systems, as aggregates of social groups, or as collectivities, but began to look to the society itself as a system of action.

Now the consciousness of the working class was perceived as the consciousness of industrial society itself, since workers' attitudes on and off the job could no longer be separated. By comparing conditions in different countries, he related workers' beliefs to specific political systems. The latter, themselves, influence methods of command, bureaucratization, and political structures. State intervention—prevalent in a number of countries—within industrial enterprises, was found to have its own impact on workers' consciousness.

Touraine expanded on these theories in the *Sociologie de l'action* (1965), defining sociology as "the science of social action."[13] At first, Touraine declared that his own sociology intends "to organize the author's thoughts" and "define the elements of a method." In the preface, Touraine thanked (among others) Lévi-Strauss, whose influence seemed plain. For, obviously, Touraine's theory of action was meant to do for sociology what structuralism had done for anthropology—to establish it as the supertheory that would explain industrial society. Touraine's language began to range farther afield as he argued, for example, that "all human conduct manifests the effects of social determinism"; as he arranged countless historical references in binary fashion; as he quoted Sartre, Fustel de Coulanges, and Ranke, swinging from philosophy to the Weberian critique and its limits of social action. But the structuralist cast of this method, in first line, addressed sociology: Durkheim, Parsons, Marx, and the sociology of work. Touraine's own sociology of action also took on a Sartrean tone:

> not a sociology of values, but a study of the creation of values considered as normative orientations of action whose *raison d'être* can only be found in the action itself, which means in the double movement by which the subject poses an object outside itself and affirms his authority over that object, thereby manifesting his capacity to act.[14]

He meant, of course, that as a result of the division of labor the actor has lost control over the object of his work and must regain control over his actions to overcome alienation. By distinguishing between forms and orientations of action systems, and by diagramming typologies of action that are once again integrated, he refined his argument. And he "humanized" his system by tying subjects directly to their action orientations, so that the study of the evolution of work would not be reduced to observation and/or categorization alone. Like Lévi-Strauss' anthropology, his sociology attempted to reach underlying structures, so that it would not simply explain phenomena, but would "construct the social sciences"[15]—social sciences that now included, in addition to the functional analysis of organization, of politics or of work, the unconscious structures of personality and collectivity. Hence, Touraine's studies of mass society, consumption, leisure, and culture (themselves components of industrial society) now dealt with the notion of work rather than with work itself.

His frequently rhetorical language addressed his Parisian peers, when, for example, he wrote of "the contradiction of the nature and of the culture in man [as] conceivable and available for study only to the extent that man is engaged in creative praxis."[16] He hoped to help create a general science of social action that would one day encompass all the human and social sciences.[17] Politics were peripheral in the *Sociologie de l'action,* although Touraine's politics were implied in his insistence that action sociology is for free individuals and cannot exist under any sort of totalitarian system—the suppression of subjective liberty always makes for alienation. Still, Touraine was as surprised as everyone else to find that his hypotheses of *La conscience ouvrière* and his *Sociologie de l'action* would so soon be tested, when in May 1968 working class consciousness and student consciousness "converged" and endangered all of France's structures.

IV

Touraine's presence on the side of the students during the 1968 revolts not only was a clear declaration that he belonged to the Left and lived by his principles, but was also an opportunity to test his theories of social movements. Had he planned to set up an experiment, he could not have constructed a better one. (In fact, since the revolts of 1968, in France and also in Italy, sociologists whose students were among the original instigators have been kept out of industrial plants: they are still accused of having planted subversive ideas in both workers and students, to have either knowingly or inadvertently activated the revolts.) Having witnessed the events from the barricades, Touraine wrote *Le communisme utopique: le mouvement de mai 1968* (1968) and *La société post-industrielle* (1969) in quick succession. The former is a descriptive analysis and the latter a theoretical exegesis with predictions for the future of modern, or "programmed," societies.

Basically, Touraine perceived the "May movement" not as a refutation of industrial society and its culture, but as the uncovering of its internal contradictions and the conflict at its core. When technocrats began to take over the university, the students "responded with a call for self-expression,"[18] to challenge the political system and power structures, to preserve society's "critical conscience," without, however, either planning or desiring to assume power themselves. France, said Touraine, was in crisis, and the May 1968 movement had been symptomatic of deep-seated social conflicts. Touraine found, as did Lefebvre, that the most militant and outspoken sectors of the student movement had accomplished nothing, and had left behind the worst destruction and the least reconstruction. In other words, this revolt (like most others) had created a backlash and had increased repression.

Opposing those who played down the importance of May 1968, Touraine argued that prevailing social values had been challenged by the best of the country's youth, who had objected to the internal transformation (and goals) of the university. They had protested the shift from "pure" learning to "technological grooming." They objected to job preparation, to the need for certification, and to obsolete courses, as much as to the fact that after graduation they would not find acceptable jobs. They wanted coherence and community rather than bureaucracy and technological ideology. Because France, stated Touraine, was full of contradictions—it was liberal and rigid, centralized and disorganized, modernist and archaic, grandiose and shabby—its universities were subject to even greater tensions than those in communist countries (despite the repression) or in privately owned institutions in the United States. Yet because French universities were controlled by the state, the state could be attacked through them by political confrontations and the questioning of values and goals, so that an organized student movement could effectively challenge the social order. According to Touraine,

> the paradox of the May movement is that, having been launched by the mystic search for a proletarian-revolutionary force and by the struggle against a rigid political and institutional system, it brought to light new opposition forces outside the university (technicians and "professionals" on the one side, young workers on the other) and revealed more than anywhere else the nature of a social power until then hidden behind reassuring illusions of modernization, rationalization and growth.[19]

In 1969 Touraine still saw this movement as a growing and viable force for change. Later on, surprised at the students' quiescence, he embarked on a study of social movements in Chile, and in the mid-1970s generally sought to place the entire phenomenon into a more global context. In *The Post-Industrial Society* (1969), however, he still perceived the student revolt in relation to French social institutions and to the changing class structure. Disenchanted with the power and centralization of business firms, students and workers wanted participation—in work and in leisure activities. But, generalized Touraine, a social movement must always:

> move beyond its internal contradictions and thus arrive at its realization and consequent disappearance. No one can forsee to what extent and under what conditions the student movement will be destroyed by its internal problems or will dominate them powerfully enough to extend its action and influence.[20]

Success or failure of a movement, maintained Touraine, depends upon the extent to which it can transcend its own group and thereby transform power relations within society. To discover their dynamics, Touraine compared student movements in various countries, examining their relation to other social forces, particularly to types of social domination.

For Touraine the process of production was central. It imposed a life-style in keeping with its own objectives and its power system; it pressured the individual into participating in work, consumption, and education in order to further the aims of production.[21] Touraine's increasingly Marxist formulations centered on the culture and the control of politics. Now dominating agencies which seduce, subvert, and enforce conformism were said to induce alienation. The media or government offices would be such agencies: they do not reduce people to misery or impose police restrictions, but they hamper people's participation in decision making. Only participation through decisions about consumption, and through attacks on centralized power and technocratic organizations can individuals free themselves. For such actions, argued Touraine, would undermine secrecy and open up debates.[22] By forging collective identity, manipulation might be resisted since individuals can no longer defend themselves singly, but only as members of a community or of a culture. Touraine again examined the emergent social order from this new perspective and, like Coser and Dahrendorf,[23] though more globally and radically, and neither from a functional nor a Weberian perspective, attempted to construct a conflict model: he wanted to enable the sociologist to undertake analyses that would integrate all theoretical models in order to examine a new type of society.

V

In *The Academic System in American Society* (1972), Touraine examined student movements in relation to their specific contexts. Analyzing the sequence of events that began in 1964 with the Free Speech Movement, he compared American university structures to those of France and Germany. He focused, for example, on the students' role in the governance of universities, on the extent of social integration within universities, and contrasted "sponsored mobility" (free and monolithic education for those who qualify) with "contest mobility" (academic and financial stratification of universities themselves).[24] He showed how the "open" American system keeps a maximum of competitors in the race, yet favors the rich. His cross-cultural data included various aspects of university life in different countries (from administration to participation, from student attitudes to faculty performance, from multiversity to small college) and illustrated their impact on both the society and the universities themselves. (Thus, for example, professors and college presidents control university policy through their philosophies of education.)

In large generalizations that included Vietnam and Cambodia, presidential politics, and racial integration, Touraine concluded that the American student movement, like every other social movement, "lacked an integrated and balanced personality . . . and oscillated ceaselessly between the twin poles of criticism and utopia."[25] Because they were both marginal and central, university-based movements had to be examined in relation to their societies, to enable them to recover control of the university's "scientific, technical and professional productive forces." Touraine thus basically reiterated the students' demands. The "technical and scientific forces," that is researchers and funds, responded by moving outside the universities to conduct sensitive research through private firms, often with university-based personnel. (Now undesirable or "subversive" work continues in organizations with fewer moral scruples and greater financial resources.) Primary research conducted in the universities still becomes part of the public domain.

On yet another level, Touraine examined the new types of class conflicts and power relations that arise as a consequence of "post-industrialism," which depends primarily on knowledge and inventiveness (orientation to individual rulers, religion or economic laws has been surpassed).[26] As American university structures changed to form multicampus systems increasingly controlled by state legislatures, they had to respond to more political pressure from minorities and unions. Touraine predicted that a new type of recruitment would become the most crucial component in creating both society's elite and its work force. He believed that

> no radical measures [were] called for, only a reinforcement of the inner life of the college or university. . . . Since the attacks against the university derive from its too numerous bonds with the economic, social and military leaders, these bonds should be cut when they are not specifically linked to the needs of academic research and teaching.[27]

In other words, Touraine wanted to reinstitute education for its own sake. Because "the university as a center of production and diffusion of scientific knowledge is increasingly becoming the main locus of the social conflicts of our time," Touraine argues, "the managers of the system should attempt to eradicate or institutionalize the fundamental conflicts that have appeared."[28]

VI

Production de la société (1973), a collection of essays written between 1969 and 1973, recapitulated in systematic form most of Touraine's previous ideas. His complicated formulations not only accounted for historical residues but duplicated the Parsonian four-cornered diagrams. Touraine included grids illustrating the interactions between people and systems, as well as structuralist notions that derive from Lévi-Strauss and allusions to "ruptures" in knowledge that resemble Foucault's theories. Touraine attempted to allow for institutional upheavals and the eruption of conflict by creating a supersystem.

With sweeping rhetoric, he postulated sociology itself as one of the social productions. (It can emerge only at a specific historical juncture.) He rejected all sociologies of values (because, he said, they pertain to individuals rather than to systems), of ideologies (because they are generated by the dominant class), and of phenomenology (because it ignores political domination). He constructed systems that incorporate conflict by providing counter-elements to allow for class conflict, because he wanted to recognize the reality of class relations by looking at actual conflicts between those who control values, norms, and policies and those who struggle against them.

One of Touraine's key concepts is historicity—the creation of a model of knowledge formed on the basis of a state of activity (in which it also interferes). Historicity is said "to transform the activity into a social system in which conduct is governed by a set of orientations, themselves determined by the society's mode of action upon itself." [29]

But historicity within a society differs and is explicable only by the meanings attributed to actions within the particular society, thereby creating its own System of Historical Action (S.H.A.). This S.H.A. is the complex of cultural orientations through which historicity operates—according to hierarchization, needs, mobilization, resources and orientation. Class relations—conflicts over the control of the System of Historical Action—are the most important components of Touraine's scheme, a scheme that was basically composed of a "type of knowledge" which results from the specific system of accumulation.

In *Production de la société*, Touraine's discussion of the political and institutional system ranged, for example, from analysis of history to organizations, from the construction of the political state to the rule of its dominant class, from government to dependence and autonomy, from institutional rhetoric to the way institutions actually operate, and from the source of social conflict to its institutionalization. Touraine found that

> the institutional system is neither the simple transposition, in political terms, of fields of historical actors, nor the locus of societal values that differentiate themselves directly in organizational norms; it has an autonomous existence, but is the locus where historicity is transformed into organization. To study its functioning, the consequences of its position must be defined in relation to the historicity and the organization of society.[30]

Simply put, the less industrialized a society, the weaker will be its historicity, the more it will rely on oral tradition, and the more likely it will be for symbolism to outweigh rationality. According to Touraine, four principal conditions (objectives, exchanges, norms, and equilibrium) would express these factors in a functioning system. He outlined all the possibilities with the help of diagrams, demonstrating the relations between historicity and organization that could occur in every type of society—in times of conflict and in times of stability.

He also returned to a discussion of the May 1968 revolts; he felt the students had not utilized their chances at the right moment and thus had not succeeded in changing the existing social order.[31] He was most original and effective when discussing the 1968 crisis; this conflict allegedly stimulated his thinking on historicity, functions, tensions, and contradictions that go into understanding "how the new is born of the old, how ancient men produce new societies."[32]

In principle, Touraine distinguished social movements (class conflicts over control of the System of Historical Action) from social change (results of war, conquest, colonization, or alteration in fundamental cultural techniques). According to Touraine, social movements can be perceived neither from the perspective of the participants, nor from the perspective of the state.[33] Instead, such movements remind us that both order and concensus are part of domination. He disagreed with the Marxists in that he believed class relations are produced by cultural rather than strictly economic forces, and showed how most social movements bring about mutations rather than revolutions. In his view, change comes about through new technology, and since technology is in the hands of the technicians, technocrats, technological experts, and scientific innovators, they become the dominant class and control the S.H.A. in postindustrial society. For Touraine, then, the main schism in the modern social order is not between worker and capitalist, but between all the participants in the production process (capitalists and workers) and those who are excluded from this process (students, the unemployed and the aged). Thus the central decision-makers who hide behind the organizations they control and are in turn controlled by them can only be challenged by those outside their reach: those excluded from the technological power structures are the only ones who could conceivably organize against it.

Touraine's essays in *Pour la sociologie*—mostly talks he delivered while working on *Production de la société*—were variations on his more global themes. He incorporated, for example, Lévi-Strauss' notions of classification, concluding that in sociology, too, relations exist behind situations[34]—relations of class, influence, hierarchy, or belligerence. And he paralleled Foucault's approach, which incorporated psychoanalytic data to show how a society identifies and treats deviancy. His theoretical problems are apparent in these essays, as he alternates between empiricism and rhetoric. He, too, suffered from the Parsonian dilemma: the more inclusive his theory became, the more removed it seemed from the phenomena it was meant to encompass. Hence, his "superintellectual" peers believed he was wasting his time, and sociologists found him too abstract.

But Touraine was less abstract and more personal in his next two books, *Lettres a une étudiante* (1974) and *Vie et mort du Chili populaire* (1973). In these studies, he mixed personal sentiment with political analyses. Theories were meshed with experience, so that Touraine himself emerged from behind his abstractions. He examined social conflicts as personal concerns; "society" seemed less of a laboratory and more of a subject for experience. According to Touraine, intellectual pursuits under fascism or Stalinism, for instance, resembled a drama or a resistance; theorizing became a luxury that people could not afford. Touraine's Chilean journal—written during the time when Allende was in power—was an especially good example of the application of sociological insight to current events, of precise analysis enhanced by personal commitment. Touraine assessed the possibilities for the success of an elected socialist government; he pinpointed the possible alternatives (a controlled economy and polity) for a beleagured socialism which would do away with idealistic and egalitarian promises; and he anticipated the consequences of an open society which would allow internal and external enemies to organize. He nearly predicted the downfall of Allende and the installation of a military junta. His report on Chili consequently remains one of the most accurate historical accounts of a period that has been reinterpreted from the most diverse ideological and political perspectives.

In recent works, Touraine's own socialist views are more clearly stated, as his system of action aims to become the "instrument of liberation from human essences, of belief in the supernatural . . . by interposing itself in social action." Touraine tries to transcend both political and economic debates (from the Left and the Right) to arrive at a cultural criticism, a criticism which itself is to evolve new categories based on new phenomena. Hence, sociology must "double back on itself," and must "act as a corrective." In examining the nature of crisis in the social order, for instance, Touraine states:

> society is reduced to a universe of objects, of rules and institutions, of signs and instruments of inequality and domination. History seems to have withdrawn from these crystal-like societies. Calculation seems to have replaced action and strategy to have eliminated politics. Society has become desocialized; we no longer have at our disposal instruments for analyzing it as society: only as order, language or technique. To move out of the crisis is to learn to feel responsible again, to rediscover the stakes of collective action. We must take this crystallized society in our hands and shatter it against the wall of our silence and our anger.[35]

Touraine's most recent works all enlarge upon this new theoretical "cultural" practice. *La societé invisible* (1977) consists of entries in his intellectual diary, from 1974 to 1976. He addresses general problems about society and social movements and particular situations in China or Algeria. Sociology and structure, historicity and Brazilian intellectuals are only a few of the topics that enter Touraine's diary. He deals with the diverse topics sociologically, focusing on change through class conflict; power and domination are the unifying themes. According to Touraine,

> class actors are oriented toward the control of historicity, knowledge, accumulation and the cultural model. . . . [But] inequality and domination penetrate into the political system itself . . . [thus] avoiding the contradiction between the classes. . . . [Instead] class conflict is inseparable from the unity of a field of historicity through which the society produces its field of practices by way of the conflict of classes.[36]

The mixture of such theory with reminiscences and of philosophy with personal insight into daily events, and the debunking of all dogmatic politics—on the right and on the left—foreshadows Touraine's current move toward the study of personal responsibility and "revolution" through the simulation of interaction in small groups of potential dissidents. In "Crisis or Transformation" (1977),[37] he argues that new paradigms must be found to comprehend the social mutations (characterized, simultaneously, by decadence and breakdown, emergence and creation) that result from multiple policies, "routes" of development, and rivalry among states. Openly dismissing functionalism and Marxism as incompatible with analyses of the "new" and emerging social order, Touraine aims to uncover social structures so that we may analyze development by opposing both "communitarian Utopian anti-technocracy and the technocratic illusion."[38] He frequently repeats such calls to political action and involvement, as he asks for the creation of a strong socialist party that would not need the union of the left—a union where communist organization under the aegis of Moscow would eventually destroy liberty.

Touraine's political actions first led to his visibility in 1968. His political concerns made him dismiss structuralism, although his search for "invisible" social structures indicates a search for what one might call a neo-structuralist sociology that would replace structuralism. As an alternative to all the existing macro-systems—to structuralism, Marxism, functionalism—Touraine's sociology aims to provide a basis for true socialism. Touraine's structures are in a society's history; and even a break (as in 1968) is located in the existing class struggle. This pits him not only against the establishment technocracy but against both Lefebvre's humanist and Althusser's scientific Marxism. And it exemplifies his call for personal engagement and against acceptance of all dogmatism.

Notes

1. Others are, for instance, Edgar Morin, Pierre Bourdieu, J. C. Passeron, Pierre Naville, Yves Barel, Jean-René Tréanton.

2. Touraine, *Pour la sociologie*, p. 15.

3. Touraine, *La société invisible*.

4. Mayo and Roethlisberger's ten-year study at General Electric was the first to recognize the limits of Taylorism and of time and motion studies as cost-saving devices in industry. This work led to conclusions about human relations and the importance of job satisfaction in work performance. (These studies would spread from Touraine's students to the Third World as well).

5. Serge Mallet, *La nouvelle classe ouvrière* (Paris: Éditions du Seuil, 1963); Michel Crozier, *Le phénomène bureaucratique* (Paris: Éditions du Seuil, 1963); Friedmann and Naville, *Traité de sociologie du travail*.

6. Touraine, "L'organization du travail" in Friedmann and Naville, p. 388.

7. Touraine, *Workers' Attitudes and Technological Change*, p. 7.

8. Touraine, *La conscience ouvrière*, p. 8.

9. *Ibid.*, p. 12.

10. *Ibid.*, p. 50.

11. *Ibid.*, p. 312.

12. *Ibid.*

13. Touraine, *Sociologie de l'action*, p. 7.

14. *Ibid.*, p. 54.

15. *Ibid.*, p. 114.

16. See my chapter 1.

17. Touraine. *Sociologie de l'action*, p. 457.

18. Touraine, *Le communisme utopique*, pp. 9–11.

19. Touraine, *Post-Industrial Society*, p. 128.

20. *Ibid.*, p. 138.

21. Here, as elsewhere, the influence of John Kenneth Galbraith, *The New Industrial State* (New York: Signet, 1967) is apparent.

22. Touraine, *The Post-Industrial Society*, p. 54.

133 Touraine: Structures Without Structuralism

23. He is not far from Coser, who argues that social conflicts that do not contradict basic assumptions tend to be positively functional for the social structure. And he is close to Dahrendorf's notion that "as conflict generates change, so constraint may be thought of as generating conflict." Lewis Coser and Bernard Rosenberg, *Sociological Theory*, 4th ed. (New York: Macmillan 1976), p. 198.

24. Touraine, *The Academic System*, p. 94.

25. *Ibid.*, p. 252.

26. Touraine, *Pour la sociologie*, p. 177.

27. Touraine, *The Academic System*, p. 263.

28. *Ibid.*, p. 279.

29. Touraine, *The Self-Production of Society*, p. 65.

30. Touraine, *Productions de la société*, p. 244.

31. *Ibid.*, p. 245. The grids and diagrams in this book resemble those by William Overholt, "Organizational Conflict Theory of Revolution," Hudson Institute (February 1976), but Touraine and Overholt do not appear to take account of each other's work.

32. Touraine, *Productions de la société*, p. 512.

33. *Ibid.*, p. 429.

34. Touraine, *Pour la sociologie*, p. 30.

35. Touraine, "From Crisis to Critique," p. 223.

36. Touraine, *La société invisible*, p. 240.

37. Touraine, "Crisis or Transformation," in Norman Birnbaum, ed., *Beyond the Crisis*, (New York: Oxford University Press, 1977).

38. Touraine, *Letters a une étudiante*, p. 59.

Bibliography

Bajoit, G. "Vers une sociologie scientifique: A propos du livre d'Alain Touraine: Production de la société." *Sociologie du Travail* (1974), 16(2):193–205.
Barel, Yves. *La reproduction sociale*. Paris: Anthropos, 1973.
Collins, Randall. "Review Essay: Productions de la société." *American Journal of Sociology* (May 1976), 81(6):1503–6.
Ellul, Jacques. *The Technological Society*. New York: Vintage, 1964.
Touraine, Alain. *L'évolution du travail ouvrier aux usines Renault*. Paris: C.N.R.S., 1955.
——*La civilization industrielle*. Paris: N.L.F., 1961.
—— *Ouvriers d'origine agricole* (with O. Ragazzi). Paris: Éditions de Seuil, 1961.
——"L'organization professionelle de l'entreprise." In Georges Friedmann and Pierre Neville, eds., *Traité de sociologie de travail*, 1:387–427. Paris: Armand Colin, 1964.

Touraine, Alain. "Pouvoir et décision dans l'entreprise." In Georges Freidmann and Pierre Naville, eds., *Traité de sociologie de travail,* 2:3–41. Paris: Armand Colin, 1964.

—— "Towards Actionalist Sociology." Archives européennes de sociologie (1964), vol. 5, no. 1.

—— *Sociologie de l'action.* Paris: Éditions du Seuil, 1965.

—— *Workers' attitudes and technological change.* Paris: O.E.C.D., 1965.

—— *La conscience ouvrière.* Paris: Éditions du Seuil, 1966.

—— *Huachipato et Lota* (with T. diTella, L. Bransm, and J. D. Reynaud). Paris: C.N.R.S., 1966.

—— *Les ouvriers et le progrès technique* (with J. Dofny, C. Durand, and J. D. Reynaud). Paris: Armand Colin, 1966.

—— "Anciennes et nouvelles classes sociales." In *Perspectives de la sociologie contemporaine,* pp. 117–56. Paris: Presses universitaires de France, 1968.

—— *Le communisme utopique: le mouvement de mai 1968.* Paris: Éditions du Seuil, 1968. Translated as *The May Movement, Revolt and Reform.* New York: Random House, 1971.

—— "Le système d'action." *Sociological Society* (1969), no. 2, pp. 221–47.

—— *La société post-industrielle.* Paris: Denoël-Médiations, 1969. Translated as *The Post-Industrial Society.* New York: Random House, 1971.

—— "Progrès et limites du traitements des conflits," *Projet* (1970), no. 49, pp. 1056–64.

—— *Université et société aux États-Unis.* Paris: Éditions du Seuil, 1972. Translated as *The Academic System in American Society.* Carnegie Commission on Higher Education. New York: McGraw-Hill, 1974.

—— "L'historicité." *Une nouvelle civilization?* pp. 3–44. Paris: Gallimard, 1973.

—— *Productions de la société.* Paris: Editions du Seuil, 1973. Translated as *The Self-Production of Society.* Chicago: University of Chicago Press, 1977.

—— *Vie et mort du Chili populaire: journal sociologique.* Paris: Éditions du Seuil, 1973.

—— "La voie chilienne." *Les Temps Modernes* (November 1973), no. 11, pp. 582–602.

—— *Lettres à une étudiante.* Paris: Éditions du Seuil, 1974.

—— "Mouvements sociaux et idéologies dans les sociétés dépendantes." *Revue Tiers-Monde* (1974), 15(57):217–32.

—— *Pour la sociologie.* Paris: Éditions du Seuil, 1974.

—— Preface to *Roland Barthes.* Grenoble: Presses Universitaires de Grenoble, 1974. (Texts of talks on television by Touraine, Barthes, Duverger, and others.)

—— Preface to F. Stendler, *L'hôpital en observation.* Paris: Armand Colin, 1974.

—— "Les nouveaux conflits sociaux." *Sociologie du Travail* (1975), 17:1–17.

—— "From Crisis to Critique." *Partisan Review* (1976), no. 2, pp. 212–23.

—— *La société invisible.* Paris: Éditions du Seuil, 1977.

—— "Transformation in Crisis." In Norman Birnbaum, ed., *Beyond the Crisis.* New York: Oxford University Press, 1977.

Structuralist Psychoanalysis

Ever since 1932, when he published his doctoral thesis on *Paranoid Psychosis in its Relation to Personality,* Jacques Lacan has been "reinterpreting" Freud and mercilessly attacking the medicalization of American psychoanalysis, American empiricism, behaviorism, psychology, scientism, and the domination of the International Psychoanalytic Association by its American members. His indictments have frequently been nasty and personal, challenging the basic assumptions of clinical theory and practice. In the tradition of Charcot and Janet, he has reinstated hysteria as the most frequently observed French neurosis; his dialectics between conscious and unconscious components of language have "modernized" Hegel; his literary forays have reinterpreted *Don Quixote* and James Joyce; and his "politics" seem to subsume Marx and eroticism. But most of all, Lacan has dramatized Freud.

Lacan was born in 1901 in Paris, where he studied medicine and psychiatry, and where he began to "retravel Freud's royal road to the unconscious."[1] In 1966, for example, he reflected that he had embarked on this road in his dissertation—when he "forgot" the customary focus on passion and emotion and looked to the "involuntary poetry" and to the language of paranoia to find out how aggressive thoughts are transformed into action. His choice of a title, too, in 1936 (*Beyond the Reality Principle*), with its echoes of Freud's *Beyond the Pleasure Principle,* is said to prove his early interest in the dialectics between language and psychoanalysis, and to demonstrate the continuity of his work.[2]

Parisian psychoanalysts and intellectuals, of course, are familiar with the typically Lacanian leaps of thought that also enhance his affinity to Freud. But for prosaic Americans the plunge into Lacanian depths is foreign. Lacan makes much of the fact that he cannot be systematized, that he cannot be "understood," that to understand him is to reify and misconstrue him, because "misunderstanding" is an inherent part of "understanding." To translate him is said to be even more hopeless, not only because the English language cannot account for French analytic idiosyncrasies of "interhuman unconscious communication," but also because Lacan's style cannot be divorced from his native and culture-bound language.[3]

This sweeping admonition deserves to be discussed on its merits. Indeed, it is intrinsic to Lacanian theory and to his training analyses. Yet, Lacan's work cannot be adequately examined outside its historical context, since it subsumes parts of Sartrean existential phenomenology, of neo-Hegelian dialectics, of romanticism, and is sympathetic to the more speculative components of Freudian philosophy. Because our Anglo-Saxon search for salvation tends to be more bounded and to gravitate toward individual solutions, while the French tend to look to politics, my "translation" must clarify both cultural and intellectual differences, as well as the disagreements about psychoanalytic theory and practice. For Lacan cannot be reduced to his psychoanalysis. Before outlining his theories, I shall describe his milieu: because he had already received some general acclaim in the 1950s, acclaim which probably encouraged his stand against the psychoanalytic establishment, it would not be accurate to divorce from the Parisian ambiance the tensions he generated within his discipline; nor would it be correct to separate Lacan from the rise of structural linguistics, which, in turn, relies on Freud. Alternately, Lacan acted as godfather, midwife, and public relations man to this movement; indeed, the French accepted Lacanian psychoanalysis almost as a corollary of structuralism. In fact, in the 1950s, Parisians had associated psychoanalysis with attitudes of secrecy and shame; yet by 1974 public attitudes had done an about-face and psychoanalysis was seen as the guide to better living.[4] To receive *une tranche d'analyse* had become fashionable.

How did such a change come about? What made for the spread of this complicated theory, or for Lacan's massive "rereading" of Freud? Does his structuralist lens really refract the light through his so-called *mirror-image* or illuminate his notion of the *imaginary*? Is he a genius or a fraud, and must the two be mutually exclusive? Has he found the clue to our universe by combining psychoanalysis with linguistics? Do his endless mental gymnastics compounded by messianic promises confuse us, so that we dare not admit that we almost cannot understand either the meaning or the need to "misunderstand"?

II

Since Freud discovered a cure for hysteria so long ago much has happened not only to psychoanalysis, to its practitioners, and to its patients, but to the culture which they all share. No one would dispute the importance of cultural influences, or deny Lacan's assertion that the European analysts who emigrated to America during World War II were integrated into American empiricism, that they adopted some aspects of behaviorism, or that the "medicalization" of the discipline was conducive to a specific clinical "scientism." But Lacan maintains that these developments led to an unhealthy adaptation to the American way of life, to narrowness and to authoritarianism. He further alleges that the very success of the American Freudians legitimates whatever they say (there are so many of them) within the International Psychoanalytic Association and allows them to reify their assumptions.[5] Hence he feels free to dismiss them as one would dismiss a provincial church whose dogma has become outdated and whose hold must be broken. In the beginning he tried to win them over; he wanted them to accept his "deviant" theoretical work on the *mirror-stage* when he presented it to the Fourteenth Congress of the International Psychoanalytic Association at Marienbad in 1936. In 1949, at the Sixteenth Congress of the Association, in Zurich, he presented another and more elaborate version of this theory.[6] By then, Lacan's insistence that ego formation occurs through distortions analogous to the reflections of mirrors within mirrors was an even greater anathema to Freudian psychoanalysts, who were increasingly relying on ego psychology. In fact, since the late 1930s, American Freudians had begun to pay more attention to the work of Hartmann, Kris, and Loewenstein (and their adherents)—and to their proposition that the functions of the ego had been neglected by psychoanalysts.[7] Thus, Lacan's notion that ego formation proceeds through inextricably confused introjections of the *I* and the *Other* in the unconscious language of the self, paralleled—on the theoretical level—the arguments that were being articulated on institutional grounds. And because Loewenstein had been Lacan's analyst, the rift took on strongly personal (some say Oedipal) overtones.

When the American psychoanalysts refused to broaden their own base or to show more flexibility, Lacan hardened his position. He argued that American Freudians had lost their touch, that they could not even recognize their own narcissism. As he got angrier, he accused them of human engineering; and he likened their view of analytic training to that of a driving school which not only claims the privilege of issuing the driving license but also wants to supervise the making of the car.[8] Classical analysts were said to usurp their privileged position in the psychoanalytic relationship, to exploit their patients by focusing on techniques. He even suggested that their mistaken scientism led them to misdiagnose their patients, to find "new" symptoms (obsessions and compulsions, and, more recently, character disorders) when, instead, the symptoms of hysteria Freud had identified are as prevalent as ever, and only the analysts' perceptions seem to have changed.

American Freudians in turn began to respond by placing Lacan in the role of the rebellious child, whose Oedipal relation to the International Psychoanalytic Association and its officiating fathers had not yet been resolved, who had not been successfully analyzed and who, therefore, could not recognize his own defense mechanisms.

By 1953, his "provocations" resulted in his inevitable break with the International Psychoanalytic Association and with the Paris Psychoanalytic Society as well. (The Société Française de Psychanalyse, Groupe d'Études et de Recherches Freudiennes was formed in opposition to the Paris Society.) Ostensibly, the rift was over questions of analytic training and of medicalization, rather than over the unbridgeable and widening theoretical gulf. The current interest in Lacan on the part of non-medical Freudians and others outside the "orthodox" associations stems at least in part from their somewhat similar relation to the Freudian establishment and from their identification with Lacan's successful separation.

Undoubtedly, present curiosity about Lacan is also related to the fact that American psychoanalysis has been losing its appeal, while its French counterpart is flourishing. Our most respected practitioners cannot even agree on whether or not psychoanalysis is dead, in decline, or a valuable resource for family therapists, encounter group leaders, experts in the helping professions, and the proponents of assorted self-help fads.[9] French psychoanalysis, on the other hand, though rent by its own divisions and disagreements, has turned Oedipus and *la psychanalyse* into popular philosophy. In any event, Lacan, the major cause of the various splits (in 1953, 1963, and 1969) remains central as the charismatic enfant terrible-cum-father.[10]

But in America, where sectarianism has led to separatism, to non-communication with the "church," and even to the use of different terminologies,[11] practitioners do not insult each other in public: they proselytize to attract specific sectors of the public. Thus a therapy-oriented population that is looking for quick salvation is presented with a succession of novel therapies. Naturally, this militates against the cult of an overall "leader." At the same time, it expresses our veneration of the new. The French, on the contrary, prefer to build on their traditions. Thus our Freudian "deviants" are more likely to disavow Freud, whereas their French brothers tend to talk of *la chose Freudienne*. So it should not surprise anyone that Lacan's innovative mixture of classical Freudian clinical techniques with his own manner of interacting in a public "seminar" is explained with a detour through philosophy and linguistics.[12] Similar practices by American psychotherapists are explained more directly. Still, the inherent concern of *all* psychoanalysts with symptomatology is inclined to direct even cultural discussions to questions of national character, to adaptations to surroundings, to personality structure, etc., as well as to clinical notions about transference and countertransference.

III

The impact of post-World War II politics, French chauvinism, and the loss of French leadership, on the development of psychoanalysis is surely complex. But it is possible to recognize the political overtones of the battle between French and American Freudians, and to see how these were related to the rise of Gaullism as well as to the psychoanalytic disagreements. The founding of a specifically French psychoanalytic school in the mid-1950s struck a chord, because this school differentiated itself from its American counterpart at a time when the French were fighting American takeover in every sphere and were meeting what Servan-Schreiber called the *American Challenge*.[13] Lacan's popularity is in part related to this challenge, and to a certain confusion between national and psychoanalytic politics.

When the International Psychoanalytic Association expelled Lacan, they "limited" themselves to questions of practice: they objected to his "flexible" psychoanalytic hour, which in some cases lasts no more than five minutes; to his socializing with patients; to his treating both husbands and wives; to his inadequate training of lay analysts; and to his opposition to the "required" didactic analysis. In focusing on these problems of professional access and uniformity of training, the Freudian functionaries forgot French practical realities—the immediate need for psychoanalysts and for training analysts, the cost and time required for their training, and the low priority accorded psychoanalysis in the general poverty and devastation after World War II. For, unlike American psychoanalysis, which had flourished since Freud's visit to Clark University in 1909, and which had resorted to medicalization in defense against quackery, the French movement had always been small. Even after World War II, French psychiatrists, for the most part, still did not want to become analysts. Thus Lacan's defiance of the American establishment was to some extent an expression of French conditions, conditions Freud had already addressed in *On the Question of Lay Analysis* (1927). And, in contrast to some of his colleagues, Lacan refused to accommodate the American contingent; he accused them all of having lost touch with Freud, of having "lost the sense of Freud."[14] But there were also other areas of disagreement.

In the *clinical* realm, Lacan's own "return to Freud," as we will see, increasingly relied on Freud's studies of hysteria, although he praised, for example, Melanie Klein's emphasis on early training and Harry Stack Sullivan's focus on interpersonal relationships—which bolster his own theories. In the *philosophical* realm, Lacan continued in the rhetorical tradition. He seemed to retain the existential components of Sartre's *Being and Nothingness,* the mediation between the individual and his surroundings; but the very idea that the unconscious rather than the existential situation would dominate contradicted Sartre's then fashionable philosophy. And he used the notion of the universality of the Oedipus complex as an added dimension, so that he was thought to some extent to contribute radical components to French phenomenology.[15] Yet the theory of the *mirror-stage,* which maintains that "the construction of the subject is not the result of pure perception but needs the image of the body as intermediary," rejects the entire Cartesian tradition from Maine to Husserl.[16] Furthermore, Lacan "fused" the mediating relationships of structural linguistics to neo-Hegelian dialectics; his psychoanalysis became part of large-scale social history; free association turned into a methodological tool to uncover both cultural and individual origins. And the Hegelian *Other,* for Lacan, increasingly referred to every *Other,* as well as to the relationship between analyst and analysand.

By the early 1960s, the radical aspects of his philosophy made Lacan persona grata for a number of Marxists who tied his ideas to revolution—ideas which in turn were bolstered by the symbiotic relationship between Lacan, idealist philosophy, and structuralism, and by Lacan's stress of Freud's early works, which paralleled the then current Parisian polemics about the early Marx. This emphasis on the early Freud did not have autochthonous origins and is not entirely accidental. The so-called "young philosophers," for example, who in the late 1920s focused, however briefly, on the young Marx, were Lacan's contemporaries.[17] In a way, Lacan's insistence that the early Freud had been neglected, that he must be revived, paralleled Henri Lefebvre's effort to reinstall the young Marx.[18] And this parallel elevates the status of Freud's early work on hysteria—itself related to Charcot and thus to French psychology. It also evokes the enthusiasm of youth that would negate the pessimism of Freud's later years, so that Lacan's new reading of Freud becomes, symbolically, part of the rejuvenation of French intellectual life.

Actually, Lefebvre's Marxist opponent, Louis Althusser, champion of the mature Marx (the Marx of *Capital*), and whose theory presents a scholarly attempt to explain Stalinism, is probably most responsible for the alleged link between psychoanalysis and revolution—in a society where Marxism remains alive. After reiterating that conventional Freudian psychoanalysis tends to perpetuate bourgeois values by socializing individuals into capitalist society, by psychologizing social conflict, Althusser praises Lacan's theory of the decentered self which shows how Freud had broken radically with psychology. Althusser posits Lacan's notion of the *mirror-stage*—on a high level of abstraction—as a possible revolutionary tool.

To Althusser, the rooting of the self at such a pre-Oedipal stage represents a possibility of interfering in the socialization process. Because infants incorporate both parental and social values and beliefs almost from birth, Lacan's focus on the preverbal formation of the self is said to hold out a new hope. Essentially, Althusser "recognizes" that even Lenin, who had struggled with the problem of resocialization, of de-bourgeoisment, had not been able to solve it. But Freud's scientific view of the unconscious together with Marx's scientific view of society—as reread by Lacan and Althusser—were to overcome all unified conceptions of ego and of self. For if we could learn how to alter the Oedipal situation, thus avoiding the typical resolution that makes for the patriarchal and bourgeois family relationships—relationships which must be undercut—then socialism would take root. Clearly, such a direct link between psychoanalysis and politics is anathema to American Freudians, as well as to their potential analysands.

IV

What is this *mirror-stage*? To what extent does it "improve" on Freud? Is it really possible to instrumentalize this event, to postulate it as a tool for change? And is it "legitimate" to declare this moment of experience as the most important psychological knot, as the locus of the self?

Basically, Lacan finds that a child's first and usually jubilant reaction to its own reflection in a mirror, which is said to happen between six and eighteen months, is of fundamental importance. It is said to reveal a libidinal dynamism which was potentially present in Freud's studies on narcissism and in the *Ichspaltung* of the *imago*.[19] This moment, alleges Lacan, is the child's initial awareness of itself as a biological organism, as an entity bound up with the human species, and as "a threshold of what it would become," at a time before it can verbalize or make sense of this experience. Because this stage, in its simplest terms, is part of the psychoanalytic problem of identification, Lacan locates the individual's anticipation of the self in this moment, and invests it with all the complex emotions and intellections that go into one's future relations between the *Innenwelt* and the *Umwelt*.[20] The moment itself is discerned as a temporal dialectic, the dialectic of a fragmented body which projects the individual into his history and which "manufactures the succession of fantasies that extend to its totality, and to the armour of an alienating identity."[21] Lacan means that the as yet uncoordinated infant cannot be aware of the perceptions it forms, cannot recognize the way it views this first glimpse of his own body (as his own), but that this first "impression" bears upon all of his future mental development, including the resolution of the Oedipus complex.

Hence the import of the *mirror-stage*, attributable to anatomically incomplete development, is said, inevitably, to set up an imaginary dual relationship: it becomes the basis for personal relationships (with all *Others*), as well as the precondition for primary narcissism and a source of aggressivity. Lacan finds proof for these assertions in psychoanalysis, when "the movement of the analysis encounters a certain level of aggressive disintegration in an analysand's dreams,"[22] or in psychopathology (i.e., schizoid and spasmodic symptoms of hysteria).

Lacanian psychoanalysis appears to be more idiosyncratic than its American counterpart. Freud's dicta to teach, practice, and amass clinical data can be valid only within the Lacanian group; Lacan tends to use the psychoanalytic techniques developed by Freud and to ignore those of his followers; and he continues to regard ego psychology as a betrayal of Freud, an example of American adaptation to social norms. But even before these disagreements led to the break in the 1950s, Lacan, unlike his American peers, had looked to the Freud of the philosophical essays, such as *Totem and Taboo, The Future of an Illusion,* particularly in following Freud's emphasis on the importance of the father in the formation of the unconscious. Lacan's concern for the larger philosophical questions allows him at times to subsume the results of some of the American empirical psychoanalytic inquiries, even while dismissing their techniques as reification.

The very range of Lacan's thought, specifically his use of the dialectic and of language, which addresses the individual's connection to the world, link him to philosophy. Less concerned with psychoanalytic techniques, or with the *mirror-image,* philosophers are intrigued with the notion that this moment could be conceptualized as the seat of metaphorical thinking, of symbolization. They look to the linking of the individual *I* with social situations, and with the *Other*—an *Other* which can refer to the Hegelian dialectic between master and slave, or, in the analytic situation, between *analyst* and *analysand.* Furthermore, philosophers of language believe that the Lacanian dissection of speech might itself provide them with a new tool.

Obviously, language would have had to be the common denominator between Lacan's politics, his psychoanalysis, his literary criticism, and his philosophy, even if structuralism had not been invented. In fact, even before structural linguistics became the favorite tool for apprehending reality—and certainly when he updated "The mirror stage" in 1949—Lacan emphasized the importance of language in fantasies at the preverbal stage. Even then he already considered speech as the most crucial element in psychoanalysis. His arguments with American Freudians, also, revolve around speech—as the tool for transference and countertransference, and when he attacks their "silences" as "loaded." Because the unconscious is said to express itself primarily through gaps, irregularities, and lapses, Lacan (like Theodor Reik who listened with his "third ear") insists that the analyst learns more from how a patient talks than from what he says. Freud, of course, was less bold. His concept of the unconscious was mediated through defense mechanisms and through the preconscious. But this difference may be only one of style. For in Freud, too, psychoanalysis and philosophy "converged" in the unconscious, an unconscious which Lacan, however, roots in "spoken" language. He states that he went back to Freud's texts,

> to the German text, and read it seriously in a contemporary framework, converted the limited, medical, and positivist approach of French analysis into something with repercussions in all the spheres of *les sciences de l'homme* . . . [and] introduced us to another Freud . . . [and] to the less than obvious fact that psychoanalysis is a language.[23]

To Lacan it is *the* language—a language that informs *all* of human activities and thought.

V

Freud's followers, says Lacan in 1953, have neglected the functions of language in psychoanalysis. Submitting current psychoanalytic theory and technique itself to the dialectic of analysis, he perceives the psychoanalysts' disregard for language as a defense and as a resistance which "is bound to recognize in this defense an alibi of the subject."[24] American Freudians, he continues, do not consider the importance of their own speech when they handle their patients' fantasies in psychoanalysis, when they discuss libidinal object relations, or when they deal with transference and countertransference. They forget that the *imaginary,* which includes the organization of "images" undisciplined by language, consists essentially of "mis-recognitions." Consequently, he suggests that they drop their customary discussions of psychoses, and of "existential phenomenology" and instead "return" to Freud's own method, to his focus on symbolization. According to Lacan,

> analysts are tempted to abandon the foundation of words, and how they are used; [in their interpretation of the imaginary, in their dealing with object relations and with countertransference] . . . and they are in danger of abandoning their own language as well . . . in favor of institutional language.[25]

To prove how psychoanalytic discourse has deteriorated, how its emphasis has shifted to technique that is handed down like a cheerless religious ritual, he cites Freud's own cases. He mentions, for example, Freud's reliance on his conversations with the parents of "little Hans"—one of Freud's famous patients—to discover how the child invented specific myths that explained his fixation at the corresponding libido stages; and with the help of language used in paranoid delusion, he shows how Freud studied the "function of the Word." Again, this attack on the professionalization of American Freudians, in its emphasis on Saussurean categories of language, can be related to the predominance of linguistics as a tool to explain social reality that began with the publication of Lévi-Strauss' "Structural Analysis in Linguistics and in Anthropology" in 1945.

Lévi-Strauss had applied structural linguistics to social phenomena by finding common elements in the telling of myths (on a sort of archetypal unconscious and "programmed" level). Lacan, however, looked to the symbols used *in* myths (both cultural and personal) to help unravel an individual's conscious and unconscious thought in its context. Therefore, some of Lacan's and Lévi-Strauss' followers began to collaborate on the mapping of natives' myths and analysands' dreams—to uncover the origins of both individual and collective nature and culture. As followers of Saussure, both Lévi-Strauss and Lacan apprehend language as *Gestalteneinheit,* as a self-sufficient system that is complete as well as historical at every moment. Structural linguistics "allowed" for an entirely new reading of Freud. Because binary relationships are postulated between the *signifier* (sound-image) and the *signified* (concept), between *langue* (language system) and *parole* (individual speech), between *phonemic* (recognized) levels of speech and abstract systems of signs (they have their own built-in oppositions), between *metaphor* and *metonymy,* Lacan can mediate, dialectically, between these dualisms. Hence, it is easy to coordinate the dualisms with all the ambivalences addressed by Freud. Now the various accepted meanings, for example, of Freud's own dreams which had "fathered" psychoanalysis could be broadened; and psychoanalysis itself could become even more complex—or at least more French. Lacan is certain that Freud who, like any other writer, had to put down myriads of simultaneous impressions sequentially, can be improved upon if only we examine his texts through "chains of signifiers." Such chains are said to link successive signifiers. For the "structure of the signifying chain discloses the possibility . . . insofar as it exists as a language, to use it in order to signify *something quite other* than what it says."[26] Thus Lacan can also discover as yet unknown components of Freud's mind, components which allegedly went into the creation of psychoanalysis. In other words, he can free-associate to Freud for the benefit of the discipline.

In principle, such updating is said to follow Freud's own practice and should be welcome. But, aside from directly attacking the clinical practice of American Freudians, Lacan resents their refusal to accept his central concept of the *imaginary* (this highly idiosyncratic concept has its roots in the *mirror-stage*, where it is said to form a "Borromean knot" with the *real* and the *symbolic*). Although Lacan himself has continually elaborated on the constantly fluctuating relationship between its three components of fundamental psychological processes, he has never quite explained how this *imaginary* functions. Constituted on the basis of the *specular ego* in the *mirror-stage*, it is said to subsume a narcissistic relation to the self, although it can exist only in a dual relation with an *Other*; it can be triggered by a particular *Gestalt*; and as a component of fantasy, it exists on the level of real *and* imagined relations.[27]

In the analytic situation, the transference introduces yet another dialectical relationship. In addition to the rapport between analyst and analysand which engages the analyst's *imaginary*, it allegedly mediates between the *signifier* of the language of fantasy (thought content) and subsequent thoughts. And every moment of this process is said to evoke emotions which make *regressive* demands on the analyst. Yet these demands are themselves responses to significations (signals) from the analyst, similar to countertransference, and reflect perceptions by the analysand. Lacan calls this interaction the *paradox of desire.* Because such paradoxes are inevitable, they lead to constant "misunderstanding" (by both analyst and analysand). American analysts are said to perpetuate the confusion by forgetting to differentiate between the *symbolic* and *imaginary* orders. Lacan proposes to overcome the problem by having the analysand analyze him, to project onto him. At one point he explains this notion with an analogy to bridge: he puts the analyst in the position of the dummy, a dummy that doesn't know what cards he holds and can therefore elicit maximum information from his partner—the analysand's unconscious. Essentially, this exchange of information between "bridge partners," takes the form of neo-Hegelian dialectics; it follows linguistic logic, a logic Lacan often illustrates through diagrams, and which moves easily from conscious to unconscious phenomena.

Ultimately, Lacan, like Freud, reaches the unconscious via dream work. Like Freud, he tries to uncover all the relationships between manifest and latent dream content, and all the omissions, pauses, and doubts by the analysand. He is especially concerned with individual speech patterns and with breaks and irregularities in these patterns. Unconscious dream thoughts and free associations as well are examined in structuralist fashion: all are part of language; they are semantic condensations of discourse and/or function as syntactic displacements; and unconscious operations such as distortion, reaction formation, denial, and the consideration of representability become equivalents of *metaphor* and *metonymy* (these exist only in "chains of meaning"). Hence, defense mechanisms at times appear to parallel literary devices; and the unconscious discovered in dreams is said to be similar to the unconscious of everyday psychopathology.

Freud, of course, had not introduced the complexities of Saussurean linguistics, so he was easier to understand. Lacan, however, insists that the use of Saussurean categories adds to our understanding of Freud:

> If what Freud discovered and rediscovers with a perpetually increasing sense of shock has a meaning, it is that the displacement of the signifier (shift of focus that changes meaning) determines the subjects in their acts, in their destiny, in their refusals, in their blindness, in their end and in their fate, their innate gifts and social acquisitions notwithstanding, without regard for character or sex, and that, willingly, or not, everything that might be considered the stuff of psychology, kit and caboodle, will follow the path of the signifier.[28]

Simply put, this is Lacan's way of reaffirming the importance of language in psychoanalysis through structuralist mediations.

Its dynamics alone are to help us apprehend the complexities of constantly changing relations and meaning with the help of binary oppositions. To complicate things further, Lacan conceptualizes language as separate from the person who uses it; even the act of speaking allegedly does not unify them. This leads him to postulate the *language of the unconscious* on a separate level or structure: it is the *language of desire*, of the id; and it is said to be irrational in the Freudian sense and to incorporate all the binary relationships of linguistics. But ordinary speech as well, which is said to be the *language of culture*, operates, separately, on structuralist principles; and there exists yet another dialectical relationship between the two languages—at every level of interaction.

It thus becomes impossible even to indicate the endless oppositions Lacan envisages. He contrasts objective and subjective meanings, meanings initially given by the symbolic order that some individuals accept and others don't. He separates unique selections of words or language into need (organic drive tied to organic satisfaction) and desire (mental image of objects of satisfaction) and then "shows" how need can be more easily satisfied than desire. For desire involves the *Other* (in the analytic situation this is the analyst) and entails the desire for a sign of recognition. This appears to be a refinement on Freud's conceptualization of wish, since Lacan again breaks wishes into their conscious and unconscious components.

The centrality of language, however, extends even further. Symptoms too become signifiers; and feelings, though not the same as their meanings (mostly not unconscious), are assembled along networks of meaning, meaning which is again organized in binary fashion.[29] This emphasis on language and on symbolism almost by necessity rules out extensions of animal studies to humans (animals don't organize chains of significations in symbolic fashion)—studies that entail empirical research and provide a basis for some of the American clinical theories. Briefly put, the centrality of symbolic language as a human activity supposedly militates against all empiricism and "scientism" and reinforces the centrality of Lacan's *imaginary*—an *imaginary* that begins in the mirror phase, as the child enters the symbolic order which is organized through language. Language, particularly spoken language, connects the child to the real world through discourse with *Others*. Since much of this discourse is unspoken, it includes fantasy and may be unconscious. Lacan calls it the language of the *id:* it (ça) talks about the other person, *it* originates in the other person, and *it* is to be thought of in terms of binary mediations in relationships *and* in linguistic structures; and this ongoing discourse includes expressed and repressed gestures, thoughts, and feelings.

But how can all this be formalized? We know that unspoken thoughts and feelings can never be anticipated, are never complete, and are bound to be distorted when written down. Lacan found that even the psychoanalytic situation, which depends upon language, is full of pitfalls. To counteract the many defenses built into this interaction, he decided to reverse the roles of analyst and analysand, to make this relationship more egalitarian. Yet when he drew the "logical" conclusions and began to insist that the analysand talk about Lacan rather than himself, he remained open to accusations of delusions of grandeur, and of narcissism.

In this context, it is important to recall that Lacan's theories almost always receive attention through his public seminars, and that these seminars often turn into "happenings," "happenings" which appear at times to become quasi-encounters. That the seminars range from literary criticism to philosophy as well as to psychoanalysis adds not only to the "suspense" but also to the confusion and the criticism. For Lacan is likely to jump from logical mathematical formulas to Swift, Kant, and de Sade; or he may shift to Oedipal free associations, to poetic insights, to "antiliteral" expressions, only to end up by inviting the audience to analyze him. Before returning to the strictly psychoanalytic controversies, it is important to describe briefly the text of a literary seminar, a text that illustrates Lacan's inimitable style—and his genius.

VI

Lacan's most famous seminar is that on Edgar Allan Poe's "The Purloined Letter."[30] Because Baudelaire had been fascinated with Poe and had translated his work, and because everyone in

France has read Baudelaire in the Lycée, this story, I believe, is particularly well suited to a Lacanian treatment. It is apropos not only in itself but because its history spans two continents; it underlines the universalism propounded by structuralist psychoanalysis; and it orients and integrates macro- and micro-structures through the linking of imaginary incidences, by means of the Lacanian symbolic chains.

Unlike other psychoanalytic commentaries on Poe, such as Marie Bonaparte's *Life and Works of Edgar Allan Poe,* which centers on the artist's psychology, and which deals with "the creator's unconscious memories, . . . with his complexes," Lacan *excludes* Poe himself from the text.[31] Instead, he explains how the focus on Poe's use of language puts this tale into an entirely new context, a context that reveals previously unrecognized meaning, and that "replaces" Poe as the *signifier.* By separating the narration of the drama from the conditions of its narration, Lacan reconstructs the scenes, the protagonists' motives for action, the maneuvers, the guiles, etc., on separate levels. The drama itself is divided into two scenes. Briefly put, the first scene takes place in the queen's boudoir, where she receives a compromising letter she must hide from the King. Minister D, noticing the Queen's distress, takes advantage of it by replacing this letter with one of similar appearance; the Queen watches this maneuver but cannot prevent it. The second scene takes place in the Minister's office; here the minister manages to fool the police, but the letter—this object of deceit and counter-deceit—is eventually stolen again, by the mysterious Dupin.

The narrative, however, is only the backdrop for Lacan's dialogue—a dialogue full of paradox that moves on various levels and focuses on repetitive actions and on "gazes" with hidden meanings (this "gaze," is an important theme in Foucault's *Birth of the Clinic*). It is full of Lacanisms, of contrapuntal devices, of made-up words, of "slights" and "slips of the tongue," of convolutions that mediate between Poe and Lacan, symbols and signifiers, and the *letter* that is understood *to the letter.* The characters in the story are taken apart, reshuffled and analyzed, first to "prove" Lévi-Strauss' relations between myths, and then, increasingly, from a literary perspective that emphasizes *metaphors* and *metonyms,* plays and alliterations. Letter, it seems, leads to litter, to literally, to Joyce's circle that "played on the homophony of these two words in English," [32] to the letter as refuse handled by the police, to a different seal on a stamp, to makers of handwriting, and on and on. Lacan opposes the possessor to the holder of the letter, ties high treason to the problems of translation, Baudelairisms, the post office, and to the circularity of letters, of social phenomena and of symbols. He speculates about the emotions, motivations and possible thoughts of all the characters, about love and hate, only to get back to Freud, to the fact that sex, the reason for all the commotion, remains hidden. Eventually, he concludes that "the sender receives from the receiver his own message in reverse form . . . that a letter always arrives at its destination. [33]

All of this is to prove, on yet other levels, that the first scene symbolizes the primal scene, while the second one is its repetition; that the author must have been aware of some of the internal ambivalences; that the narration "doubles the drama with a commentary without which no *mise en scène* would be possible;" [34] and that "the unconscious is the discourse of the other." Lacan does not consider that Poe may not have wanted to introduce sex overtly, whether for psychological reasons or for the sake of plot or suspense; that he may have been a product of his time, or that he may have been observing the conventions of a literary genre. Lacan ignores such considerations, not only because they may be defenses, but because literary structuralism elevates texts over their individual authors. We are to read only Poe's text, to interpret it as arising from the expression of Poe's talent and his social and cultural milieu. And Lacan submits this text to a Freudian treatment insofar as he looks at it the way Freud looked at a psychoanalytic patient.

Essentially, Lacan treats every seminar as a "living" text, a text whose public character undercuts the privacy of the psychoanalytic hour, and whose written record becomes yet another and "narrower" text. Still, an individual's defenses are not broken down as they would be in psychoanalysis. The public character of a seminar exhibits Lacan's performance, a performance full of *languisteries,* that is, of newly-coined words, and of new meanings which are said to overcome existing boundaries of language. Like Barthes, Lacan is intent on creating new meta-languages to explain subtle meanings, plays on words, etc., that would add eroticism, symbolism and unconscious knowledge to our vocabulary. His seminar *Encore* (1975) is full of these word games; for example, he contrasts *d'eux* with *deux,* or associates *etourd-it* with the Freudian *id.*[35] Elsewhere, he splits "existence" into "exsistence"—the "eccentric" place where the unconscious is located.[36] Lacan's allusions undoubtedly enrich the French language and create a language that cannot be translated. This is why he is thought to have reinvented Freud. In any event, the witticisms and puns do not overcome the obstacles to understanding Lacan's work.

But it would be unfair to overemphasize his abstruseness, which is due to the complexities of structuralist psychoanalysis, a psychoanalysis which, in addition to everything else, aims to free the analysand for enjoyment (*jouissance*). This is yet another task Lacan shares with Barthes, who invites the reader to free-associate with his (or her) own emotions and intellect to his *writerly* text. For both Lacan and Barthes sincerely expect to create a new language of enjoyment, a language which will include fantasy, and which, by eliminating the repressive components of our existence, is said to liberate us. In this endeavor lies his radicalism.

VII

Lacan's psychoanalytic colleagues, however, are less concerned with this component of his work than they are with his influence on psychoanalysis. For his performance in the seminars not only attracts serious disciples who are analysed by the master and then become recognized Lacanian analysts, but others who, because they are able to play on words, begin to think of themselves as analysts and to solicit patients. Psychoanalysts also criticize his flamboyance, his style, and his clinical practices; the most serious objections, however, have to do with various aspects of Lacan's theory. He has sparked hair-splitting discussions about the applicability of specific parts of language in clinical practice and about the possible consequences of his techniques not only on his patients psyches but on their use of language. Some of these discus-

sions are about the effect of the popularity of the seminars themselves, which are said to "simplify Oedipus." Others are
exceedingly technical and intrinsic to the psychodynamic processes of individuals. Still others extrapolate from Freud's philosophy and/or his literary style. It is hard to convey the flavor of
the debates, for their "intertextuality"[37]—fragmentary allusions
to other texts such as music, politics, poetry, psychology—legitimates all the free associations. By arranging these free associations in binary fashion and by moving back and forth, for instance, between a selective fragment of Freud and any one of a
psychoanalytic patient's dreams, Lacan's psychoanalysis becomes
an impressive linguistic performance.

One of Lacan's major critics is André Green who earlier
had been a disciple. He has devoted an entire volume, *Le discours vivant* (1973), to refuting Lacan's position on the question
of affect. Basically, he attacks the centrality of signifiers, that is of
concepts (signifieds) announced or declared through speech—a
chain of signifiers—in the meaning of affects. For if affects are
derived from representations in language, he wonders, then how
can Lacan explain displacement of affect which can avoid language altogether, or intellectualization, which obfuscates affect.

Jean Laplanche and Serge Leclaire split from Lacan and
joined the Association Psychanalytique de France, because they
opposed him on yet another fundamental question of language.
They postulate "the unconscious as the condition of language"
rather than "language as the condition of the unconscious."[38]
Basing themselves on George Politzer's forgotten neo-Marxist critique in *Les fondaments de la psychologie* (1928), which attacks
Freud's metapsychology for its abstraction and realism but retains the radical meaning of *the unconscious,* they juxtapose this
"phenomenology of consciousness" to the "psychoanalytic unconscious" (it is similar to Hegel's "unhappy consciousness" and
"beautiful soul").

None of this makes sense unless we remember that Laplanche and Leclaire, too, operate according to structuralist di-
chotomies, so that they subsume the notion of a third dimension
of time (it mediates between past and present, that is, between
synchronic and diachronic time). And because this temporal dialectic is believed to parallel the clinical process insofar as thought

and free association also collapse time, they agree with Lacan. But Leclaire and Laplanche's unconscious is perceived as "an organized structure of self-apprehension" which exists both in its infinite separate moments as well as in its coherent totality.[39] Hence for them the distinction between "consciousness" and "second consciousness" as a radical division between conscious and unconscious components of meaning breaks down when the unconscious becomes conscious. They argue that Lacan fudges the distinction between the unconscious and language when he insists that the unconscious is structured like a language. They go on to illustrate how Lacan, in dream analysis, fails to differentiate between primal language and primary process (psychosis), so that they not only invalidate his clinical practices but consider themselves the "true" descendants of Freud. Simultaneously, they reinforce the connection between language and the unconscious text as central to psychoanalysis. When they argue whether language precedes the unconscious, or, vice versa, whether the unconscious comes first, it is also very clear that these controversies are far removed from American psychoanalysis.

This fact is underlined by Leclaire's other books, *Démasquer le réel* (1971) and *Psychanalyser* (1968), which deal, for the most part, with data gathered in psychoanalytic practice. But, again, Leclaire's is a search for the linguistic "knot" of the unconscious or for "theoretical ensembles of letters" rather than for a more direct unraveling of interpersonal emotions. More than Lacan, Leclaire roots his theory in his practice, in the analyst's office, in "the game between the couch and easy chair." He, too, stresses a personal descent from Freud:

> The zero-sum game and its representation, or the relation of the subject to the lack he underlines in the ensemble in which he nevertheless takes part, call this the 'primal scene' where Freud taught us to situate the space of the impossible knowledge of 'the origin of each one'."[40]

Questions of space (and of time) once more get back to the French literary debates, to questions of writing, and of history in structuralist theory. Leclaire seems to address, for the most part, Barthes' notion of the "zero degree of writing," that is, the space between words and the silence that modifies them, and that must be "read." Clearly, this is another example of "intertextuality," of the interpenetration of texts, texts that emphasize, in this instance, psychic liberation, the history of literary criticism, and the unconscious. Linguistic psychoanalysis and literary criticism, it seems, replicate the proverbial chicken/egg problem: together they open up to all thought associations, to new investigations. So Leclaire is inspired to "recuperate the pleasure principle in adulthood," to advocate more instinctual living, and to "transfer" the pleasure Barthes finds in the relationship between the *readerly* and the *writerly* to that between analyst and analysand.

J. B. Pontalis—a "dissident" Lacanian and a long-standing intimate of Sartre—for his part, locates enjoyment in the analyzed individual, in the status he (or she) has gained through analysis.[41] For unlike "Little Hans," who told Freud fifteen years after his analysis that he "remembered nothing," Pontalis finds that today's analysand "remembers everything." To be analyzed is to his economic advantage, he argues, because the analyzed person is perceived as strong by all *Others,* even though this new strength eventually backfires as defenses rigidify.[42] In his dictionary of Freudian concepts, *The Language of Psychoanalysis* (1967), Pontalis (with J. Laplanche) carefully traces the evolution of Freud's ideas to the present (including, for example, Reich's orgone box, Moreno's psychodrama, Lacan's Desire, and so on.). But even Pontalis focuses on the language of psychoanalysis rather than on clinical observation. Lacan has set the tone for Parisian psychoanalysis in which language dominates, even for the detractors who emphasize its repressive character that "perpetuates the Oedipal triangle" and hence the socialization into bourgeois culture. Thus Deleuze and Guattari's *Anti-Oedipus* (1972), which assails the entire "Oedipal machinery" as repressive and introduces a "schizoanalyse" to shatter all psychoanalytic and societal myths—an anti-psychiatry that engages the individual unconscious directly in politics—indirectly upholds the Lacanian structures it attacks.[43] Except for Piaget, who cautions that, so far, only the "initiated" perceive how Lacan's "new transformation rules . . . [allow] for the irrational ingredients of the unconscious and the ineffable features of private symbols to make their entry into a language really designed to express the communicable,"[44] few "structuralists" question the methodological assumptions which seem to go hand in hand with socialist ideas. Their mission, it appears, derives directly from Freud, as it bypasses the attempts of Reich, Fromm, or Marcuse to fuse Freud and Marx, to create a theory of practice based on the currency of psychoanalytic language.

VIII

To what extent, we must ask, can this new language induce social change? Neither Lacan nor the other structuralists who produce only texts of texts of texts have provided an answer. But Lacan's promises of personal liberation were enhanced, inadvertently, when in response to the events of 1968 he "descended into the street" to show allegiance to the dissident students who had contested all political structures and authorities. This act seemed to underline the revolutionary potential of Lacanian psychoanalysis, or, at least, to show how the psychoanalyzed individual "coincided" with Marx's unalienated man (or woman). Consequently, no one ever seriously challenged Lacan's revolutionary bent, if only because his "radicalization" of Freud had turned psychoanalysis itself into a new social movement.

Lacan, however, in spite of his revolutionary image, bypasses politics, even when he holds forth on the politics of *parole* and *désire*, that is, roughly, on speech and self-actualization through manifestation of the *Other*. Still, because Lacan and his disciples were physically in the street, they were deemed radical, while the analysts who psychologized about the events in their offices were considered conservative. This contrasting behavior mirrored the previous stereotype that identified French psychoanalysis as revolutionary and its American counterpart as reactionary. But even though the Lacanians' sympathy for the students was overestimated—they were thought to have abandoned "bourgeois ideology" and were hailed as the bearers of social change—these political judgments themselves politicized psychoanalytic practice.

As Lacan's call for the "return to Freud's meaning" was increasingly heeded, and as books in *le champ Freudien* became a major industry, the strong existentialist and socialist background of the French psychoanalysts—they had been weaned on Marx rather than on Freud—gained the upper hand. Lacan now not only attacks American Freudians for adapting the individual to the culture but actually expects to reverse this process of adaptation as he exposes the *politics of speech*. This philosophical rhetoric is far removed from our own psychoanalytic heresies, from the derivative therapies such as, est, encounter, biofeedback, primal therapy, etc. For even our phenomenological therapies lean on empiricism and on observation; they lack the structuralist and Marxist bases whose conventions of discourse are alien to our own pragmatism. This is not to say that Lacanianism may not become yet another one of our therapeutic fads, or that our psychoanalysts might not adapt some aspects of Lacan's clinical notions, but only that Lacan will not become an *American* Freud.

No one, it seems, who has even dabbled in Lacan remains neutral. Whether he is Freud's heir, a genius, or an egomaniac, his linguistic analysis has become a movement that combines theoretical formulations with some sort of participatory potential. Thus, to the man in the street who may attend his seminar or who may watch his performance on television, Lacan holds out equality, "cheap" psychoanalysis, or even salvation. To French intellectuals, of course, he promises the highest form of truth. But to American psychoanalysts he is an enigma, an enigma they are only beginning to explore. To them, and to our intellectuals, however, a dose of Lacan could be extremely useful—not in its full strength, but at least as an antidote against fragmentation and over-professionalization.

Notes

1. Lacan, *Écrits I*, p. 66.

2. *Ibid.*, pp. 81–88.

3. Pamela Tytell, "Lacan et l'anglais tel qu'on le parle," *Magazine littéraire* (February 1977), no. 121, pp. 14–18. Tytell states, "from the first reading, the American must sense the nuances of the French (more difficult than to understand, read or talk) and be able to resist translating into English: language too comfortable, full of cultural sense and pitfalls."

4. Serge Moscovici, *La psychoanalyse, son image et son public* (Paris: Presses Universitaires de France, 1961), examined the social context, definitions, and areas of intervention of psychoanalysis in the 1950s from a sociology of knowledge and social psychological perspective. Sherry Turkle, *Psychoanalytic Politics,* p. 194, examined the impact and diffusion of psychoanalytic ideas in French society in 1974. She discovered that over half of her representative sample of Parisians found psychoanalysis to have become more important in the general culture.

5. Lacan formulated this statement in various ways, but he is probably most succinct in the preface and the introduction to "The Function and Field of Speech and Language in Psychoanalysis," Report to the Congress of Rome, 1953, in *Écrits: A Selection,* pp. 30–39.

6. Lacan, "Le Stade du miroir comme formateur de la fonction du Je telle qu'elle nous est révélée dans l'expérience psychanalytique," translated by Alan Sheridan as "The mirror stage as formative of the function of the I as revealed in the psychoanalytic experience," in *Écrits: A Selection,* pp. 1–7.

7. See Heinz Hartmann, "Ego Psychology and the Problem of Adaptation," translated by David Rapaport (New York: International Universities Press, 1958), originally published in German, in 1939; Heinz Hartmann, Ernst Kris, and R. M. Loewenstein, "Comments on the Formation of Psychic Structure," *The Psychoanalytic Study of the Child* (1946) 2: 11–38.

8. Lacan, *Écrits: A Selection,* 33.

9. This was particularly apparent at a gathering of psychoanalysts and intellectuals. *Partisan Review* (1979), no. 4, pp. 501–41.

10. Essentially, the split in 1963 came about because the French Psychoanalytic Society (Association Psychanalytique de France) was unable to deal with the wish of many of its members to belong to the International Psychoanalytic Association (students from other countries came to be trained in Paris, despite the association's refusal to admit Lacan. When the international body recognized the anti-Lacanian group that had formed, the Association Psychanalytique de France, and gave them the right to train analysts, Lacan moved his seminar to the École Normale Supérieure, and in June 1964 founded the Freudian School of Paris (École Freudienne de Paris).

In 1969, another split occurred as a result of Lacan's insistence that "pure psychoanalysis" was equivalent to a training analysis, because it was the only way one could examine the tangled "knot" of the transference to the analyst. When Lacan clung to this position, a number of analysts left to form The Fourth Group (Le Quatrième Groupe). For details of these events, see Turkle, *Psychoanalytic Politics,* pp. 104–29.

11. Joseph Barnett, "A Structural Analysis of Theories in Psychoanalysis," *Psychoanalytic Review* (Spring 1966), 53(1):85–98.

12. Lacan's *séminaire* differs from our conception of seminar. It is a lecture delivered to the general public and to students under the auspices of the École Normale Supérieure. Lacan draws many hundreds to his *séminaire;* people are known to line up for hours beforehand in order to get in.

13. Servan-Schreiber, *The American Challenge.*

14. Lacan, *Écrits I,* p. 213.

15. Shands, "Anthony Wilden, The Language of the Self," *Semiotica* (1971), no. 3, p. 284.

160 Lacan: Structuralist Psychoanalysis

16. Palmier, *Lacan*, p. 24. Ricoeur, in *Freud and Philosophy* maintains that no reflective philosophy has come as close to the Freudian unconscious as Husserl's phenomenology, but that in the end it fails, because "by dissociating the true beginning from the real beginning or natural attitude, phenomenology reveals the self-misunderstanding inherent in immediate consciousness" (p. 377).

17. By all accounts the most brilliant of these, George Politzer, proclaimed in *Les fondements de la psychologie* that "materialism is no more than the scientific understanding of the universe," but he later split with Henri Lefebvre over the importance of Freud (quoted in Poster, *Existential Marxism in Postwar France*, p. 47).

18. Politzer, *Les fondements de la psychologie*; see also Lefèbvre, *La somme et le reste*.

19. Lacan uses the German word for the "split in the ego;" again, because he wants to avoid the broader use of "ego" in English; he refers only to the temporal phenomenon in the *mirror-image*, at least in this context.

20. Palmier, *Lacan*, p. 24.

21. Lacan, "The mirror stage," *Écrits, A Selection*, pp. 3–5.

22. *Ibid.*, p. 4.

23. Wilden, *Language of the Self*, p. 310.

24. Lacan, *Écrits I*, p. 3.

25. Lacan frequently comes back to this theme; see the introduction to "Function and field of speech and language," *Écrits I*, p. 118; also Wilden, *The Language of the Self*, p. 4.

26. Lacan, *Écrits, A Selection*, especially, p. 155.

27. In this context the definition by Laplanche and Pontalis in *The Language of Psychoanalysis*, p. 210, is particularly helpful: ". . . from the intersubjective point of view, a so-called *dual* relationship based on—and captured by—the image of a counterpart (erotic attraction, aggressive tension)." For Lacan, a counterpart (i.e., another who is me) can only exist by virtue of the fact that the ego is originally another.

28. Wilden, *Language of the Self*, quoted in Stanley A. Leavy, "The Significance of Jacques Lacan," pp. 206–7.

29. Leavy, "Significance of Lacan," p. 209.

30. Lacan, *Écrits I*, pp. 19–75; also in *Yale French Studies*, (1972), no. 48, pp. 39–72.

31. Bonaparte, "Poe and the Function of Literature," in William Phillips, ed., *Art and Psychoanalysis*, pp. 54–88.

32. Lacan, *Yale Studies*, p. 55.

33. *Ibid*, p. 72. Were Althusser to analyze this story he might come up with a nearly identical summary, but he would find social inequalities, potential revolutionary situations, the oppression of the masses, and possibly of women.

34. *Ibid.*, p. 41.

35. Lacan, *Le séminaire, livre XX, Encore*, pp. 19–27. *D'eux* (of them) and *deux* (two) or the ending of *etourd-it* (deafened) and *id* use the same sound images yet share no meaning.

36. Jeffrey Mehlman, Introductory note to "Seminar on 'The Purloined Letter,'" *Yale French Studies*, (1972), no. 48, p. 39.

37. This term, coined by Julia Kristeva, expresses the fact that none of the structuralist literature may be taken partially; that everything, all the time, refers to everything else; that all thought associations and traditions may, legitimately, become part of a text; that every text is open to new readings with yet other associations; and that texts refer to one another.

38. This theme of Lacan's "The function and field of speech and language in psychoanalysis" is, again, central.

39. Jean Laplanche and Serge Leclaire, "The Unconscious: A Psychoanalytic Study," *Yale French Studies*, (1972), no. 48, pp. 118–175.

40. Leclaire, *Psychanalyzer*, p. 174.

41. J. B. Pontalis, *Après Freud*.

42. *Ibid.*, p. 12–13; Turkle, "Contemporary French Psychoanalysis," has elaborated on this phenomenon.

43. Gilles Deleuze and Felix Guattari, *L'Anti-Oedipe*. Guattari combines a militant Marxism with the practice of psychoanalysis; Deleuze is a philosopher. Their theme is: Desire is revolutionary and, at the outset, invests the social world and production. They tie this proposition to the primary production of the so-called *desiring machines*, whose energy is said to be the libido. So they propose a new method of analysis: schizo-analysis. Thus, they focus on Freud's notion of energy, which Lacan allegedly has left out.

44. Jean Piaget, *Structuralism*, p. 87.

Bibliography

Althusser, Louis. *"Lenin and Philosophy" and Other Essays*. London: New Left Books, 1971.
—— *For Marx*. New York: Pantheon, 1969.
Anzieu, Didier. "Oedipe avant le complexe." *Temps Modernes* (1966), 22:675–715.
Auzias, Jean-Marie. *Clefs pour le structuralisme*. Paris: Éditions Seghers, 1967.
Bär, Eugen. "Understanding Lacan." *Psychoanalysis and Contemporary Science* (1974), 3:473–544.
—— "The Language of the Unconscious According to Jacques Lacan." *Semiotica* (1971), 3(3):241–68.
Baliteau, Catherine. "La fin d'une parade misogyne: la psychanalyse Lacanienne." *Les Temps Modernes* (1975), 30(348):1933–53.
Barthes, Roland. *Le degré zéro de l'écriture*. Paris: Éditions du Seuil, 1953.
Bonaparte, Marie. "Poe and the Function of Literature." Excerpted from *Life and Works of Edgar Allan Poe* (London: Imago, 1949). In William Phillips, ed., *Art and Psychoanalysis*. New York: Criterion Books, 1957.
Calogeras, Roy C. "Lévi-Strauss and Freud: Their 'Structural' Approaches to Myths." *American Imago* (Spring 1973), 30:57–79.
Chalumeau, Jean-Luc. *La pensée en France*. Paris: Fernand Nathan, 1974.

162 Lacan: Structuralist Psychoanalysis

Clement, Catherine B., Pierre Bruno, and Lucien Sève. *Pour une Critique Marxiste de la Théorie Psychanalytique.* Paris: Éditions Sociales, 1973.

Corvez, Maurice. "Le structuralisme de Jacques Lacan." *Revue Philosophique de Louvain* (May 1968), 66:282–308.

Deleuze, Gilles and François Lyotard. "Les exclues du département de psychanalyse de Vincennes." *Temps modernes* (January 1975), p. 856–63.

Deleuze, Gilles and Felix Guattari. *L'Anti-Oedipe.* Paris: Éditions de Minuit, 1972. Translated as *Anti-Oedipus* by Robert Hurley, Mark Seem, and Helen R. Lane. New York: Viking, 1977.

Domenach, Jean-Marie. "Oedipus in the Factory." *Salmagundi* (Summer 1975), no. 30, pp. 120–28.

Ehrmann, Jacques. *Structuralism.* New York: Doubleday Anchor, 1970.

Francioni, Mario, "La psicolinguistica Freudiana secondo Lacan." *Filosofia* (1973), 24(1):35–52.

—— "I significanti nell'inconscio secondo Lacan." *Filosofia* (1973), 24(4):425–52.

Freud, Sigmund. *On the Question of Lay-Analysis.* New York: Norton, 1950.

Gautier, Yvon. "Language et psychanalyse." *Dialogue* (March 1969), 7:633–38.

Green, André. *Le discours vivant.* Paris: Presses universitaires de France, 1973.

—— "The Borderline Concept." In Peter Hartocollis, ed., *Borderline Personality Disorders,* pp. 15–46. New York: International Universities Press, 1977.

Grent, Paul B. "Science, nescience, conscience." *Revue Thomiste* (July 1972), pp. 439–54.

Hale, Nathan G. Jr. *Freud and the Americans.* New York: Oxford University Press, 1971.

"Healing Words." *Times Literary Supplement,* January 25, 1968.

Hefner, Robert W. "The Tel Quel Ideology." *Sub-stance* (1974), no. 8, pp. 127–38.

Kristeva, Julia. "Polylogue." *Tel Quel* (Spring 1974), no. 57, pp. 19–56.

Kurzweil, Edith. "Structuralist Psychoanalysis." *Partisan Review* (1978), no. 4, 642–46.

Lacan, Jacques. *Écrits I.* Paris: Éditions du Seuil, 1966.

—— *Scilicet,* vol. 2/3. Paris: Éditions du Seuil, 1970.

—— *Le séminaire, livre XI, Les quatres concepts fondamentaux de la psychanalyse.* Paris: Éditions du Seuil, 1973. Translated as *The Four Fundamental Concepts of Psychoanalysis.* J. Jacques-Alain Miller, ed. New York: Norton, 1978.

—— *Télévision.* Paris: Éditions du Seuil, 1974.

—— *Le séminaire, livre I, Les écrits techniques de Freud.* Paris: Éditions du Seuil, 1974.

—— *Le séminaire, livre XX, Encore.* Paris: Éditions du Seuil, 1975.

—— *Écrits II.* Paris: Éditions du Seuil, 1971.

—— *Écrits: A Selection.* New York: Norton, 1977.

"Lacan, Jacques." In *Encyclopedia of the Social Sciences,* pp. 6897–98. New York: Macmillan, 1971.

163 Lacan: Structuralist Psychoanalysis

Lavers, Annette. "Some Aspects of Language in the Work of Jacques Lacan." *Semiotica* (1971), 3(3):269–79.

Laplanche, Jean. *Life and Death in Psychoanalysis*. Baltimore: Johns Hopkins University Press, 1976.

—— *Hölderlin et la question du père*. Paris: Presses Universitaires de France, 1969.

Laplanche, Jean and J. B. Pontalis. *The Language of Psychoanalysis*. New York: Norton, 1973.

Leclaire, Serge. *Démasquer le réel*. Paris: Éditions du Seuil, 1971.

—— *Psychanalyser*. Paris, 1968.

Leclaire, Serge et al., eds. *Psychanalyse et politique*. Paris: Éditions de Seuil, 1974.

Leavy, Stanley, A. "The Significance of Jacques Lacan." *Psychoanalytic Quarterly* (1977), no. 2, pp. 201–19.

Lefebvre, Henri. *La somme et le reste*. Paris: La Nef, 1959.

Lévi-Strauss, Claude. *Structural Anthropology*. New York: Basic Books, 1963.

Marcus, Steven. "Freud and Dora: Story, History, Case History." *Partisan Review* (1974), no. 1, pp. 12–23 and 89–108.

Mehlman, Jeffrey, ed. "French Freud." *Yale French Studies* (1972), no. 48.

Meissner, W. W. "Freud's Methodology." *Journal of the American Psychoanalytic Association* (April 1971), 19(2):265–307.

Mitchell, Juliet. *Psychoanalysis and Feminism*. New York: Pantheon, 1974.

Morris, Christopher D. "Barth and Lacan: The World of the Moebius Strip." *Critique* (1975), 17(1):69–77.

Moscovici, Serge. *Essai sur l'histoire humaine de la nature*. Paris: Presses Universitaires de France, 1961.

—— *La psychanalyse, son impact et son public*. Paris: Presses Universitaires de France, 1961.

Mounin, Georges. "Quelques traits du style de Jacques Lacan." *La nouvelle revue Française* (January 1969), 17:84–92.

McDougall, Joyce and Serge Lebovici. *Dialogue with Sammy*. New York: International Universities Press, 1969.

Nelson, Benjamin. "Phenomenological Psychiatry, Daseinsanalyse and American Existential Analysis." *Psychoanalysis and the Psychoanalytic Review* (Winter 1961–62), 48(4):1–25.

—— "The Psychoanalyst as Mediator and Double Agent. An Introductory Survey." *The Psychoanalytic Review* (Fall 1965), 52(3):45–60.

Palmier, Jean-Michel. *Lacan*. Paris: Éditions universitaires, 1968.

Pontalis, J. B. *Après Freud*. Paris: R. Julliard, 1965.

Politzer, Georges. *Les fondements de la psychologie*. Paris: Éditions Sociales, 1969.

Poster, Mark. *Existential Marxism in Postwar France*. Princeton: Princeton University Press, 1975.

Piaget, Jean. *Structuralism*. New York: Harper & Row, 1970.

Ricoeur, Paul. *Freud and Philosophy*. New Haven: Yale University Press, 1970.

Roussel, Jean. "Introduction to Jacques Lacan." *New Left Review*, (1968), no. 51, pp. 63–77.

Said, Edward W. "Linguistics and the Archeology of Mind." *International Philosophical Quarterly* (March 1971), no. 11, pp. 104–34.

Sartre, Jean-Paul. *Search for a Method.* New York: Vintage, 1963.

Sebag, Lucien. *Marxisme et structuralisme.* Paris: Payot, 1964.

Servan-Schreiber, Jean-Jacques. *The American Challenge.* New York: Pelican, 1969.

Safouan, Moustapha. *Études sur l'Oedipe.* Paris: Éditions du Seuil, 1974.

Saussure, Ferdinand de. *Course in General Linguistics.* New York: McGraw-Hill, 1966.

Shands, Harley C. "Anthony Wilden, The Language of the Self." *Semiotica* (1971), 3(3):280–87.

Spiegelberg, Herbert. *Phenomenology in Psychology and Psychiatry.* Evanston, Ill.: Northwestern University Press, 1972.

Turkle, Sherry. "Contemporary French Psychoanalysis." *The Human Context* (Summer 1975), 7(2):333–42.

—— "Contemporary French Psychoanalysis." *The Human Context* (Autumn 1975), 7(3):561–69.

—— *Psychoanalytic Politics: Freud's French Revolution.* New York: Basic Books, 1978.

Wery, Claire. "Les analyseurs arrivent." *Les Temps Modernes* (December 1972), pp. 1025–76.

Ysseling, Samuel. "Structuralism and Psychoanalysis in the Work of Jacques Lacan." *International Philosophical Quarterly* (1972), 10:102–17.

Wilden, Anthony. *The Language of the Self.* Baltimore: Johns Hopkins University Press, 1968.

Literary Structuralism and Erotics

Roland Barthes' work has gone through many phases. He has been an existentialist, a Marxist, a structuralist, a linguist, a textual critic; and he has combined sociology with literary criticism. But all along he has been debunking every reality we tend to take for granted, constantly pushing his own thought to "overcome its previous limits" and to escape disciplinary classification. He has rejected every type of systematization, so that sociologists cannot deal with him easily—even though he himself frequently refers to his own sociology. Without using customary sociological methods, Barthes nevertheless attempts to uncover the relation between thought and society, his now characteristic "method" (the term perhaps is too narrow) being to focus on the language of texts. But Barthes goes much beyond texts to find irrational and illogical connections: he free-associates and creates words and meanings to embroider on both the texts and on what presumably lies behind them. He wants to expose all false notions and ideologies. And for a while he attempted to construct a comprehensive frame capable of integrating all past and future creative acts and works through the language used in writing. Like Georges Bataille, who cannot, Barthes believes, be classified as novelist, poet, essayist, economist, philosopher, or mystic, Barthes is somewhat of an enigma.

In *Barthes by Barthes* (1977), he indicates that he had a happy childhood, full of serenity (even though his father died when he was an infant), and that this "solid beginning" carried him through a difficult adolescence spent in and out of sanitoriums for tuberculosis. But this autobiography is itself a piece of his work and an exercise of his *imaginary*. (It is written in the third person, to avoid confession and revelation.) And it is not the book of his ideas, [but] the book of the *I*, the book of my resistances to my ideas; it's a recessive book, . . . as if written by a character in a novel—or by a few of them . . . [it is] the prehistory of the body that made its way toward the labor and the pleasure of writing.[1]

Barthes' philosophy of language, and his writing, have undergone many changes. At one point his work paralleled the views of Robbe-Grillet and Sarraute, as well as those of Sartre. By stripping literature and ideas of a false rhetoric, of every unnecessary construction, he expected to get to "rock bottom in style," and thereby to discover a sort of archetypal unconscious. His notion of "zero degree"—the enclosed and silent space between the written words that is open to interpretation in a dialectical relationship to these words and that neutralizes a language that can never be truly neutral—was to answer Sartre's famous 1948 query "what is literature?"

Along with Sartre and the other Left intellectuals, Barthes wanted to transcend his own petit bourgeois origins by expressing his humanity with the help of a *littérature engagé*.[2] Notwithstanding their various theoretical disagreements, they all believed that the social and political impact of writers would revolutionize society. Their Marxist convictions, when combined with *l'écriture blanche* (writing stripped of accepted notions) such as Camus ostensibly had used in *The Stranger,* were to be the ultimate expression of a *passion de l'écriture* that would tear apart bourgeois consciousness, and, at the same time, would reinvest writing with a meaningful voice, and would show that even "objective literary form and style contain the moral of their language."[3] In other words, Barthes had not yet arrived at his current emphasis on the inclusion of *all* subjectivity, when, in *Le degré zéro de l'écriture,* in 1950, he began to prove the subjectivity of the so-called "objective" literature. In his "existential" phase, Barthes set out to develop a new literary form that would express the revolutionary changes occurring in society. Caught up in the longing for basic renewal—social, political and intellectual—after 1944, he dreamed of an imminent and radical social transformation that would come about with the help of writers' commitment in everyday life.[4] Barthes shared with Sartre and the group around Les *Temps Modernes* a passion to expose the sustaining myths of bourgeois life, while remaining critical of the Communist Party.[5] Whether he argued, for instance, against Althusser's "scientific" Marxism, or against Lefebvre's or Garaudy's Marxist "idealisms," he avoided heavy philosophical discussions because he focused on writing; his method was irony, a method that was soon to be overlaid with structuralism.

Gradually, as the Communists appeared to become more and more bankrupt, and as Sartre came to focus increasingly on his existential Marxism, Barthes, along with other French intellectuals, became intrigued with Saussure's general science of signs, or semiology.[6] Since Lévi-Strauss had applied the methodology of structural linguistics to social phenomena, and had introduced a third—and mediating—dimension between *synchronic* (structural) and *diachronic* (historical) dimensions in language, it seemed even more appropriate to study literature in this new way. Barthes proposed to extend this method to study *all* philosophical and cultural traditions. Lévi-Strauss, we recall, had planned to prove the common origins of *all* myth and thought[7] by distinguishing between *langue* (the abstract language system) and *parole* (individual speech), as well as between the phonemic (recognized) levels of speech and abstract systems of signs (they have their own dual aspects of concept and sound image). Barthes', whose own perspective had always been somewhat peripheral to existentialist and Marxist views, was fascinated by the promise of Lévi-Strauss' ideas and opened up increasingly to the structuralist debate around him. Eventually he went beyond it.

In addition, Saussure's rejection of language as absolute in favor of this mediating relationship between existing language and its actual use struck a chord. Barthes had been searching for a similar dimension in his preoccupation with what happens to the space between written words, a silent space that "both speaks and is absolute"; and structuralism promised to "resolve" these contradictions. Structuralism also was to shed light on the problems faced by a bourgeois writer whose revolutionary writing cannot transcend its own loaded language, who cannot bridge the gap between his life and literature. Yet, from the beginning, he claims to have thought of language as only one of various systems of signs—images, gestures, musical sounds, objects, etc., and associations to them are other systems.[8] His extremely complex ideas, ultimately unprovable, eventually led the more conventional writers to accuse Barthes of polemicism, of dogmatism, and of inventing an ideological impressionism. Thinkers as diverse as Ricoeur, Lacan, or Lefebvre, we noted, agreed that language, because it is everywhere, could illuminate every sociological and literary phenomenon, and therefore ought to provide the clue to all knowledge.

II

Barthes begins *Le degré zéro de l'écriture* (1953) by reflecting upon the historical condition of literary language, upon the fact that all language is constricted by its previously ascribed meaning, that it exists in a specific culture and therefore is always full of implicit assumptions about social reality. Classical French literature, for instance, was rather uniform, an innocent reflection of the alleged inevitability of the bourgeois order which shapes reality in its own image and thereby "encodes" its values. (In Barthes' scheme, Balzac is the last classical writer and Flaubert the first modern one.) With the disintegration of that order, around 1850, there emerged a multiplicity of writing styles. Barthes documented the "fragmentation" in writing, as Foucault documented the fragmentation in knowledge (linked to scientific breaks) within the society, and found that modern writing, in response to the shift in romantic, poetic, and bourgeois mentality and conscience, reflects this fragmentation.[9] The writer must rely on what Barthes calls "the private components of a social ritual," or "the biology of his life."[10]

But this does not explain any given genius or talent. Nor does it explain how such nearly contemporary writers as Gide and Queneau, Claudel and Camus, belonging to the same society and the same class, use such profoundly different language. "Vulgar" Marxist literary criticism never faces this problem, argued Barthes, as he attempted to explain the individuality of a writer's style in terms of a "secret source," a "decorative voice," or some sort of supra-literary operation that is "transposed to the threshold of power and magic."

Little by little, he changed his notion of writing: it became *all* style, supplanting even the possibility of becoming an "open passage for the intention of language," or an "objective" social means of communication. To overcome a writer's bourgeois origins, Barthes found it increasingly useful to examine literary creation through the writer's language and to distinguish between historical dimensions of language, the speech of specific texts, and the roots of this language. Structuralist methodology was to help uncover these roots.

By 1953, Lacan's linguistic psychoanalysis had begun to challenge Freudianism.[11] Lévi-Strauss' anthropology was about to spread far beyond Paris; Althusser was subjecting Marx's texts to his "rereading." Thus it seemed natural for Barthes to speak, for example, of *le regard* of writing in the manner of Foucault's *regard* by doctors, a *regard* which tries to take in everything at once. Barthes argued that a writer can only express his ideas sequentially and must, therefore, for the sake of a cohesive argument, make more or less incidental choices of sequence and of words. He wanted to "liberate" texts from such accidental choices and to integrate various ideas and feelings in texts into his structuralist system. Rules of opposition and transformation were to coordinate every facet of a literary work into complicated grids that would, eventually, interrelate them all, along with their authors. Concurrently, he planned to disentangle the many notions about style and content and to demonstrate that *writing* has a life of its own, apart from its *author.* He proceeded to violate every tradition of literary criticism by incorporating them all. He never thought that literary structuralism itself might add as many problems as it solved, that it might increase the chaos it set out to cure. Nor did he foresee that his view of the author as "no more than a talented instrument of his time" would (as it has in recent years) again be replaced by an emphasis on subjectivity, by what he calls "the return of the author."

III

Barthes did not anticipate that *Elements of Semiology* (1968), his emerging semiology for literary structuralism, would take so long to complete. He had intended to conceptualize total language experience (*la langue moins la parole*) by interpreting every sign associated with spoken and written language. But because signs also transmit capitalist ideology, he had to "demythologize both the language and its message" along with the dialectical relationship between customary language usage and the specific use of a word. He began by "inserting every writer into his language" (this means into his social milieu), to account for his haphazard (though not arbitrary) choice of words. Finding Saussurean linguistics inadequate for this purpose, Barthes added concepts which would make language "more formal" and "words more social." This involved his adapting parts of Hjelmslev's, of Martinet's, and of Jakobson's theories.

From Hjelmslev [12] he "borrowed" the notion of three levels within language: 1) its scheme (this refers to phonological requirements of a particular language, such as the French 'r'); 2) its norm (this is already defined by social realities but is still independent of them, such as the pronounciation of the French 'r'); and 3) its usage (this is the ensemble of social customs, such as the pronunciation of the French "r" in a certain region). From Martinet he adopted the division of the signifier into *articuli:* this allows the more important aspects of language to be emphasized over others.[13] Phonology and phonetics are thus distinguished in relation to what they are meant to convey. And he accounted for the idiosyncracis of a text by way of Jakobson's *idiolect,*[14] a notion that allows for "aberrations"—of a linguistic community, a writer's style, or an aphasic's speech. The inherent ambiguity of these linguistic concepts was to prove that the dual nature of language/word can be identified with the dual nature of code/message, and that their double structure itself allows for *shifters*—they explain double meanings of words in writing. "*I* go," for example, can refer to my own departure; it can become "you go," when *I* conjugates the verb "go," or it can be associated to "ego." (On one level, this parallels Lévi-Strauss' shifting time and space referents when natives tell their myths. On another level it refers to literature and to an author's arbitrary selection of words which come to his mind while writing— the phonetic free associations of his *imaginary*.) These *shifters* "help" Barthes push beyond existing "frontiers of language" into avant-garde literature; they account for the experimental double meanings of his own writing and for his "meta-languages."

Barthes' refinement of Saussurean linguistics also allows for sociological "conclusions," insofar as a speaker's use of language, and especially of articulation, by indicating place or class of origin, level of education or personal idiosyncrasies, and the existence or absence of specific words in a language, itself, points to what is important to its culture. Hence, Barthes could talk of "the emission and the reception of the message"—a message that is said to be a product, a channel and an autonomous object.[15] Gradually, he became more experimental, and focused on the problems connected to the multiplicity of messages.

But in the *Elements of Semiology,* he argued how language and speech in their reciprocal relation complement Durkheim's concept of collective conscience; and how Merleau-Ponty's philosophy, by opposing *parole parlante* (significative intention of the word at its nascent state) and *parole parlée* (spoken word) elaborated on Saussure's system; or how Lévi-Strauss correctly connects unconscious components of language with the exchange of women between tribes. And he showed how Lacan, for whom desire itself is said to be a system of signification—a process that binds the signifier and the signified in a sign whose floating relationship (at certain anchorage points) represents the repression of the signified[16]—differs from Saussure.

Inevitably, Barthes was carried along by the structuralist tide as he, too, wanted to locate the importance of unspoken (and unconscious) language in writing. Desire and emotion as part of written texts were examined in relation to politics and social life. But even before then, in short, sparkling essays (published monthly between 1954 and 1956 and collected in *Mythologies* (1957), Barthes had focused on hidden (and unconscious) messages by the mass media that promote capitalist ideologies. He had attacked not only the myths of the right but also those of the "established" Left. Unmasking all ideologies to destroy their effectiveness, Barthes had found that both capitalist and revolutionary languages perpetuate their own myths. Barthes' devasting irony moved from bourgeois history to the identification of petit bourgeois man, from tautology to "neither-norism" as verbal devices, from the quantification of quality to the love of proverbs. Claiming an eye (since childhood), for the "falsely obvious," he had ridiculed the "bourgeois' promoting of mountains" in the *Guide Bleu,* where "the scenery is picturesque any time the ground is uneven," or the Parisian striptease, where "the woman is desexualized at the very moment she is stripped naked" (eroticism is nullified and becomes a sport, a national pastime). And he had poked fun at moviemakers, wondering for example, why all the men in Mankiewicz's film *Julius Caesar* wear fringes— curly, straggly, tufted, oily and always well-combed ones—and concluded that they want to remind us of their Roman-ness. In one essay, Garbo's face was said to signify the Platonic ideas of the human creature; in another essay, Einstein's brain was perceived as an unusual piece of machinery that would disclose relativity when "dismantled" after his death. The semiological duality of code/message became an additional device to point out the contradictions in modern society; it was another aspect of Barthes' attempt to "Marxify the Sartrian engagement." [17] These clever exposés did not draw serious fire. But the application of this method in *Sur Racine* (1963) got him into a full-blown literary and academic war.

IV

Barthes' application of structuralism to Racinian drama attacked the very basis of academic critical discourse and the politics implicit in it. Previous reexaminations of Racine (and Pascal and other figures), in the 1950s, had reopened questions of politics, morals, and religion. (Marxists had found anticipation of pre-revolutionary influences and ideologies.) But Barthes wanted to subject classic writers to his own type of textual reading. He purposefully avoided both the biographical approach that specializes in recounting details of life and Goldmann's sociological one that connects Racine's tragic vision with the ideology of the Jansenist group who had supported the *noblesse de robe* of the day. [18] Nor did he want to "duplicate the work of Charles Mauron's psychoanalytic study of Racine." Instead, he used his own method and opened with an admirable evocation of the Racinian landscape:

> The great tragic sites are arid lands, squeezed in between sea and desert. . . . Troezen, where Phèdre dies, is a scorched knoll fortified by rubble. . . . Even outside the house, there is no real breath of air; there is scrub, the desert, "unorganized space."
>
> The "unorganized space" of the desert is contrasted with the constricted space of the "chamber" where the tragedies are enacted, where the characters are dogged by "hidden Power" lurking in the shadows. The basic situation is freedom in flight and meeting death administered stealthily by poison or strangulation, or violently by the sword.[19]

According to Barthes, Racine's theater is not about love but about force within an erotic situation. His emphasis on the types of aggression used in Racine's world, on the conflicts that arise when moral codes are broken, and on the reversal of fortune that frequently overtakes the hero, goes much beyond the use of structuralist methodology let alone beyond the more traditional commentary on Racine.[20]

> Racine's plays appear not as the polished vehicles for a moral view of the world as approved by the French literary establishment, but as the basis of a "Racinian anthropology" whose complex highly patterned system of thematic oppositions generates a variety of hitherto unheard-of (or suppressed) psychological structures."[21]

Barthes' rereading of Racine led Raymond Picard, a more orthodox Racine scholar at the Sorbonne, to attack "a variety of Marxist . . . existentialist . . . phenomenological, and structuralist tendencies" in a nasty leaflet, *Nouvelle critique ou nouvelle imposture* (1965). Barthes responded in *Critique et vérité* (1966) and lumped all "conventional" critical methods under "Lansonism" (after a respected literary critic of the beginning of this century) or university criticism, as he tied the latter to positivist bourgeois ideology and to political and intellectual conservatism. The ensuing quarrel, which involved every self-respecting Parisian intellectual, turned Barthes into a celebrity and led to his own institution, the École Pratique des Hautes Études, being associated with left politics and thought, with progress, while the

Sorbonne (traditionally conservative) and everyone connected with it became, by implication, reactionary or even fascist.

Eventually, every intellectual and journalist felt compelled to take sides. Only a bourgeois ideologue would avoid this "quarrel," in which increasingly personal attacks pretended to discuss the reading of literary texts alone. Looking at characters in a work, at their psychology, at genres, at motivation, at myth, or at "literary sociology," branded one conventional, whereas the acceptance of Barthian techniques turned one into a radical. In the end, Picard dismissed the "new criticism" as bad, as a cause that "replaced the life of the mind with automatic affirmation of [structuralist] prefabricated ideology." [22]

Barthes' previous effort to search for an author's existential base in his writing had been *Michelet par lui-même* (1954). But at that time structuralism was still obscure enough so that the uncovering of Michelet's "structures of existence," his "organized network of obsessions," or his "internal contradictions" did not threaten Picard or anyone else. Yet this "petit bourgeois without an original political idea" had been found critical of his time and contemporaries, had been preoccupied with themes of conflict, with blood, death, passion, revolution, and androgyny. Barthes had perceived Michelet as

> destined to approach woman as confidant rather than as ravisher, [he] had to be both man and woman. He saw dual sexuality as an ideal, and androgynous man as complete. For Michelet the two sexes of the mind are no other than the male force of an idea, coupled to the female milieu of the instinct.[23]

This focus on sexuality, pleasure, and adrogyny became much more central later on, especially after 1968, when in the aftermath of the failed student revolts, preoccupations with personal fulfillment, with sexual freedom and "narcissistic" pursuits grew more dominant in Paris as well as in New York.

Barthes' *Michelet* had been his first attempt to present ideas in the form of sections of one or more paragraphs, headed by a descriptive caption (they are called *divagations*) to allow the customary reading to be "transcended." These *divagations,* however ("Goethe-dog," "suspended state," "yes and no," etc.) were not yet as purposeful as the alphabetical order ("Affirmation," "Babel," etc.) of the later *Plaisir du texte* (1973). And the alternation of passages from Michelet's works with his portraits, and with Barthes' associations and commentaries, were not yet as subtle as those in his recent *Barthes by Barthes* (1977).[24] Nevertheless, Barthes was already pointing to the technique he was to perfect later to attack the duplicity of literature and to unmask the signs that, in addition to their meaning, project the bourgeois world view.

During a good part of this time, Barthes also dabbled in what he called his sociology, that is, in the application of *semiology* to the "linguistics of fashion." In *Le système de la mode* (1967) he analyzed the ideologies conveyed in fashion magazines. He wanted to know, for instance, how the wearer of a hat or dress communicates the current fashions; what a wide or a narrow belt and its specific color, texture, and material could mean for a sport coat, an evening gown, or a morning costume; and he meant to reconstruct

> a simulacrum of the object, in which the rules according to which they were designed become evident. His primary concern (always) is with the process by which objects come to signify rather than with what they signify.[25]

By the time the book was published Barthes found *Le système de la mode* a dated and naive experiment in linguistics. He did state that he had ignored the way one speaks about fashion, and had looked only at the social implications of fashion magazines, at their codes and hidden messages. But his endless fashion inventory, and the many oppositions and transformations mediating between the signs and the meanings of fashion, that invented new connections and meta-languages, in the end overshadowed his many interesting insights.[26] Intrinsically, this work was an extension of his critique of the media, of mass culture, where fashion writing occupies a distinct location in petit bourgeois culture, apparently replacing the books young girls used to read.[27]

The "literature" of fashion that Barthes analyzed constituted a specific type of literature—bad literature with poverty stricken poetics that he found to be in quasi-parasitic rapport with the vulgarizations typical of horoscopes, palmistry, or elementary

graphology.[28] Illustrations and verbiage intend to sell goods, as
fashion camouflages its market orientation and hides its repressive and prescriptive nature.[29] By "proving the repressiveness of
this system" (in over three hundred pages), Barthes had expected
to help revolutionize French society and to uncover universal
givens in the literature of both "high" and "low" culture. To this
end, in 1966, he joined "semiological, Lacanian and Althusserian
themes" in *Les Cahiers pour l'Analyse.*[30]

At the time, Hugh Davidson, attempting to explain Barthes'
work, had suggested that we could

> begin to understand the critical position of Roland Barthes
> by paying attention to four things he does: (1) he places liter-
> ature in the general context of language rather than of things
> or of thought; (2) he identifies it specifically as the intransi-
> tive and symbolic use of language; (3) he assigns to the critic
> the task of giving a sense, not *the* sense, to the work, realiz-
> ing as he does so that other senses will be found as rivals to
> his own and that all senses are subject to replacement; (4) he
> integrates criticism into a scheme that includes the unex-
> pressed gift of sense to a text, which is reading, and the
> study of polyvalent language, which is the science of litera-
> ture.[31]

But the events of 1968 made criticism of this kind less convincing, and less prevalent. For the breakdown of political and
social structures, also, questioned structuralism's implications of
stable traditions. So the various structuralist thinkers rethought
their positions. It is hard to say whether the "quarrel" with Picard had cleared the air, or whether the criticism and the "practice" from the Left simply relegated it to the sidelines. Serge
Doubrovsky, in *Pourquoi la nouvelle critique* (1969), attempted
to clarify all the underlying assumptions.[32] But by then Barthes'
structuralist methodology had shifted ground and had abandoned its links to formalism. He increasingly devoted himself to
textual analysis. And by 1973, Richard Howard found that
Barthes had come full circle. He had forgotten about semiological
theory and had "given himself up to an inevitably random succession of fragments, facts, aphorisms, touches and shoves,
nudges, elbowings, bubblings, trial balloons . . . of an arbitrary
design that aspires to catch pleasure out, to attain bliss."[33]

V

Barthes' drift into texts represented a further depoliticization. Since the "revolt" of May/June 1968 had fragmented the Left by pointing to the "futility" of political action, left intellectuals increasingly tended to retreat into particularistic and/or academic pursuits; or they became interested in abstruse literary activities. Barthes himself now set out to create a theory that would "liberate" the theorizer and "pluralize" criticism, "dissolving" chronology and "dividing" texts according to their *readerly* and their *writerly* qualities.[34] According to Hawkes, Barthes'

> *readerly* texts (usually classics) are static, virtually "read themselves" and thus perpetuate an "established" view of reality and an "establishment" scheme of values, frozen in time, yet serving still as an out-of-date model for our world; *writerly* texts require us to look at the nature of language itself, not *through* it at a preordained "real world." They thus involve us in the dangerous, exhilarating activity of creating our world *now,* together with the author, as we go along. Where *readerly* texts presuppose and depend upon the presumptions of innocence outlined above, and with them the unquestioned relationship between signifier and signified that those presumptions reinforce, saying "this is what the world is like and always will be like," *writerly* texts presume nothing, admit no easy passage from signifier to signified, are open to the "play" of the codes that we use to determine them. In readerly texts the signifiers march: in writerly texts they dance.[35]

Given the predictable quality of *readerly* texts, Barthes finds *writerly* texts of primary interest. For in these texts he can locate themes and textual typologies, and he can extrapolate much beyond such texts themselves.

How does Barthes select the themes and anti-themes, or "establish a primary typology of a text"? First of all, he posits the existence of five codes—hermeneutics, semantics, symbolism, action, and reference—which are said to modify, determine, and generate a plethora of meanings every time a text is read. The best illustration of this method is *S/Z* (1970), the essay on Balzac's novella *Sarrasine. S/Z* is divided into 561 numbered *lex-*

ias (segments varying from one word to several lines) that are arranged into 93 *divagations* (each between a short paragraph and two pages). The first lexia, *Sarrasine,* for instance, raises questions that will not be answered until lexia 153, "is an enigma," and therefore part of hermeneutics; its connotation of feminity "is a signifier," which also makes it part of semantics. The next lexia—the beginning of the story—has eight words ("I was deep into one of those daydreams"), and others extend over a few sentences.[36] Barthes' whimsy seems to determine the length of each lexia, as he uses his own and his students' free associations to imagine how Balzac might have constructed the story of Sarrasine, the painter who sees the world through its clichés, who falls in love with an Italian castrato; believing he/she is a woman because he/she acts like one; is eventually killed by the castrato's protector; and dies, literally, from his belief in stereotypes.

This book, says Barthes, was the result of "productively" listening to the text's inner sounds. For writing (*écriture*) allegedly activates certain noises in listening readers, so that an encounter with the reader becomes an open-ended "theater."[37] Each new reading produces new interactions and interpretations. Such a *writerly* text, whose "plurality of interpretations" encourages exploration, relies upon some sort of unconscious, "gives in to play," "succumbs to the spell of the signifier," "seeks to sketch the stereographic space of writing,"[38] and "draws the text out of internal chronology to recapture mythic time."[39] Most texts, however, are aimed at consumers who reject or accept them, and thus cannot be "rewritten" as they are being read. Here Barthes refers to purposeful texts, to advertising, to manipulation by the media. But whereas previously, in *Mythologies* and in *Le système de la mode* he used such texts as the basis of his critique, he now condemns them. He focuses on the *writerly* texts, because he sees them as reaffirming the centrality of literature to collective life, and as maintaining fluidity, openness, and coherence through time and space.

This notion of *writerliness,* which would make for social cohesion even in the case of solitary reading (Barthes' *Sarrasine,* as the product of a seminar with students, also includes "intellectual" socializing) provides a multitude of links and meanings that the writer (in this case Balzac) took for granted and may only have alluded to. In other words, Barthes' attempt to find intertextuality[40] unveils the story's self-contained structure much as Foucault (see chapter 8) tries to comprehend everything that is seen, said, heard—consciously and unconsciously—by the writer and by every reader, at all times. Thus Barthes reconstructs the social and cultural fabric of Balzac's *Sarrasine* in his *writerly* text, a text that is to include pleasure and erotics, that is to be seductive and sensuous, that is to encompass the reader's emotions, and that is to provide new enjoyment with each reading. But what do we make of literary criticism that is itself a piece of creative writing and is more than seven times as long as the classic it discusses? Some of the experts—Barthes' reviewers—approve. Michael Wood, for instance, likes *S/Z;* he finds its logic effective, though dubious,

> because Barthes's entire morality is behind it, and it says what he wants to say. Stereotypes can kill. This is a highly literary notion, but . . . . Barthes's enemy is, finally . . . the loss of freedom, pictured in *S/Z* as a loss of life, which we suffer whenever our language ceases to be our own.[41]

Peter Brooks thinks it is

> a tale which is itself framed within another relation of frustrated desire between a teller and listener . . . . and of itself implies almost all that one needs to consider in discussing fictionmaking as a dialectics of human desire.[42]

To Barthes himself, these comments would prove *S/Z*'s *writerly* qualities, its openness to interpretation, and its success. No doubt, this is a stimulating and enjoyable essay, with a special combination of suspense and seduction that comes closer to poetry than to criticism. The very excitement it creates seems to stem from Barthes rather than from Balzac.

VI

S/Z appears to have been a transition to Barthes' subsequent works—*Sade Fourier Loyola* (1971), *Le plaisir du texte* (1973) and *Barthes par Barthes* (1975)—in which "the text becomes a pure object of pleasure."[43] Increasingly, he separates *plaisir* (pleasure) from *jouissance* (enjoyment or bliss), so that the pleasure of a text is associated with its more or less intellectual message, while the enjoyment is an *intransitive* mode of pleasure that implies privacy, satisfaction, and sexual fulfilment. For the private fantasies of the *Marquis de Sade* are not about actual sex or cruelty but about the enjoyment Barthes derives through Sade's language. Fearful that some dimension of the pleasure/enjoyment might escape him, that he might, inadvertently, treat a text as a purely intellectual object, Barthes introduces his organizing codes in "a new language that is traversed by natural language, but open to semiological definition of a text . . . which has recourse to self-isolation . . . articulation . . . and ordering." [44] And "the pleasure of this text also includes the amicable return of the author . . . an author who has no unity, who is a plural of charms." [45]

Barthes now wants to bridge the gap between subjective philosophical and esthetic theories and the formalism of linguistics; he plans to eliminate value judgements and yet retain artistic judgment by "joining Sade, Fourier and Loyola." Aware that linking these three figures might itself be construed as provocation, he states that he wants only to show how all three are founders of a language that creates new meaning. Barthes "liberates" them to make them "bearable."

> From Sade to Fourier, sadism is lost; from Loyola to Sade, divine interlocution. Otherwise, the same writing; the same sensual pleasure in classification, the same mania for cutting up (the body of Christ, the body of the victim, the human soul), the same enumerative obsessions . . . the same image practice . . . the same erotic, fantasmatic fashioning of the social system. [46]

Barthes wants to show the similarities of their differences by illustrating how neither the evil writer, the great utopian, nor the Jesuit saint are bearable, since all three make pleasure, happiness, and communication dependent on an inflexible order. [47] He brings them together to show that each of them has created a new language, a language we can decipher with the help of semiology. Their languages are said to arise from a material vacuum, a vacuum that is articulated through distinct signs.

> Fourier divides mankind into 1,620 fixed passions, combinable but not transformable; Sade distributes ejaculation like the words in a sentence (postures, figures, episodes, seances); Loyola cuts up the body (successively experienced by each of the five senses) as he cuts up the Christian narrative. . . . And their discourse is always provided with an Ordainer or a Master of Ceremonies, a Rhetorician who . . . regulates their rituals.[48]

Because linking these three figures is itself sacrilegious and shocking and is bound to titillate the reader's senses, we are aware of various levels of irony when tantalizing significations evolve from oppositions, from the writer's imagination, and from his "theatricality." Barthes excites the reader's fancy, when, for example, he links Sadian practice, eroticism, and the devil to show the orderly organization of space, time, language, morality, work, etc. into a system; or when he divides the population into amorous classes—storytellers, fuckers, troops of Vestals, Youths and Favorites of both sexes.[49]

As in *Sarrasine* and in *The Pleasure of the Text*, he suggests that episodes be "starred," so that the reader may be able to create converging and diverging sequences. Each reading is to challenge the reader's "circular memory." The text becomes a personalized intertext rather than a final or definitive text and is said to emerge from "the impossibility of living outside the infinite text, whether this is Proust, the daily newspaper or the television screen. The book creates the meaning, the meaning creates life."[50] Simply put, the reader interprets a text in his own way. Thus Barthes, for example, finds that the extensive travel in Sade's novels leads only to solitude, to "libertine solitude as a duality of existence," a sensual pleasure of being that desocializes crime and plans everything in relation to vice.[51] Or he perceives Loyola's *Exercises* as "obsessional neuroses" that "break up ascetic matter" and force the sinner to account for his sins and for his lapses during atonement; his impatience with God and himself is said to end up in narcissistic awareness, the modern sin of enjoyment.

The enjoyment of this text appears to derive in part from Fourier's utopia. Barthes stresses that Fourier's *Harmony* promised happiness, that children, for instance, would be raised on sweets which are cheaper than bread, that a palatable counter-sugar would save their health; or that the coffee break would be a sign of civilization in bureaucracy.[52] But whereas Fourier's pleasure had been in the inventing of this imaginary community, Barthes' pleasure seems to be in the imaginary connections he makes, in the signifiers he detects in the imaginations of these authors and, most of all, in his own. Anything goes.

In fact, Barthes' entire endeavor can be understood only with the help of psychoanalysis, which allows for simultaneous phonetic, contextual, and symbolic associations. Yet he never psychoanalyzes individuals, only their *texts;* and he frequently stresses unusual associations—and prefers outrageous ones. When he talks of the "language of the unconscious," he follows Lacan, who in turn has adopted a neo-Barthian textual approach, especially in his famous "Seminar on 'The Purloined Letter.'"[53] Both Lacan and Barthes read the texts of contemporary society, they declare, by elevating the notion of *signifier.* But whereas Lacan claims to uncover the unconscious, Barthes first "unites a text, rediscovers its unconscious categories," and then teases out every possible link to its reader. That is how he "revolutionized" the *sign* and the *signifier.*

At about this time, he became the leader of the *Tel Quel* group.[54] Their "cultural revolution," however, after its rather brief fling with Maoism, turned toward a concern with intertextuality and with the power of language. Under specific circumstances this power of language is to be used and created to reshape itself and the culture and is to be adapted to political ends.[55] Barthes' own practice, too, has gained currency in France, where the rereading of a classical text as an open-ended jigsaw puzzle is seen as a way of connecting tradition with innovation and of reaffirming both. Barthes avoids political engagement, even though he calls himself the *"arrière-garde de l'avant-garde,"*[56] as his language games, increasingly removed from his semiology are given over to hedonistic enjoyment. The gap between the master and his disciples may, however, be only superficial. For even the post-facto analyses and the creation of language for political ends may simply express the political abdication of the intellectuals: they appear to have abandoned even the pretense of Sartrian engagement.

During the last few years the semiological enterprise seems to have splintered. According to a report by Jean-Loup Rivière on the Congress on Semiotics held in Milan, in 1974,

> the history of the first *semiologie* is that of its Oedipal conflict with structural linguistics . . . that was paradoxically blocked by the very instrument that created it: the sign. . . . [But it seems to have] engendered 'specific' semiotics. . . . semiotics that still lack a theory of the relations between semiotic systems. . . . (Specific semiotics are architecture, music, gestures, etc.) [57]

Basically, semiotics looks at the interstices of disciplinary language, that is, at the point of contact between the languages of various scientific fields and consequently rejects Barthes' earlier *zero degree;* it rejects his *utopia* in favor of an *atopia* and its *regard* focuses on the "addition" of knowledge rather than on the "text." [58] Some of Barthes' former colleagues continue the scientific study of language he himself now rejects. But, to a large extent, the new semiotics are dominated by Jacques Derrida, the philosopher whose "writing under erasure" attacks Barthes' structuralist base in order to "deconstruct" language.

VII

Barthes himself, while he continues to flesh out the French language, to create new meanings, seems to have retreated from direct social critique to semantic games. He goes on thinking up new connotations and denotations, adding new words at the "frontiers of language." He writes of today's Werther who, seated behind his table in the coffeehouse, dreams that the language of the *Other* responds to him and intolerantly rejects the discourses of Marxism, of Christianity, and of psychoanalysis. [59] Freed of these ideologies, Barthes can devote himself to language alone, to teasing unconscious content from conscious language, to creating more meta-languages for new texts; or he can abandon himself to his pleasures. Because he enjoys reading (Zola, Proust, *Montecristo, Les mémoires d'un touriste,* or even Julien Green), the "raw material" for his work is part of his pleasure.

So he can "depoliticize what is apparently political, and politicize what is not." Or he can cast "the Text [as] that disengaged *persona* that shows its behind to Père Politique," in a tongue-in-cheek parody of the Lacanian discourse which at one point postulated various Oedipal fathers.[60]

Like Lacan, Barthes has become ever more disrespectful and acerbic, more ironic and self-indulgent, a tendency that is said to be part of his search for authenticity, as is the addition of a third textual dimension:

> [This] would be the *irreadable* that catches on, the burning text produced outside of all probability, and whose function—visibly assumed by its writer—would be to contest the merchandising constraints of the written. . . . It is received like a fire, a drug, an enigmatic disorganization.[61]

Such criticism is designed to undercut all absurdity, all psychological subversion by the media, and to amalgamate psychoanalytic, social, and cultural criticism in literature. Essentially, this was how he had analyzed the media in *Mythologies* (1956), although at that time he had not yet constructed the theory to explain his practice. Now "the notion of text redoubles the notion of 'literature': literature *represents* a finished world, the text imagines the infinite of language: without knowing, without reason, without intelligence."[62]

Barthes dazzles with his particular mix of rhetoric, charm and knowledge. He never questions the assumption that culture *is* French. Although he has by now discarded all of his pretensions at social science, structuralist formulations still creep in and spark his *imaginary,* which, together with the real and the symbolic as the root of individual being, is said to have learned to free-associate systematically. Barthes' eroticized prose is enjoyable. Nonetheless, even those who ultimately dismiss it as drivel, or as nonsense must, along with those who take it too seriously, deal with Barthes' challenge to "coherent" literary criticism which tends to be more concerned with the historical continuity of thought. In his disrespect for conventional history, Barthes negates all linear continuity. He prefers to "explode" texts, to make them modern, in order to liberate the individual. This

makes him the anarchists' god, the conservatives' devil, the dilet-
tantes' idol, and a brief moment in the history of criticism. For
Barthes' *divagations,* as a result of their fragmentary nature and
their quality of free association, attack every previous notion of
the separation of form and content while uniting them, and also
deny the existence of such catetories as fiction, criticism, poetry,
and biography. For genre, Barthes substitutes text, text that is
continuously created, that has no dimensions of time, that retains
the qualities of structuralism even as structuralism itself is repudiated. In his attempt both to free himself of the text, and to
associate himself with it, he searches for constant renewal. He expects to avoid paralysis by recognizing the *Doxa*—popular opinions, clichés, pieties—as "wrong objects," and by attributting a
paradox to each *Doxa.* When the *paradox* turns bad and itself
becomes a new *Doxa,* Barthes searches for yet another *paradox.*
This is how he claims to put himself into a text. Even so, he finds
that the text tends to degenerate into prattle—*babil.*[63]

Clearly, Barthes escapes categorization. This appears to explain at least in part why sociologists either avoid him or do not
know what to make of him. In addition, his search for truth by
extending literature and the "creative spirit" beyond what is
known, is in itself anathema to empirical inquiry. For Barthes,
according to the French sociologist of art, Jean Duvignaud, is
dealing with the *imaginary*—"the existential force which through
symbols and signs, tries to gain possession of the widest experience that man can undergo . . . evoking emotions of the future
. . . and of freedom."[64]

American social theories, however, because of their bent to
categorize, to define, and to quantify, through their very nature
tend to produce only *readerly* texts, texts closed off to *writerly*
interpretations, to *jouissance,* which would, when achieving "clo-
sure," not only be uninteresting and/or ideological, but would
lack the necessary intertextuality. So the customary animosity between sociologists and literary critics is again reaffirmed. In current French (and neo-structuralist) terminology, Barthes might
say that the life of his own textual analysis would be the death of
its sociological counterpart, and *mutatis mutandis,* the life of
"American" methods would be the death of Barthian criticism.

Yet the two methods, though mutually exclusive, both aim to explain the relation of thought to society: the one through ponderous systems, the other through the play of wit.[65]

Notes

1. Barthes, *Barthes by Barthes*. Quotations are from the introduction to the descriptions of pictures of Barthes' childhood and youth, which constitute the first forty pages, and from the chronological biography that follows his text.

2. Jean-Paul Sartre, *Search for a Method* (New York: Vintage, 1963), p. 160.

3. Barthes, *Le degré zéro de l'écriture*, p. 12.

4. For an excellent discussion of this period see Poster, *Existential Marxism in Postwar France*. Poster argues that Hegelianism, with minor exceptions, arrived in France only toward the end of World War II, and until then the leading philosophers had been Brunschvig and Alain, both steeped in the idealism of Descartes and Kant (p. 76). Henri Lefebvre elaborates this point in *La somme et le reste*, and in "Le Marxisme et la pensée française," *Les Temps Modernes*, 13:137–48. Simone de Beauvoir, in *Memoirs of a Dutiful Daughter*, p. 243, states that "at the Sorbonne, my professors systematically ignored Hegel and Marx."

5. *Les Temps Modernes*, conceived by Sartre while he was still in the Resistance during World War II, and launched immediately afterwards with Camus, Merleau-Ponty, de Beauvoir and others, was of tremendous importance—politically and intellectually.

6. de Saussure, *Course in General Linguistics*.

7. See especially Claude Lévi-Strauss, *Structural Anthropology* (New York: Basic Books, 1963), *The Savage Mind* (Chicago: University of Chicago Press, 1966) and chapter 1 in this book.

8. Barthes, *Elements of Semiology*, p. 9.

9. Barthes, *Le Degré zero de l'écriture*, p. 86.

10. *Ibid.*, p. 17.

11. See especially Jacques Lacan, "The Function and Field of Speech and Language in Psychoanalysis," (Report to the Congress of Rome, September 1953) in Alan Sheridan, ed., *Écrits, A Selection* (New York: Norton, 1977), p. 30–113; Sherry Turkle, "The Roots of the Psychoanalytic Culture" in *Psychoanalytic Politics* (New York: Basic Books, 1978); see also chapter 6.

12. Louis Hjelmslev, *Essais Linguistiques* (Copenhagen: Nordisk Sprog-og Kulturforlag 1959).

13. André Martinet, *Elements of General Linguistics* (London: Faber and Faber, 1960).

14. Barthes, *Elements of Semiology*, p. 21.

15. Barthes, *Image Music Text*, p. 15.

16. Barthes, *Elements of Semiology*, p. 49.

17. Barthes, "Réponses," *Tel Quel,* no. 47, p. 92.

18. Lucien Goldmann, "The Sociology of Literature: Status and Problems of Method," in Albrecht, Barnett and Griff, eds., *The Sociology of Art and Literature.* Essentially, Lucien Goldmann's genetic structural sociology is based on Marx's dialectical materialism in the tradition of Georg Lukács. His concepts of "mental structures" and of "collective consciousness" also recall Durkheim, as do the "structuralist" discussions. But Goldmann's method consists of the dissection of a work in order to discover the underlying group consciousness, or *Weltanschauung.*

19. Turnell, "The Criticism of Roland Barthes," p. 35. It is important to remember that this style of criticism was fashionable at the time; that Louis Althusser found similar themes in Bertolazzi and Brecht; that Lacan had conducted his seminar on "The Purloined Letter," (*Yale French Studies,* vol. 48); and that Lefebvre and Goldmann had reinterpreted Racine, Pascal, Musset, and others from a Marxist perspective.

20. Turnell, "The Criticism of Roland Barthes," p. 34.

21. Terence Hawkes, *Structuralism and Semiotics* (Berkeley: University of California Press, 1977), p. 111.

22. Picard, *New Criticism or New Fraud,* p. 12.

23. Barthes, *Michelet par lui-même,* p. 131.

24. *Barthes par Barthes* was itself a parody from the "par lui-même" series on classical authors, a genre Barthes somewhat transcended.

25. Funt, "Roland Barthes and the Nouvelle Critique," p. 330.

26. According to Barthes, the various levels of a language system and the systems themselves (they all consist of content, expression and relations between them) can only be conceptualized by a meta-language. Analogous to Hegel's affirmation, negation, and the negation of the negation—it is itself a new affirmation—each meta-language is negated in a new connotation and generates yet another meta-language. Magliola, "Parisian Structuralism Confronts Phenomenology," p. 239, compares Barthes' use of structural linguistics to Paul Ricoeur's and finds that "whereas for Ricoeur the sign consists of signifier, signified and referent, the sign for Barthes is composed of signifier and signified alone. Nor is there any chance that Barthes' signified includes reference to the real."

27. Olivier Burgelin, "Le double système de la mode," *L'Arc,* 56:11.

28. Barthes, *Le système de la mode,* p. 257.

29. *Ibid.,* p. 265.

30. Barthes, *Essais critiques,* p. 7.

31. Davidson, "The Critical Position of Roland Barthes," p. 374.

32. According to Robert Magliola in "Parisian Structuralism Confronts Phenomenology," Doubrovsky argued that "the structuralists had been cooked in their own stew. They had without justification negated the origins of meaning, viz., self and world, and then, with curious blindness, lamented the very loss of the meaning they had occasioned. Gerard Genette answered that structuralism does not isolate language from experience. On the contrary, it postulates that 'language and experience are one ond the same.'"

33. Barthes, *The Pleasure of the Text,* p. 7.

34. Barthes, *Essais critiques,* p. 276.

35. Terence Hawkes, *Structuralism and Semiotics* (Berkeley: University of California Press, 1977), p. 114.

188 Barthes: Structuralism and Erotics

36. The lexia differ from Lévi-Strauss' constituent units insofar as their length is determined by Barthes' literary judgment and depends upon a certain sense, or internal coherence, while Lévi-Strauss allegedly uses the "shortest units."

37. Barthes, *Essais critiques*, p. 276.

38. Barthes, *S/Z* (English translation), p. 15.

39. *Ibid.*, p. 16.

40. This notion originated with Julia Kristeva. Intertextuality, says Barthes, serves to fight the law of context, and there are always at least two contexts, so that the rest of a phrase, by following the one possible sense leaves out the other. The intertext includes the influences, sources, origins, etc., to which one must compare a work, an author—it is the *traverse de l'écriture;* it is the text to the extent *qu'il traverse et est traversé.*

41. Wood, "Rules of the Game," pp. 31–32.

42. Brooks, "An Erotics of Art," p. 38.

43. Barthes, *Sade Fourier Loyola* (English translation), p. 7.

44. *Ibid.*, pp. 3–5.

45. *Ibid.*, p. 8.

46. *Ibid.*, p. 3.

47. *Ibid.*, p. 5.

48. *Ibid.*, p. 4–5.

49. *Ibid.*, p. 114.

50. Barthes, *Pleasure of the Text*, p. 36.

51. Barthes, *Sade Fourier Loyola*, pp. 15–19.

52. *Ibid.*, p. 92.

53. See Lacan's "Seminar on 'The Purloined Letter.' "

54. This group of radical left intellectuals committed to political action, whose current leaders are Julia Kristeva and Phillipe Sollers, continues to look to Barthes—even though their approach to language as a means of analysis now diverges from Barthes' own.

55. Gouldner, *The Dialectic of Ideology and Technology*, p. 149, addresses this problem from another persepective, from Habermas's theory of communicative competence, and from his own critical sociology: "The politics of a linguistically grounded critical theory raises the question how change in a linguistic code or a communication practices can be achieved as a matter of *political* effort."

56. Barthes writes in "Barthes puissance trois," p. 3, "to be avant-garde means to know what is dead; to be rear-garde means to go on liking it."

57. Rivière, "Le congrès internationale de l'association sémiotique," p. 24.

58. *Ibid.*, p. 24.

59. Xavier Delcourt, "Les mille façons de dire 'Je t'aime,' " *Quinzaine Littéraire* (May 1–15, 1977), no. 255, p. 4.

60. Gardair, "Le plaisir du texte," p. 109. André Green, the Parisian psychoanalyst who accuses Lacan of omitting the field of affect, still considers Lacan's emphasis on the Oedipal father of theoretical importance. (See bibliography in chapter 6.) Barthes, clearly,

is intent on accounting for affect, enjoyment, and pleasure as well as for Oedipal relations.

61. Barthes, *Barthes by Barthes* (English translation), p. 118.

62. *Ibid.,* p. 119.

63. *Ibid.,* p. 71.

64. Duvignaud, *The Sociology of Art,* p. 144.

65. Karl Löwith, *From Hegel to Nietzsche* (New York: Doubleday Anchor, 1967), p. 342. In discussing Voltaire's attack upon the Bible and Hegel's dissolution of religion, Löwith contends that they are doing the same thing, "the Frenchman with wit, the German with pedantic seriousness." American sociology of knowledge, of course, tends to overcome the problems inherent in all cultural biases.

Bibliography

Albrecht, Milton C., James H. Barnett, and Mason Griff, eds. *The Sociology of Art and Literature.* New York: Praeger, 1970.

Barthes, Roland. *Le degré zéro de l'écriture.* Paris: Édition du Seuil, 1953.

—— *Michelet par lui-même.* Paris: Éditions du Seuil, 1954.

—— *Mythologies.* Paris: Éditions du Seuil, 1957. Translated as *Mythologies.* New York: Hill and Wang, 1972.

—— *Sur Racine.* Paris: Éditions du Seuil, 1963.

—— *Essais critiques.* Paris: Éditions du Seuil, 1964.

—— *Critique et vérité.* Paris: Éditions du Seuil, 1966.

—— *Le système de la mode.* Paris: Éditions du Seuil, 1967.

—— *Éléments de semiologie.* Paris: Éditions du Seuil, 1964. Translated as *Elements of Semiology.* New York: Hill and Wang, 1968.

—— *L'empire des signes.* Geneva: Skira, 1970.

—— *S/Z.* Paris: Éditions du Seuil, 1970. Translated as *S/Z.* New York: Hill and Wang, 1974.

—— "Changer l'object lui-même." *Esprit* (April 1971), pp. 609–12, 613–36.

—— "Languages at War in a Culture at Peace." London: *Times Literary Supplement,* August 10, 1971, pp. 1203–4.

—— *Sade Fourier Loyola.* Paris: Éditions du Seuil, 1971. Translated as *Sade Fourier Loyola.* New York: Hill and Wang, 1976.

—— *Tel Quel* (Autumn 1971), no. 47. Entire issue.

—— *Le plaisir du texte.* Paris: Éditions du Seuil, 1973. Translated as *The Pleasure of the Text.* New York: Hill and Wang, 1975.

—— "De la parole à l'écriture." *La Quinzaine littéraire,* March 1–15, 1974.

—— *Barthes par Barthes.* Paris: Éditions du Seuil, 1975. Translated as *Barthes by Barthes.* New York: Hill and Wang, 1977.

—— "Barthes puissance trois." *La Quinzaine littéraire,* March 1–15, 1975.

Barthes, Roland. *Magazine littéraire* (February 1975), no. 97. Entire issue.
—— "Pourquoi j'aime Benveniste." *La Quinzaine littéraire,* March 1–15, 1975.
—— *Image Music Text.* New York: Hill and Wang, 1978.
—— *A Lover's Discourse.* New York: Hill and Wang, 1978.
Beauvoir, Simone de. *Memoirs of a Dutiful Daughter.* New York: World, 1959.
Brooks, Peter. "An Erotics of Art." *New York Times Book Review,* September 14, 1975, p. 36.
Calvet, Louis-Jean. *Roland Barthes.* Paris: Bibliothèque, 1973.
Chalumeau, Jean-Luc. *La pensée en France de Sartre à Foucault.* Paris: Fernand Nathan, 1974.
Champagne, Roland A. "La Chanson de Roland: A Study of Roland Barthes' Le degré zéro de l'écriture." *Delta Epsilon Sigma Bulletin* (October 1972), 17:78–87.
Coser, Lewis A. and Bernard Rosenberg. *Sociological Theory.* New York: Macmillan, 1957.
Curtis, James E. and John W. Petras, eds. *The Sociology of Knowledge.* New York: Praeger, 1972.
Davidson, Hugh M. "The Critical Position of Roland Barthes." *Contemporary Literature* (Summer 1968), no. 3, pp. 367–76.
Derrida, Jacques. *Of Grammatology.* Baltimore: Johns Hopkins University Press, 1974.
Doubrovsky, Serge. *Pourquoi la nouvelle critique.* Paris: Mercure de France, 1966.
Duvignaud, Jean. *The Sociology of Art.* New York: Harper and Row, 1967.
Flaubert, Gustave. *Bouvard and Pécuchet.* New York: New Directions, 1954.
Fourier, Charles. *Design for Utopia.* New York Schocken, 1971.
—— *Actualité de Fourier.* Henri Lefebvre, ed. Paris: Anthropos, 1975.
Fowler, Roger, ed. *Style and Structure in Literature.* Ithaca: Cornell University Press, 1975.
Funt, David. "Roland Barthes and the Nouvelle critique." *Journal of Aesthetics and Art Criticism* (Spring 1968), no. 26, pp. 329–40.
Garaudy, Roger. *Le grand tournant du socialisme.* Paris: Gallimard, 1969.
Gardair, Jean Michel. "Le plaisir du texte." *Paragone* (1973), no. 24, pp. 109–12.
Gouldner, Alvin. *The Dialectic of Ideology and Technology.* New York: Seabury, 1976.
Harari, Josue V. "The Maximum Narrative: An Introduction to Barthes' Recent Criticism." *Style* (Winter 1974), 8(1):56–77.
Koch, S. "Melancholy King of the Cats." *Saturday Review,* 5:32–34, 1978.
Lefebvre, Henri. *La somme et le reste.* Paris: La Nef, 1959.
LeSage, Laurent. *The French New Criticism.* University Park: Pennsylvania State University Press, 1967.
Lotringer, Sylvère. "Argo-Notes: Roland Barthes' Textual Trip." *Boundary* (Spring 1974), 2(3):562–72.
Luccioni, Genni. "Le mythe aujourd'hui." *Esprit* (April 1971), pp. 612–16.
Magliola, Robert. "Parisian Structuralism Confronts Phenomenology: the Ongoing Debate." *Language and Style* (1973), 6(4):237–48.

Mannheim, Karl. *Ideology and Utopia.* Harvest Books, 1936.
Molina, David Newton de. "Le plaisir du texte." *Modern Language Review* (April 1974), 69(2):362–65.
Moreau, Jean A. "Heurs." *Critique* (July 1973), 24:583–95.
Norris, Christopher. "Les plaisirs des clercs: Barthes' Latest Writing." *British Journal of Aesthetics* (Summer 1974), 14:250–57.
Pachet Pierre. "Une entreprise troublante." *La Quinzaine littéraire* (November 1–15, 1974), pp. 19–20.
Perrone-Moises, Leyla. "Le language de Roland Barthes." *La Quinzaine littéraire* (July 16–31, 1974), pp. 23–24.
Pettit, Philip. *The Concept of Structuralism: A Critical Analysis.* Berkeley: University of California Press, 1975.
Picard, Raymond. *Nouvelle critique ou nouvelle imposture.* Paris: Pauvert, 1966. Translated as *New Criticism or New Fraud.* Pullman: Washington State University Press, 1969.
Poster, Mark. *Existential Marxism in Postwar France.* Princeton: Princeton University Press, 1975.
Rimmon, Shlomith. "Barthes' Hermeneutic Code and Henry James' Literary Detective: Plot-Composition in 'The Figure in the Carpet.' " *Hebrew University Studies in Literature* (Autumn 1973), vol. 1, no. 2.
Rivière, Jean-Loup. "Le congrès internationale de la sémiotique et la Piazza del Duomo." *La Quinzaine littéraire* (July 16–31, 1974), p. 24.
Saussure, Ferdinand de. *Course in General Linguistics.* New York: McGraw-Hill, 1966.
Scholes, Robert. *Structuralism in Literature.* New Haven: Yale University Press, 1974.
Turnell, Martin. "The Criticism of Roland Barthes." *Encounter* (February 1966), no. 26, pp. 30–36.
Vannier, Bernard. "Balzac à l'encan." *Critique* (July 1972), no. 28, pp. 610–22.
Wood, Michael. "Rules of the Game." *New York Review of Books,* March 4, 1976, pp. 31–34.

VIII. Michel Foucault:

Structuralism and Structures of Knowledge

Michel Foucault, professor of History and Systems of Thought at the *Collège de France,* was born in 1926. This makes him the youngest of the figures in this book. Along with Alain Touraine he did not, as it were, grow up with existentialism and into structuralism, but came of age intellectually during the struggle between these two ideologies—which may account for a certain evenhandedness toward both, and for Foucault's distance from official Marxism. In fact, there is hardly a mention of Marx in Foucault's earlier works, although he did later incorporate Marxist ideas implicitly, insofar as his critical analyses subsumed class interest and false consciousness.

Foucault received his degree in philosophy from the Sorbonne in 1948, his degree in psychology in 1950, and a diploma in psychopathology in 1952. Such training itself would explain his initial interest in *Madness and Civilization*—the topic and title of the book which catapulted him to fame. Since then, his additional studies of deviance, which are also histories of psychiatry and psychopathology, of medicine, natural history, economics, grammar, linguistics, criminology, and sexuality, have necessarily become more complex as they have reexamined every facet of society and thinking. And as Foucault's detailed descriptions of bizarre behavior and sadistic torture, of chastisement and maiming (descriptions that border on the ghoulish) link humanity with inhumanity, they add to our scientific knowledge of delinquency. But, unlike most American experts, who tend to analyze conditions in order to improve them and who propose either to humanize the deviants or the society, Foucault perceives deviance as a social fact, a function of the normal, and focuses on how it is dealt with, and by whom, during various historical periods. He thus avoids traditional analyses, either Marxist, functional, or pragmatic; instead, he uses them all to cut through the language and to arrive at underlying beliefs or structural codes of knowledge. His work reflects his personality; he is a loner in touch with his admirers, a theoretician attuned to practice, and a historian deviating from conventional views of history.

We can trace Foucault's own evolution through his books. They initially concentrated on methodology and the establishment of his epistemological epochs of knowledge; then on the theoretical linguistics; and, most recently, on the locus of power during each epoch. This type of schematization, however, led at least one reviewer to accuse Foucault of having written the same book over and over again. True, he becomes repetitious, but each book deals with a different central topic and refines the previous works. Thus *Madness and Civilization* (1961) recreates the existence of mental illness, folly, and reason in its time, place, and social perspective, while *The Birth of the Clinic* (1965) focuses more explicitly on the rise of the doctors' power. Both books stress the relationship between the signifying and the signified components of the many texts on madness and disease, so that the sane and the insane, the healthy and the sick are always discussed in connection with each other. Such a search for structures of knowledge, however, when combined with Bachelard's concept of "scientific ruptures" (they roughly resemble Kuhn's notion of scientific revolutions), tends to "dehistorize" history.[1] But Foucault introduces "historical blocks of time," arguing that this allows him to study "periods dominated by a specific knowledge," while moving back and forth in time and space within each of the periods he defines as selfcontained. This conception of history allows him to "outflank" the debate between Sartre and Lévi-Strauss.

Foucault's early books clearly left him open to attacks—attacks to which he responded with his next works. Here, deviance and history, social needs and political expediency, ideologies and scientific beliefs became the backdrop, or the foil, for what might be called his "Grand Historical Code of Knowledge." In *The Order of Things* (1966) he observed how culture absorbs and expresses similarities and relationships between things, the order of their arrangement; the *Archeology of Knowledge* (1969) expanded this order and concentrated on the history of thought. But once he got past the questioning of teleologies and totalizations, consciousness and orgin,[2] the philosophical problems in relation to structural continuities and discontinuities receded into the background, while he examined a single concrete case of "madness-crime" in *I, Pierre Rivière, having slaughtered my mother, my sister, and my brother . . .* (1975). Inevitably, his review of this crime through all the available records—including the madman's—with the contradictory discourses and opinions by lawyers, doctors, journalists, and other experts, not only proved to Foucault the irrationality of rationality in 1836, but implicitly showed why we still cannot differentiate between madness and crime. Foucault's subsequent book, *Discipline and Punish* (1977), had to be about the treatment of prisoners—again from the 16th to the 20th century. His most recent work is *The History of Sexuality*, vol. 1 (1978).

Popular interest in madness, disease, and crime undoubtedly helped make Foucault a best-seller, so that he has been (and is) read by people who could not possibly understand his theories but who liked his tales of madness and his mad tales. As in the case of Lévi-Strauss, the popular success of a new system of thought dressed in scientific cloth preceded Foucault's appointment to the Collège de France. His lectures are always mobbed, as he spins out the intricate connections between society's need for deviance and the deviant's responses and "counter-needs." His intellectual peers respect his scholarship; like Althusser and Barthes, he used structuralist methods but, since about 1969, takes offense at being called a structuralist; and his theoretical arguments with Barthes, Althusser, Lévi-Strauss, or Sartre, as well as his insights, keep him at the center of intellectual discourse.

Foucault's codes of knowledge, initially focused on religion, then on philosophy and science, and exposing the changing role of priests, lawyers, judges, and doctors, are refinements on Saint-Simon, whom Foucault might introduce as one of the first great thinkers of our own era of man. Because Foucault also anticipates the end of this era—as "an end to history" or "an end to man"—the popular media often depict him as a millenarian. But

he is really talking about the end of our "scientific" and fragmented world views, which he himself attempts to bridge.

For Foucault, Marxism's emphasis on economics, psychoanalysis's (French-style and Lacanian) isolation of the individual,
structuralism's unconscious structural unity, and existentialism's
focus on the relation between subject and object, all create "partial" theories that end up as ideologies. Foucault sets out to
uncover their underlying unity—the historical code of
knowledge—which is an "archeology" rather than a history.[3] His
system, like Durkheim's, stresses the malaise of societies according to the magnitude of deviance. But he goes beyond Durkheim
when he includes the scientists themselves in his diagnosis, as
both symptom and cure: they create the knowledges and languages, and they wield the power to implement and to perpetuate
the very deviance they set out to eradicate. That is how Foucault's ironic vision, which Northrop Frye calls the detachment
from detachment, has made him the guru of the human sciences.

II

What then are Foucault's theses and themes, his tales of horror
and predictions of doom? In what way does he "update" history
and make it relevant to a general public? What problems does
he tackle, and how do the themes evolve from one work to another? And how do they relate to the rest of his intellectual community? In other words, what do Foucault and his system promise, what theoretical problems do they solve?

In *Madness and Civilization,* he painstakingly documented
how the definition of madness among the elite depended upon
the composition of this elite itself, upon society's need for out-
casts, and upon the examination of madness as a phenomenon
only when leprosy disappeared. All societies need deviants,
argues Foucault, because their exclusion and the act of their exclusion make for everyone else's feeling of inclusion—for social
solidarity. Thus Foucault describes the spectacle of the *ships of
fools* that "displayed" madness until the end of the Middle Ages.
He keeps reiterating that the fate of these fools was less important than the act of their expulsion: they would serve as exam-

ples, so that their exclusion would, symbolically, purify the society.

Because everyone was fascinated by madness, continues Foucault, its very ambiguity, its existence at the edge of experience, helped men to deal with their anxieties about death. In literature and art, the madman seemed to know both more and less than the sane. But rather than asking the customary questions that connect madness to the creative mind, Foucault looks at the mad in relation to the sane. Because the madman seemed to be able to look into the future, he was frequently cast in the role of prophet or placed at the midpoint between life and death: "his laugh could anticipate the macabre he had disarmed," and painters could "appreciate" him as a vehicle for their interpretation.[4] Bosch's *Ship of Fools,* for example, has a mast in the form of an uprooted tree of knowledge, and the fool's pleasure in the victory of the Antichrist seems a manifestation of his position as mediator between God and the Devil, passion and delirium—emotions which suddenly were perceived to exist in every man. Thus, Erasmus, says Foucault, saw madness "from the heights of his Olympus" as a "disorderly use of science, as the truth of absurd knowledge, as the comic punishment of knowledge and its ignorant presumption," while the painters were less "earthbound."[5] Still, at that time, all creative works seemed to use the mad as the means to depict the proximity of heaven and hell, sanity and insanity, if only because the mad appeared to have access to a symbolic, and completely moral, universe.[6]

But at the end of the Middle Ages, Foucault argues, a new code of knowledge emerged that made people fear the very duality of madness as they listened to its moral messages, identified with the fool, and went to see performances of *Don Quixote.* Foucault quotes novels and satires, Shakespeare and Cervantes, to reinforce his point, perceiving authors themselves as transitory links—as well as ruptures—between the earlier view of madness as inhuman and the emerging seventeenth-century view of madness as all too human. Carefully and credibly, he reconstructs from the archives the social climate and the prevalent beliefs about madness, revealing how changing ideas and needs led to the confinement of the mad in the hospital after 1656, when the Hôpital Général of Paris was founded.

Confinement, often in reconverted leprosariums, Foucault concludes, marked the beginning of a new age: madness still preserved its ambivalences and appearances but was also tied to the rise of scientism and to the loss of religious values. Now the mad were available for discussion and treatment, for legal regulation and scientific diagnosis, even though it was not until the nineteenth century that they were separated from thieves and criminals, squanderers and beggars, vagabonds and unemployed. Their separation from other deviants became a scientific question occupying doctors, lawyers, and police. Both *I, Pierre Rivière, having killed my mother, my sister and my brother . . .* and *Discipline and Punish* concentrate on medical, legal, and administrative authority and on the growing relationship between medical knowledge and legal power, while *The Birth of the Clinic* examines medicine and doctors. Once more Foucault looked at the functions of deviants and noted that their confinement not only condemned the idle, the beggars, the poor, and the mad, but also provided a source of cheap and forced labor.

Even though Foucault has since then sharpened these insights, his thrust was already evident when he described the earlier conditions of horror to which the mad were condemned, or the later total domination by the hospital directors, whose "power of authority and direction, administration and commerce, police and jurisdiction, correction and punishment," allowed them to use "stakes and irons, prisons and dungeons."[7] Chained, exposed to rats, in wet and sewerless cells, the mad often acted as if they deserved mistreatment and brutalization. But these conditions, stated Foucault, themselves might have driven anyone insane. Outside the asylums, however, madness began to be tied to passion, which now was thought to exist in everyone, and to "radiate to both the body and the soul."[8] Doctors treated the passions of the well-to-do—who paid them—outside the hospitals, gradually learning about the connections between, for instance, romantic love and mental states.

Foucault contrasts sanity and insanity from the vantage point of the new scientific *Zeitgeist* that led to investigations of madness and to differentiations between hallucinations, delirium, mania, depression, and general derangement. Foucault's lively case histories indicate that the imagination of the doctors, as they reintroduced madness as a disease, as a human condition, resembled the imaginings of the fools. The very construction of their medical reports formed a new language of signs and symbols that allows Foucault to perceive "language [as] the first and last structure of madness, its constituent form."[9] Foucault mediates between insanity and sanity, in the way that Lévi-Strauss mediates between myth and reality. And, like Freud, he links the language of delirium to the language of dreams. But this link between "words that are blind and abandon reality" in turn could bring about "a rational hold over madness to the very degree that madness was nonreason."[10] In other words, because the structure of madness is mixed up with the structure of language, Foucault examines the relation between them within specific epochs of knowledge. Thus the advance of scientific thought during the Classical Age was found to have initiated its own end.

This advance came primarily from the treatment of the insane outside the institution, where doctors consolidated spirits and nerves through purification (e.g., the mad ate soap, quinine, tartar, or vinegar; were ritually immersed in water; or had their "bad" blood replaced) or hired actors to embody a hallucinatory subject which could then be "exorcised." These new methods, based on the realization that melancholia, for example, was not due to animality, that non-being or delirium was not caused by spirits, that mania could not "pierce new pores in the cerebral matter,"[11] and that hysteria was not a displacement of the womb, often led to far-reaching conclusions. Women, for instance, now acquired "frail fibers, were easily carried away in their idleness by the lively movements of their imagination, and were more subject to nervous disease than men who were more robust, drier and hardened by work."[12]

Foucault's method does not allow him to draw "direct" conclusions to current issues; his links are all in the past, as he ties mental illness to feelings and consequently to nervous complaints and to the morality of the day. Now the person became both more innocent and more guilty, as mental disease was tied to passion, to leisure, and to irritability—that is, to the rich. Enter psychological medicine and language as the link between reason and unreason, the forerunner of the "talking-cure." And language itself as part of the cure, was altered by the new scientific knowledge it incorporated and created.

Eventually, treatment of the not-so-mad outside the asylums was extended to the confined mad. Their plight was reexamined in keeping with the principles of the French revolution; they were "rediscovered," and their human rights were affirmed through the creation of asylums without doors. Foucault explains just how, when philanthropic doctors applied the techniques they had used on the rich to the poor, patients began to be managed through fear rather than through physical constraints, and how wardens became the new social authority—both as judges and as representatives of sanity. Now the madman could expiate his sins through work and could return to God's commandments, be rewarded and punished, as the lawyers increasingly restructured madness, and as the asylum became a religious domain without religion.[13] Foucault examines the evolving authority structure and shows how it not only dominated the fools who were legally and emotionally reduced to children, but how it made for the rise of patriarchy and of the bourgeois family—as control through manipulation became the norm.

Inside the asylum, the keeper's new "scientific" language "taught" the mad about their madness by pointing out the irrationality of their fellow inmates. Here Foucault applies Lacan's concept of the *mirror-image* that is said to reflect everyone's madness.[14] Thus madness, a pure spectacle and an absolute object, was demystified; it was constantly called upon to judge itself in interaction. Now the madman could be punished with justification when he did not fit in. Foucault finds that he learned to comply and to repress transgressions.

That is how madness became a disease to be treated by doctors, with the help of language—the major tool of psychiatry. Foucault concludes that psychiatric practice itself "remystified" madness, because once more the sane and the insane were separated as the doctor-patient relationship became more personal and as the patient had to surrender to the psychiatrist "in advance" by accepting the latter's reputation and prestige. In this manner, language "served" to explain, to cure, and to structure madness, and prepared the ground for Freud, for whom language became the structure of madness itself.

III

In *The Birth of the Clinic,* Foucault dropped madness to focus on disease and on a medical power that "emerged" roughly between 1794 and 1820. This work is "about space, language, death and the act of seeing" [15]—the *regard medical* or *gaze.* Even though he has since discarded this notion, it was meant to examine the deepest structures of medicine and of disease, of clinical discussion and medical reports, of historical records and scientific literature from a structural perspective.

Foucault analyses eighteenth-century medicine through its concern with "species" of illness that were present in (or represented by) a patient. Such species had their natural state and ideal processes, which gave the doctor a chance to watch and diagnose the reciprocity between patient and disease—in its natural environment. [16] He links the space and place of medical practice to the state of knowledge as it changed in response to social needs. Thus he finds that medicine expanded along with its language; after the French revolution there were more patients who needed more hospital care and more doctors—doctors who were bound to create more medical knowledge in their talk of metastases and metamorphoses, of sympathies or of "distinctions between the convolutions of an epileptic with cerebral inflammation and the hypochondriac with congestion of the viscera." [17] In general, disease became circumscribed, medically invested, isolated, and divided. Foucault discusses bodily regions in relation to geographic regions; he compares the many debates about illnesses to debates over the need for hospitals, usually in the context of the revolution and of equality. Because doctors began to link epidemics to poor housing and sanitation, to inadequate education and political negligence, because they learned from the new statistical supervision of health that the poor got sicker and died more frequently than the rich, they were frequently cast as the saviors of both individuals and of society.

Foucault brilliantly describes the doctor's ambiguous role—as crusader for social reform and as advocate for medical power.

In any case, the need for experimentation and for the unification and expansion of medicine put the doctors in a privileged position—in a society that had just abolished privilege. Political equality had crowded existing hospitals, had made them impersonal and costly, so that they had become breeding grounds for communicable diseases. At this point, when it became preferable to send the sick back to their families, Foucault discerns shifts in revolutionary rhetoric. He argues that doctors' and politicans' needs converged when it became cheaper to keep the sick at home (they were often poor), especially when they were entitled to state support. Now "humaneness" became expedient; doctors were to make housecalls. For Foucault this indicates a new epoch of knowledge: medical space changed; disease moved out of the hospitals; and hospitals became research-oriented. Doctors who had accused the state of negligence and of furthering "disease-producing conditions," now asked the state to provide laws, funds, and the climate for research. That is how the clinic was born. Inside the clinic, just as inside the asylum, the poor were inevitably the guinea pigs. This was justified because the rich subsidized their treatment, and because science was to benefit everyone. Doctors were to keep track of diseases, the government was to keep track of doctors, regulate medicine, and get rid of quacks and charlatans. This division of functions, says Foucault, led to the disappearance of the institutionalizing of disease, and of the "medicine of space."

From then on, "knowledge was to be empirically derived and tested in a radically restructured clinic."[18] Foucault compares the doctors' lectures about disease to the philosophers' descriptions of countries they have never seen likening them to the blind whose vision is suddenly restored.

They now had to find cures for the many diseases caused by de-hospitalization, quackery, and epidemics. For the first time, the sick were observed in their beds and became a subject of structured curricula for students. Simultaneously, the clinics controlled professional access; Foucault shows that social and professional stratification based on scientific knowledge began when criteria for licensing of health officials, doctors, and paraprofessionals were established. Essentially, he says, the doctors helped build a structure that would preserve the hospitals, strengthen their own privileged position, and incorporate liberal political principles.

Together, these factors produced new codes of knowledge, and new laws favorable to medicine. The dissection of corpses, for instance, was legalized at the doctor's instigation; they could then begin to "gaze" at death. For Foucault, these circumstances became the basis of the new knowledge, knowledge he once more examines through structuralist oppositions, where the dialectic of disease parallels that of linguistics, where the relationships between disease and its progress, and the doctor's diagnosis and his treatment, are subsumed in a clinical method that "distinguishes between signs and symptoms," recognizes their constituent rights and the effacement of their absolute distinction." When he talks of "the signifier (sign and symptom) [as] . . . transparent for the signified, whose essence—the heart of the disease—is entirely exhausted in the intelligible syntax of the signifier, . . . [and when] the symptom abandons its passivity . . . [to] become a signifier of the disease," then the reader has a preview of his subsequent works.[19] Foucault's theory becomes even more abstruse when his philosophy "unites" language and perception in the clinic to distinguish visible and invisible components of a disease in "a language that is at one in its existence and its meaning with the gaze that deciphers it—a language inseparably read and reading."[20]

Here Foucault borrows from Barthes,[21] as he compares in many texts the clinician's gaze to the philosopher's reflection, searching for analogies and frequency of occurrences, for degrees of certainty and probability, even while affirming that these logical analyses, which follow a mathematical model, cannot work. He says that his own structural linguistics is free of mathematical ideology, that his clinical gaze can "hear a language" as soon as it "perceives a spectacle," as he mediates between hospital domain and teaching domain, medical experience and hospital field, visual and oral investigation, patient and symptom, sickness and its progress, prescription and intervention. Eventually he subsumes it all in the doctor and his utterance—the énoncé.

No summary can do justice to Foucault's complexity or to what seems to be his philosophical mission. When, for example, he points out to us that autopsies and the dissection of corpses heralded the new scientific era, when dead tissues could be examined apart from the individual's death, or when disease could be restructured from the corpse so that new knowledge could be discovered, then we are aware of Foucault's strange and somewhat disturbing genius for always picking on the unusual and weird only to make it seem inevitable and true. Documentation of the changing discussion about the communication or impermeability among tissues, and about the invention of the stethoscope, which added ear and touch to sight, crisscrosses with philosophical conclusions about "death as a disease made possible in life," until "deviation in life is both the order of life, and life that moves toward death."

Foucault uses the stethoscope to bridge technological as well as moral obstacles for the doctors. The doctors, he claims, became ever more differentiated from ordinary mortals when they were thought to know all about life and death, when they began to write about their new techniques, about fevers and their roots, about pathological causes and physio-pathological processes. He finds this abrupt change already evident in Broussais's *Traité*, which focused, in 1816, on the sick organism and the *new way to see (le regard medicale)*. This event represents for Foucault the scientific break in medicine that inaugurated the discourse of our own age. For the doctors' insights and observations had progressed from an "anato-clinical" method to the "historical condition of positive medicine;" their gaze "rested upon the stable, visible, legible basis of death." [22] Typical of the general debates on science since Comte (positive science in France has remained more an ideal construction than empirical study), Foucault links death, as viewed at the end of the eighteenth century, to life and to medicine, just as he had tied madness to psychiatry. Both incorporated the new moral methods that arose in response to the social conditions and needs created by the French revolution and gave birth to a "science of the individual."

IV

In *The Order of Things* he seems to outdo both Comte and Lévi-Strauss in his at-once sweeping and narrow explications of our universe, moving from medicine to psychiatry, from economics to physics and technology, to unearth a unified structure of knowledge by means of his structural-linguistic framework. For him, the texts of doctors and human scientists, of artists and philosophers are there to be deciphered; "the very constitution of medicine or biology [becomes] a poetic act, a genuine 'making' or 'invention' of a domain of inquiry."[23] As he strips away linguistic representations and games, trying to get at the underside of discourse and at structures of knowledge, and as he unveils the strategies that sanction the "conceptualizing rituals," his systematic search for order is, in effect, upsetting conventional history. Sequential events are transcended; his sophisticated free associations take over as events, authors, and their works bolster and "prove" the theories. Like Lévi-Strauss, he promises order at the end, after all representations have been unveiled—when the codes of knowledge of each of his periods will be clearly known. Like Lévi-Strauss, he uses a four-cornered system, his "quadri-lateral of language" (proposition, articulation, designation, and observation), whose "segments confront each other in pairs," and whose diagonal relations place the name at the center. (See illustration.) This scheme, applied to all literature from fiction to science, is meant to show the relation between all written texts, to prove the unity of language itself, and to put syntax into historical context, linking it genetically to nature. At that point, analysis and space are said to have met at the end of the Middle Ages and to have emerged as the prose of the world—a prose that is treated like madness and disease.[24]

Foucault maintains that language in its original form, when given to men by God himself, was clear, because rooted in signs. But its clarity of signs was destroyed as languages became separated and took on many new meanings and symbolic functions. Originally, argues Foucault, language was rooted in resemblances through adjacency, convenience, analogy, and sympathy. In written language, however, there are complex interactions that reflect social and cultural conditions and changes in language.

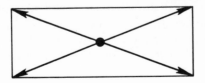

Signs began to be arranged in binary fashion as the connections between *signifieds* and *signifiers*,[25] and chains of resemblances led to signatures (recognitions and similitudes, or signs that tie resemblances) as "intermediate forms of the same resemblances," or "marks of sympathy," to delimit the world and to form one vast single text for those who could read."[26] Foucault tries to reconstruct universal history by getting back to the roots of language—with the help of a structuralist analysis of everything written about nature and animals, grammar and syntax, verbs and plants, and about whatever one comes across.

As Foucault "articulates" and "designates," "speaks" and "classifies," he demonstrates that the resemblances that governed until the Renaissance were suddenly changed and reorganized as doctors replaced natural classifications by comparative anatomy, as political economists talked of labor and production rather than of wealth, and as general grammar gave way to historical philology. Yet Foucault does not focus on these transformations, but only on the new consciousness and the codes that emerge from them—codes that can be known only, as it were, after the fact and that depend upon a combination of available language, the representations and signatures of which act back upon themselves to underline the disjunction in these epistemic codes. Such disjunctions, are, once more, "demonstrated" through literary works like *Don Quixote,* whose analogies and ambiguities first "introduced" literature. With his advent, "the written words and things no longer resembled each other, as between them Don Quixote wanders off on his own,"[27] as madness and sanity are united in him, and as language gets separated from things, in order to return *only* in literature that no longer "speaks."

This novel reading of texts, that is to lead us to the codes of knowledge is then tied to changes that occurred in other fields. Analysis of commodity and wealth, for example, was replaced by analysis of monetary systems so that economic knowledge, too, changed its space, became discontinuous, and broke with its past. By locating the discontinuity in economic knowledge rather than in economic conditions, Foucault bypasses the inevitability of Marx's potential revolution and Althusser's Marxism, although he increasingly emphasizes economic factors as crucial. Foucault connects economic conditions to the new understanding by man of his own situation, and to the way in which capital and labor, production time and wages were now related to new means of production. Although he does not discuss it as such, alienation appears to be "knowledge" that surfaced at the end of the Classical Age.

Yet everything, Foucault keeps reiterating, depended upon language. He traces language from archaic analyses of inflection and cries, through language development, to general grammar, because, in fact, language was created along with the ideologies and the biases it incorporated.[28] Addressing the philosophical discussions at the time, Foucault argues that the Kantian critique that questioned its own limits brought us to the threshold of modernity, where positivism had to give way to the modern episteme; and that after Fichte, Hegel's phenomenology led us back to the interior of consciousness, which could then reveal itself as spirit. Thus Hegel is said to have paved the way for Husserl and for all subsequent phenomenological reflections on subjectivity.

But Foucault's archeology must reject subjectivity. Authors, works, and language are said to be objects in search of a logic independent of grammars, vocabularies, synthetic forms, and words.[29] Man thereby becomes the subject of his own discourse, as both the object of knowledge and the subject that knows.

Foucault exemplifies how man is outside his discourse when, for example, he shows how the king in Velasquez's painting is both slave and sovereign: seen through a mirror, his real presence is excluded, and his "finitude is heralded" insofar as he knows that the painting both immortalizes him and anticipates his death.[30] That is when modernity allegedly begins, as "the human being begins to exist within its organism, inside the shell of its head, inside the armature of his limbs, and in the whole structure of his physiology; when he [is] the center of his labour; . . . [and] when he thinks in . . . language much older than himself."[31] In the new modern age "pre-critical naïveté" and scientific advance allegedly meet, when man appeared as an "empirico-transcendental doublet."

On this level, Comte and Marx become "archeologically" indissoluble, so that Foucault does not directly confront them when he questions man's being, the relation between the thought and the unthought—a new form of "reflection removed from both Kantian and Cartesian analysis." He leads up to Freud, when his unconscious is "the unthought" that articulates itself upon thought, or when he talks of "the Other that is not only a brother but a twin, not of man, nor in man, but beside him and at the same time, in an identical newness, in an unavoidable duality."[32] Foucault goes on—through Hegel and Marx, Sade and Nietzsche, Artaud and Bataille—to "prove" that thought can now no longer be theoretical, but is in itself a perilous act. He ends up by opposing doubles that "unveil the same"; the thought *and* unthought; the empirical *and* the transcendental.[33]

This search for the ultimate explanation of our universe ends in "three faces of knowledge": mathematics and physics; the sciences of language, life, production and distribution of wealth; and philosophical reflection. The human sciences are said to exist at the interstices of them all, because they lend relevance to the others and follow three constituent models, based on biology, economics, and language, which operate in interlocking pairs: function and norm, conflict and rule, signification and system. And history, the customary *bête noire* in the structuralist polemics, is perceived as the oldest of the human sciences that existed long before *man* who appears only at the beginning of the nineteenth century. Hence, history "constitutes the environment for the human sciences," which means that Foucault "must limit its frontiers" to coincide with his epochs of knowledge—related to codal periods rather than to chronological events.

Yet, even though he views psychoanalysis and ethnology as the sciences of the future that "form an inexhaustible treasure-hoard of experience and concepts, of contestation and criticism," he admonishes Lévi-Strauss for "defining ethnology as the study of societies without history" and for remaining within the categories of thought of Descartes and Kant. Since Lévi-Strauss' "anthropological quadrilateral," he argues, derives from mythology in non-developed societies and is, thus, in effect, asleep,[34] his theory ought to be overcome in its very foundations; and ethnology ought to deal with unconscious processes that characterize the system of a culture. For Foucault wants to find the relation between conscious and unconscious thought, between nature and culture that questions all knowledge; and that spans the sciences "dissolving" man.

V

The inclusiveness of Foucault's propositions was bound to evoke criticism. Some of the comments led Foucault to reevaluate a number of his basic postulates. His *Archeology of Knowledge,* he says, answers theoretical objections by extending his previous works and reexamining old concepts.[35] Former categories such as the "experience" of *Madness and Civilization,* the "gaze" of *The Birth of the Clinic,* and the "episteme" of *The Order of Things* are altered as his new focus becomes the enunciative function (*énoncé*). Now he sets out to reorganize, to recover in controlled and methodical fashion, what he had previously done blindly.[36] As he proceeds systematically to account for each aspect of spoken and unspoken language he tries to uncover autochthonous transformation. By this he means that when, after a rupture, a new knowledge begins, it is unrelated to previous knowledge. He wants to get away from cultural totalities, so that he can "impose the forms of structural analysis on history itself," while constructing a method of "historical analysis freed of anthropology," in a "blank space that is slowly taking shape in a still precarious discourse," or at "a particular site defined by the exteriority of its vicinity."[37] As he refutes both the continuity of history as subject and the structural discontinuity of its ruptures, he is inventing a structuralist methodology without structures or history that is to uncover "pure" language and that resembles a Barthian textual reading.

Naturally, Foucault's continuous circling of language and blank space, in a manner analogous to the cat's chasing its tail, becomes heavy and dull. Madness, disease, and crime are more fascinating than this linguistic excursion into history and into the impersonality, regularity, and dispersion of thought itself, especially as examples are piled up to illustrate scientificity. Foucault says that his archeology of dead monuments, inert traces, and objects without context works from its interior, so that progress of conscience and evolution of thought, themes of convergence and accomplishment become invalid. "Global history" fades away as "general history" emerges, with series, ruptures, limits, chronological specificities, and types of relations. Foucault says that his history operates from anti-anthropologist, anti-humanist, and anti-structuralist premises, so that he pits himself once more, against most other "grand theorists." His linguistic practice undercuts the Marxists by avoiding political engagement and refutes Lévi-Strauss by attacking anthropology's floating languages and unconnected themes. And when he repeatedly rejects the author as the specific creator of a work, arguing that creative works arise from their context (of culture and knowledge), he sides with Barthes, and, simultaneously, reinforces his own adaptation of Bachelard's epochs.

In sweeping statements, Foucault spans our entire intellectual universe, cuts through "historical successions that exist behind revolutions, governments and famines, to other pasts, hierarchies and networks whose internal coherences constitute and maintain themselves." [38] Because his task requires a "pre-systematic system" to accommodate this history of thought and knowledge, of philosophy and literature, he accumulates "stratified ensembles" and "discursive regularities" and unites "discursive strategies" for the sake of order between objects and concepts, choices and enunciations. Thus he arrives at his new, and basic, enunciative unit in language, which (on the level of methodology) would roughly compare to Lévi-Strauss' constituent unit in myth.

These enunciative units are said to produce relations and a play between relations and are defined without reference to their foundation. Instead, they exist in relation to "a body of rules proper to discursive practice." [39] Accordingly, the doctor, for example, is related to his "institutional site," is part of his object-oriented discourse inside his enunciative field[40]—a field dominated by a strategy with its own ideas and ideality, a strategy that is to be circumvented through linguistic rules. This means that doctors constructed their own mystifying and scientific lingo, by separating the symptom from the sickness, the signifier from the signified. Foucault extends this translation from linguistics to definitions of "statements. . . . to their functions and descriptions. . . . [and] to discursive formations." [41]

And as this linguistic theory-to-be gets murkier, his enunciative unity—a function of existence that presents itself as a positivity between language and thought—becomes part of "verbal performance" and of the "ensemble of signs produced by a natural or artificial language." Like a disease, an ensemble of signs is neither hidden nor visible, is hard to recognize, does not decipher a "fundamental muteness," and facilitates "the transcendental ends of a form of discourse that is opposed to all analysis of language." Yet, as Foucault gazes into the depths of consciousness and of "un-thought thought" and into the relations and roots of every thought, he continues to insist that he must also free himself of the limits of linguistic structure. Hence, his "blank space" becomes independent of phrases and grammar, of propositions and logic, or of psychology. Even his subjects have no special importance,[42] because they are linked to the present and the past through recurrences which relate to antecedent elements in the form of selective memories and to larger ensembles. These ensembles are Foucault's "archives," the repositories of myriads of unique relationships that play the role of his "historical a prioris"[43]—the constructs that determine the reality of the enunciative units which help us understand internal points of contact, insertions, or the emergence of disciplines of knowledge. They provide Foucault-like history, in that they exist only to be remembered under specific circumstances. The archives also control the appearance of enunciative units; regulate what can be said and what is to be left unsaid; and form distinct configurations, compositions, and rapports. But because the archives of a culture are never complete and emerge only in fragments, Foucault creates "a general horizon" for them all—his "archeology."[44] This archeology is chiefly described by what it is not. It is "neither a search for beginnings" nor a geology that attempts to define discourse itself. It is not a history of ideas, because it is not interpretive, does not look for transformations, and has no slow progressions; it does not try to grasp moments on its horizon, nor does it attach itself to sociology, anthropology, psychology, or creation. It never reconstitutes what was thought, wanted, or proven, but is "the systematic description of a discourse-object itself," on a horizon "entangled in unique interrelationships of relations" (interpositivities).[45] Hence, Saussure's, Keynes' and Darwin's systems, for example, are able to operate in different fields of "enunciative regularities that characterize enunciative formation," and yet use the same grammar and logic. This example illustrates enunciative homogeneity, through placing the three systems into three different knowledges *during* an epoch. Nevertheless, archeological observation has no "deductive schema" and does not attempt any "totalitarian periodization."[46]

Endless archeological examples tie irregularities and contradictions in language, on all kinds of levels, to coherences that are said to show similarities between chronological discourse (such as *Madness and Civilization* or *Birth of the Clinic*) and lateral discourse (such as *The Order of Things*). They differ from the customary approach, claims Foucault, in that they do not try to reconstruct a particular domain or rationality, a specific classification or causality; their aim is to "reveal" the relations between well-determined sets of discursive formations. Consequently, Foucault can talk of the Classical Age even as he denies the Classical spirit; as his archeology refutes symbolic projection, expression, and reflection; and as he gets away from a traditional history.[47] Actually, Foucault "freezes" history, in order to make his discontinuities viable. He seems to reach for the farthest corners of his horizon, while descending into the deepest reaches of language, as his archeology "disarticulates the synchrony of breaks, does not use the epoch, the horizon or its objects as basic unities, but only as discursive practice."[48]

Foucault ends *The Archeology of Knowledge* with a discussion he has thus far managed to avoid: the relation of science and knowledge to ideology. As we would expect, ideology for Foucault springs from the discursive formations and becomes a unique relationship cutting through all kinds of practices—discursive, political, and economic.

VI

In *I, Pierre Rivière, having slaughtered my mother, my sister, and my brother . . .*, Foucault demonstrates this (ideological) practice by analyzing a single instance of murder and appears to "update" parts of *Madness and Civilization*. In this edited work of historical documents (from June 3, 1835 to October 22, 1840), Rivière's own account of his crime and its motives contributes to the analysis. Half of the experts had found this strange and ignorant peasant insane, and the jury could neither acquit nor condemn him. For Foucault, Rivière provides the "excuse" to examine power structures and social institutions, to question the scientificity of medical science, and to delineate the chaos of values and beliefs, of knowledge and power as it existed 150 years ago—a chaos we have not yet eliminated. But now, says Foucault, we can examine the evidence impartially and can reconstitute the knowledge of that time by putting Rivière's memoir in its proper place. In his search for the perfect crime to study, Foucault found that although parricide itself was not rare at that time, Rivière's memoir was unique. It made "the murder and the narrative of the murder consubstantial."[49] Its text became an "exhibit in evidence," an element in Rivière's rationality or irrationality, because it "did not relate directly to the deed." Memoir and murder are found, however, to be intricately interwoven, to support each other, and to "carry one another in ever-changing relation." In this kind of narrative—Foucault's applied archeology—"the text was to surround the murder," as Rivière free-associated from minute descriptions of family relations and circumstances, interpreting his emotions from his a priori intention to write the plot (*before* the murder took place) to the actual writing, afterward, in prison.

Rivière's brutal act (he used a pruning bill on all three victims) was premeditated, but was Rivière sane or mad when he decided that his father had to be "delivered from all his tribulations?" Judges and lawyers, doctors and psychiatrists did not know, yet produced "expert" opinions: opinions rooted in the new knowledge about madness. Foucault does not know either, but reconstructs the "archeological horizon." He notes that only a few years before a similar crime would not have engaged the "experts," since insanity had not yet become a disease to be cured, and had not yet been separated from crime. The trial, the legal and medical opinions were themselves product and precedent of new practices. Rivière provided a pivot for the crystallization of a new power structure based on "scientific" pronouncements.

Psychoanalytic hindsight might interpret the murder as the acting out of arrested Oedipal attachment—an act of insanity. Some neighbors, townspeople, and journalists reached a similar conclusion: only a madman could have committed such a beastly act (even though many thought that Rivière's mother could have driven anyone insane). For the lawyers, it was parricide and ought to be punished like regicide, that is, more severely than a run-of-the-mill murder, if sanity could be proven. Foucault, including all pronouncements, language, and positions, finds that these are reflections of changing political, social, and economic relations, of the new rights and obligations related to family and property after the revolution, when legal equality began to expand knowledge and to express it in a new code.

With his colleagues, Foucault deciphers this code by looking at the same texts from different angles: madman vs. animal, extenuating circumstances, power of medicine vs. law, and "intermittences of rationality." This multidimensional textual analysis resembles Barthes' treatment of Balzac's *Sarrasine*. Foucault omits quantitative data as he teases out all possible information from one case, insisting that this method, too, is scientific. He leaves the generalizations to the reader. In any event, he shows how current legal language (that is, particulars, circumstances, explanations, and occurrences) arose at that time to explain the grotesque, the gruesome, or the despicable. The new words, he contends, helped to make the transition from the familiar to the remarkable, from the everyday to the historical at a time when, suddenly, the act of writing could turn gossip into history. Starting then, he says, the histories of street brawls and murder "joined" the histories of power, and "murder was at the intersection of the segments of language." It was set to music in popular lyrics, reports Foucault—in the form of lamentations by the dead person about his guilt, his expiation through punishment, and his isolation. "Pierre Rivière filled his place in this fictional lyricism by a real murder," and "came to lodge his deed and his speech in a defined place in a certain type of discourse and a certain field of knowledge." His parricide was paid for in the glory he sought, and was sung in the fly sheets.[50]

Foucault illustrates clearly that deviance is still dealt with in similar fashion—either when we blame the system that produces the deviant, or when we advocate law and order. For Foucault it "proves" that the symbiotic collusion between medicine and law has become the norm: in England, where mental institutions are increasingly used to punish crime, in the U.S.S.R., where they have become political prisons,[51] or, I might add, in America, where proof of insanity—however brief—"excuses" crime.

VII

Discipline and Punish, the sequel to *Rivière,* links crime to madness and politics in formal and central fashion and traces it, just as we would expect, in France, from the eighteenth century to the present, and from the "punishment of the body to that of the soul." The book begins, dramatically:

> On March 1757 the regicide was condemned 'to make the *amende honorable'* . . . he was taken and conveyed in a cart, wearing nothing but a shirt, holding a torch of burning wax weighing two pounds, to the Place de Grève, where on a scaffold that will be erected there, the flesh will be torn from his breasts, arms, thighs and calves with red-hot pincers, his right hand, holding up the knife with which he had committed the parricide, burnt with sulphur, and on those places where the flesh will be torn away, poured molten lead, boiling oil, burnt with sulphur, burning resin, wax and sulphur melted together, and then his body drawn and quartered by four horses and his limbs and body consumed by fire, reduced to ashes and his ashes thrown to the winds.[52]

Foucault's detailed description of Damien's punishment and of witnesses' reports affects the reader today, much as the public was affected then. Actually he once again indicates how his concept of epistemological ruptures holds up—on this occasion for the study of crime, as it had earlier for madness and disease. Mediating between crime and punishment to show that they were public rather than secret, physical rather than mental, and violent rather than "civilized," he finds a new subject for an old theme: crime is shown to be another deviance within the social fabric, as judges and lawyers, police and public, create the new system that needs and produces them.

Until the turn of the eighteenth century, says Foucault, punishment for crime had been a theater of torture and pain that destroyed the body and served as social control. Since then, attitudes have changed; cruelty was replaced by pseudo-leniency; our penal operation "charged itself of extra-juridical elements and personages" now judging the soul rather than the body. But, observes Foucault, that has not altered the judges' qualifications; it helps merely to absolve them of responsibility—to veil their power. (Naked power exists exclusively inside the prisons.) The authorities now use psychiatric knowledge to chastise, while they justify and strengthen their own hidden power, power they effectively mask under the law they help create. For Foucault, this *new* type of punishment, along with the *new* "technology of power," serves *new* social, political, and economic ends. He argues that in the prevailing system of production, "the punished provide a supplementary work force that constitutes civil slavery."[53] Psychological punishment is an adjunct to a penal system that incorporates psychiatric and medical knowledge in order to legitimate the legal power, that now can establish "truth" even in the absence of the accused. Foucault means that a crime can now be legally reconstructed and evidence can be produced, so that the criminal can then confess, post facto and "spontaneously," to this legally induced truth.

Thus, once more, Foucault combines data from various fields to provide new insights, including both Marxist and capitalist premises in the construction of his "horizon of crime." New rituals are compared to previous ones, arbitrary sovereigns are contrasted with the new "egalitarian" legality, and old-style executioners with modern and anonymous electric chairs. He even juxtaposes the people's solidarity against "real" criminals to their newly discovered affinity with the post-revolutionary delinquencies—delinquencies that are investigated by the new class of inspectors and police. And he finds that as property crime increased it became more and more differentiated from blood crime. The latter, it seems, fascinated the people who then glorified criminals and executions, so that Rivière could, posthumously, become a neo-saint.

Foucault even links the decrease in blood crimes and the increase in property crimes to the systematization of punishment that now had to be universalized and that had to differentiate illegalities from suppression. Crime was punished in relation to its damage to the social pact, so that Foucault can talk of an economy of punishment by politicians that is based on a "technology of representation."[54] An offender's intent was judged along with the crime, and "the length of pain was integrated to the economy of pain." But whereas previously torture—days of pillory, years of banishment, or hours on the wheel—had been prescribed, now the condemned would expiate his crime through work. In other words, a pseudo-Marxist Foucault talks of productions of crime and punishment—productions that, analogous to madness, turn into knowledge that is tied to "manipulable" guilt. But guilt changed only the "quality" of crime and of punishment.

Punishment, Foucault indicates, necessitated the construction of new prisons—prisons that were modeled after the Walnut Street prison of Philadelphia.[55] He describes scientific rationality involved in the allocation of space (hierarchically organized in line with the offense), and talks of the regimentation and control of work and guilt that was to modify behavior inside these institutions. He then compares control in prisons to similar controls in schools, in the army, and in the factory: time was strictly organized, surveillance was efficient and uninterrupted. These rules and obligations became part of the new apparatus of knowledge that never deterred crime but merely regimented criminals.

Foucault illustrates how the aim of perfecting society resulted only in the perfection of punishment. He describes the machinery of punishment, with its concomitant coercion, docility, and regimentation that gradually turned people into cases, until hierarchic surveillance became the norm. Power became anonymous and functional. Foucault finds that this new disciplinary system "celebrated" the deviant, the child, and the mad, because individualization proceeded by singling out inherent differences, defects, childish traits, or secret follies. Yet this "individualism" helped to hide a disciplinary society in which a centralized police force was attached to political power. Of course, Foucault is not the first to describe the total institution, the solitary confinement, the accompanying disciplinary measures, coercions, and ideologies, or the total power of the staff.[56] But his endless excursions through prisons and the process of incarceration, through the Panopticum and delinquency, through the rules and penitentiary conditions, enliven his erudite "transformational interactions"—interactions that integrate everything, from comportment to isolation, from pain to work, from education to control by "specialists," from word to language, and from there to his dialectics between language and thought, conscious and unconscious.

His trenchant insights relating the police to the organization of prostitutes—from their health and houses to their regulated passages through prison, and the relations between informers and participants—do substantiate how financial profit from illicit sexual pleasure was funneled back into the society. When Foucault shows how morals were lost as moralization increased, when he concludes that "the delinquent milieu was in complicity with an interested puritanism" in setting a price for pleasure and in making a profit on the repressed sexuality, or when he relates illegalities and crime to bourgeois illegalism that was both punished and fostered, he is at his best. Political expediency, bourgeois pretension, and power itself, he argues, "constantly mixes up the art of rectifying with the right to punish,"[57] so that legality and nature are constantly confused. Essentially, he shows just how legal experts, with the help of medical experts, have created the very knowledges and norms they then hold up as "normal." And when, in this confusion, judges "indulge their enormous appetites for medicine and psychiatry . . . which in turn allows them to babble about the criminology they forget to judge,"[58] then they are bound to hand down therapeutic verdicts and readaptive sentences that help to perpetuate the norms of corrupt power along with crime. Foucault's indictment of this power is devastating.

VIII

Foucault's most recent book, *The History of Sexuality, vol. 1* (1978), examines how this power corrupted even sexuality. In the seventeenth century, argues Foucault, frankness was common: sexual practices had little need of secrecy; codes regulating the coarse, the obscene and the indecent were lax; and bodies made a display of themselves.[59] But the Victorian bourgeoisie transformed freedom into confinement, relegated sex to the parental bedroom, and banned it from speech and thought. The resulting

repression, which Freud later on demonstrated so well, remains. Circumspection, medical prudence, and "scientific guaran-
tee of innocuousness" brought sex to the psychoanalyst's
couch—to yet another "whispering on a bed."[60] To expose
Freud's conformism, continues Foucault, as Reich or Fromm did,
could not eliminate the discourse of repression. For talk of sex,
the demand for sexual freedom, or for knowledge about sex was
separated from sexual feelings, only to become a part of the
repressive power structure.

According to Foucault, the affirmation of sexuality and the
exposure of the relationship between sexuality and the power
structure (in legal codes and in the treatment of "deviant" sexuality, from homosexuality to sodomy and childhood sexuality) can
never obliterate the repression that is rooted in our institutions
and in our modes of behavior. Again, he focuses on discourse,
discourse he relates to the sermon against hypocrisy we have
been accustomed to since the end of the Middle Ages—a great
sexual sermon. Our "will to knowledge" has made us accept
(and construct) a science of sexuality. "The agencies of power are
determined to speak about it, to hear it spoken about, and to
cause *it* (the Lacanian *id*) to speak through explicit articulation
and endlessly accumulated detail."[61] Sex was "taken charge of,"
tracked down, legally exposed, discussed in relation to norms,
became both public and private, so that the state was allowed to
penetrate the private (and silent) bedroom.

"Gazing" at sexuality in the emerging institutions, Foucault
discerns manifold mechanisms in the areas of economy, peda-
gogy, medicine, and justice that are said to incite, extract, distrib-
ute, and institutionalize the sexual verbosity that had become the
order of the day. Sex began to be managed. Children's sexuality
was being eradicated through rules against masturbation,
through corrective discourses, and the induction of guilt; perver-
sion became codified; observation in hospitals, prisons, schools,
and homes regulated the boundaries of sexual pleasure for
parents, children, wives, criminals, and for people of every age.
Sexuality proliferated as the power over it was extended, as the
persistence of this power took hold and spread, along with the
sites for sexual pleasures (more sex in more places).

But all this talk was only a screen discourse, as Freud

showed. It was screened by scientific pretensions, asserts Foucault, and by its adherence to medical power, which initiated a *scientia sexualis*—the knowledge-power that emerged when confession rituals were moved from church to couch. For "scientific sexuality" is said to have produced interrogations, consultations, autobiographical narratives, literature, letters, dossiers, and commentaries that add up to a great archive of the pleasures of sex, a record of people's pleasures. (Inevitably, the Marquis de Sade has become a popular hero for both Barthes and Foucault.) Even erotic art was subverted into a pleasure in confiding secrets, into the search for truth, and into "the specific pleasure of the true discourse on pleasure." [62]

"Sexual strategies" (hysterization of women, pedagogization of children's sex, socialization of procreative behavior, and psychiatrization of perverse pleasure) from the eighteenth century onward are examined to prove how the deployment of sexuality was gradually centered upon the family. Finding parent-child relations at the heart of sexuality (Oedipus, etc.), Foucault argues that psychoanalysis helped keep sex in the family even when its technical procedure (confession) placed it outside. Since this practice is said to have resulted in a saturation of desire (the center of Lacan's concerns) in social institutions, our current preoccupation and openness about sex are seen as tactical shifts in the uses of sexuality rather than changes in the power structure. Once more, Foucault's indictment of this power is devastating.

IX

Some American historians are currently addressing similar issues by examining the effect of Puritan morals on political structures; they are searching for a sociological synthesis between politics and psychology that can explain the present in relation to the past. Their focus, however, is primarily on America while Foucault easily crosses oceans, moves from American prisons to French morality, and from physical torture to psychological guilt. In a way, his theory, like his mind, is a sponge, capable of absorbing all of the specialized and fractured knowledges.

As we follow Foucault, we can accept his conclusions, his

"archeology." In a police state police do not even know whom they are policing; and in a repressive society citizens, thinking they are free, do not for the most part even have the capacity to recognize their own delusion. Foucault locates the reasons for this false consciousness in the production and the perpetuation of surveillance by the legal-medical powers. Social workers and therapists, for instance, who help individuals to adapt, are cast as unwitting accomplices of this power. But socialist society—itself a failure and a victim of the police state in a more conscious form—never presented a solution for Foucault. This pits him directly against Althusser, whose inquiries lead to different results. For Foucault, the only salvation—if there is to be any—will come through knowledge, knowledge that grows on the ruins of our own epoch. Although he does not predict just how this will happen, he seems to imply that his own type of object-subject relations and his method will be instrumental, the method he demonstrates in his search for the locus of power that even Marx and Freud did not find—power that is both visible and invisible, present and hidden, and invested everywhere.[63]

Foucault's Marxist critics, of course, object to his claim that "archeological practice" is an enterprise not very different from historical materialism. Foucault is merely using words, argues Lecourt, since he has no answer to his own questions about the rapport between infrastructure and ideology; and Foucault does not say how practical ideologies are represented in the theoretical ones, or how the eruption of science *in* knowledge is inserted into social formation. Foucault's archeology is missing a class viewpoint, concludes Lecourt, and forgets the answers historical materialism (Althusser-style) can supply; this lack makes an ideology of the archeology itself. Although Lecourt may be correct, his conclusion that historical materialism has the answer not only seems to be a counter-ideology,[64] but omits what might be the basis of Foucault's assertions. For Lecourt forgets that Foucault's Marxism stems, at least in part, from observation, from disillusionment with Soviet society as well as with capitalism, from his concern with the freedom of the individual—a freedom that he found to be lacking when he visited Soviet hospitals and prisons.[65]

All in all, then, Foucault refutes the critics from the left by attacking conditions in Russia. Other critics, who like his approach to the history of thought, doubt that its dogmatism, its selectivity of disciplines, its autonomy, or its location within the history of ideas, hold up. Some question the object-subject relations—mostly in *The Archeology of Knowledge*—of this speculative enterprise itself: this history of science, with its "grounds" of positivity and epistemology, scientificity and formation, appears too simple to them and less scientific than Foucault claims.

Some American sociologists have found Foucault's approach particularly useful in studying deviance, and to broaden their social perspective, or their pseudo-neutral language. In such a context, his theories are often used to bolster radical views. But Foucault is not really radical in the Marxist sense, although his trenchant exposure of juridical and medical practice in relation to modern power structures and belief systems could, conceivably, be used by radicals.

Foucault challenges not only Marx's ideas, but also Durkheim's notion that social solidarity increases with an increase in written laws. He shows instead, however indirectly, that the myriads of laws—laws engendered with the help of medicine—made doctors and lawyers our new "priests," who have legalized and medicalized us into increasing anomie. And, like their predecessors, they perpetuate their own mystification. Their high remuneration "expresses their worth"—a worth achieved through strong professional organizations that prohibit access to many and indoctrinate the "elected" few—in a society whose values, as Simmel said long ago, are all eventually expressed through money. The Patty Hearst trial, for instance, with its show of celebrity-seeking psychiatrists, who were to prove her guilt or innocence, exemplifies Foucault's themes. The very presence of such professionals, together with the actor-lawyers, is our modern spectacle. Like Damien's fate, Patty's fate became a public show that served to perpetuate authority and social solidarity. But whereas the Damiens and Rivières exposed their pain and subsequently their sins, our Patty Hearsts plead their guilt and/or insanity as both reason for and expiation of their crimes. Foucault would argue that it is part of our code of knowledge.

If I understand him correctly, he foresees the end of our age, because there seems no way out: our very therapeutization, linked up with legalization in the interest of social order, has intensified the chaos of modern life, allowing chaos to become the norm. By now, crime is "everybody's business," and business crime is as normal as the therapy that "eases" its accompanying guilt and helps "adaptation." Ever more therapy and more police are needed and "produced"; as manipulation takes over, as every action requires legal advice, as crime has reached even to the American presidency, and as the honest person has gradually taken the place of the fool. Analogous to Foucault's fool of the Renaissance, the honest person is uninfluential, poor, and marginal: he might well be taken for the prophet, predicting the doom of our scientific era.

Foucault himself, with his non-historical approach that looks at a process, at a continuum that is bound to be broken, seems to be one of the prophets. Whether we "gaze" at his fools, his criminals or his geniuses, at Don Quixote or at Velasquez, his dialectic of language, just because it covers everything, leaves no loophole. We are in for a break, not only in knowledge, but in practice. Foucault's millenarian predictions appear to be solidly grounded. If he is correct, if the "era of man" is ended, his analysis already carries the seeds of the next "epoch." And Foucault's own marginality, objectively assessing and "transcending" all of philosophy and knowledge, turning back upon itself with irony, avoiding oversimplification and reduction, marks him as one of the giants of our time—even if his codes of knowledge remain forever buried.

Notes

1. The resemblance of these concepts is superficial only. Whereas Thomas S. Kuhn, *The Scientific Structure of Revolutions* (Chicago: Chicago University Press, 1962) essentially argues that the testing of scientific hypotheses takes place in a certain context (there are *paradigms* for each context which preclude others), Bachelard postulates scientific epochs dominated by specific scientific knowledge. Communication across Kuhn's paradigms is, inevitably, partial. Bachelard postulates a rupture. Foucault, accepting this notion of rupture, nevertheless perceives some communication between epochs by postulating the seeds of a new knowledge at the end of a previous epoch—an idea which is in line with Marx's concept of the progression of history.

2. Michel Foucault, *The Archeology of Knowledge*, p. 3–5.
3. Foucault, *The Order of Things*, p. xxii.
4. Foucault, *Madness and Civilization*, p. 16.
5. *Ibid.* p. 28–29.
6. *Ibid.*, p. 27.
7. *Ibid.*, p. 59.
8. *Ibid.*, p. 91.
9. *Ibid.*, p. 100.
10. *Ibid.*, p. 107.
11. *Ibid.*, p. 126.
12. *Ibid.*, p. 156.
13. *Ibid.*, p. 257.
14. See my discussion of Jacques Lacan in chapter 6.
15. Foucault, *The Birth of the Clinic*, p. ix.
16. *Ibid.*, p. 10.
17. *Ibid.*, p. 14.
18. *Ibid.*, p. 62.
19. *Ibid.*, pp. 91–92.
20. *Ibid.*, p. 96.
21. See chapter 7.
22. *Foucault, The Birth of the Clinic*, p. 196.
23. White, "Foucault Decoded," p. 45.
24. Foucault, *The Order of Things*, p. 116–120.
25. *Ibid.*, p. 42.
26. *Ibid.*, p. 34.
27. *Ibid.*, p. 48.
28. *Ibid.*, pp. 240–42.
29. *Ibid.*, p. 312.
30. *Ibid.*, p. 313–14.
31. *Ibid.*, p. 318.
32. *Ibid.*, p. 326.
33. *Ibid.*, p. 328.
34. *Ibid.*, pp. 378–87.
35. Foucault, *The Archeology of Knowledge*, pp. 16–17.
36. *Ibid.*, p. 17.
37. *Ibid.*

38. Russo, "L'archéologie du savoir," pp. 69–105.

39. Foucault, *The Archeology of Knowledge*, p. 48.

40. *Ibid.*, p. 59.

41. *Ibid.*, p. 114.

42. *Ibid.*, p. 122.

43. *Ibid.*, p. 127.

44. *Ibid.*, p. 131.

45. *Ibid.*, p. 140.

46. *Ibid.*, p. 148.

47. *Ibid.*, p. 165.

48. *Ibid.*, p. 177.

49. Foucault, *I, Pierre Rivière, having slaughtered . . .* , p. 200.

50. *Ibid.*, p. 210.

51. Foucault, "Table ronde," pp. 678–703.

52. Foucault, *Discipline and Punish*, p. 3.

53. Foucault, *Surveiller et punir*, p. 32.

54. *Ibid.*, p. 106.

55. *Ibid.*, p. 127.

56. See Erving Goffman, *Asylums* (New York: Doubleday Anchor, 1961); "Bureaucracy," in Gerth and Mills, eds., *From Max Weber* (New York: Oxford University Press, 1958), pp. 196–264; and the literature on the sociology of medicine and criminology.

57. Foucault, *Surveiller et punir*, p. 310.

58. *Ibid.*

59. Foucault, *The History of Sexuality*, p. 3.

60. *Ibid.*, p. 5.

61. *Ibid.*, p. 18.

62. *Ibid.*, p. 71.

63. This is a recurrent theme that appears more and more obvious as it is spelled out in *Surveiller et punir*.

64. See Lecourt, "Sur l'archéologie du savoir," pp. 69–87.

65. Foucault, "The Politics of Crime," pp. 453–59.

Bibliography

Amiot, Michel. "Le relativism culturaliste de Michel Foucault." *Les Temps Modernes* (1967), 22:1271–98.

Benoist, Jean-Marie. "Le champ de la modernité." *La Quinzaine littéraire* (October 16–31, 1975), p. 21.

Chalumeau, Jean-Luc. *La pensée en France de Sartre à Foucault*, pp. 48–64. Paris: Fernand Nathan, 1971.

Corvez, Maurice. "Les nouveaux structuralistes." *Revue philosophique de Louvain* (1969), 67(96):582–605.

Deleuze, Gilles. "Un nouvel archiviste." *Critique* (1970), 26:195–209.

Foucault, Michel. *L'histoire de la folie*. Paris: Gallimard, 1961. Translated as *Madness and Civilization*. New York: Random House, 1965.

—— *Raymond Roussel*. Paris: Gallimard, 1962.

—— *Naissance de la clinique*. Paris: Presses Universitaires de France, 1963. Translated as *The Birth of the Clinic*. New York: Pantheon, 1973.

—— *Les mots et les choses*. Paris: Gallimard, 1966. Translated as *The Order of Things*. New York: Pantheon, 1970.

—— *L'archéologie du savoir*. Paris: Gallimard, 1969. Translanted by A. M. Sheridan Smith as *The Archeology of Knowledge*. New York: Pantheon, 1972.

—— *Moi, Pierre Rivière ayant égorgé ma mère ma soeur et mon frère . . .* Paris: Gallimard, 1973. Translated as *I, Pierre Rivière, having slaughtered my mother, my sister, and my brother . . .* New York: Pantheon, 1975.

—— "Un dossier, un entretien." *Magazine littéraire* (June 1975), no. 101. (This entire issue is devoted to Michel Foucault and contains an excellent bibliography of his writings up to that date.)

—— *Surveiller et punir*. Paris: Gallimard, 1975. Translated as *Discipline and Punish*. New York: Pantheon, 1977.

—— *La volonté de savoir*, vol. 1. Paris: Gallimard, 1976. Translated by Robert Hurley as *The History of Sexuality*, vol. 1. New York: Pantheon, 1978.

Foucault, Michel, Jacques Proust, and M. J. Stefanini. "Correspondance: à propos des entretiens sur Foucault." *Pensée* (1970), 139:114–19.

—— "Table ronde." *Esprit* (1972), no. 4, pp. 678–703.

—— "What is an Author?" *Partisan Review* (1975), no. 4, pp. 603–14.

—— "The Politics of Crime." *Partisan Review* (Fall 1976), no. 3, pp. 453–59.

Karol, S. K. "Un entretien avec Michel Foucault." *Le Nouvel Observateur* (January 26, 1976), pp. 34–37.

Kurzweil, Edith. "Michel Foucault: Ending the Era of Man." *Theory and Society* (1977), 7(3):395–420.

—— "Law and Disorder." *Partisan Review* (1977), no. 2, pp. 293–97.

—— "The History of Sexuality." *Theory and Society* (1979), 8(2):422–25.

Le Bon, Sylvie. "Un positiviest désepéré: Michel Foucualt." *Les Temps modernes* (1967), vol. 22, pp. 1299–1319.

Lecourt, Dominique. "Sur l'archeologie du savoir." *Pensée*, no. 152, pp. 69–78.

McMullen Roy. "Michel Foucualt." *Horizon* (August 11, 1969), pp. 36–39.

Pelorson, Jean-Marc. "Michel Foucault et l'Espagne." *Pensée* (1970), no. 152, pp. 88–99.

Russo, François. "L'archéologie du savoir du Michel Foucault." *Archives de philosophie* (1973), vol. 36, pp. 60–105.

Starobinski, J. "Gazing at Death." *New York Review of Books* (January 22, 1975), pp. 18–22.

White, Hayden, V. "Foucault Decoded. Notes from the Underground." *History and Theory* (1973), no. 12, pp. 23–54.

Conclusion

My purpose in writing about the most important trends in French social theory since the decline of existentialism, has carried me through the structuralist debate—a debate that dominated French intellectual history from about 1955 to the early 1970s. During this period, many intellectuals, in confronting the questions raised by Saussurean linguistics, for the most part turned to semiology, the general science of signs which was to help uncover the roots of human thought and behavior. Today, however, semiology has to a large extent been superseded by semiotics, whose foremost exponent, Jacques Derrida, defines graphic and phonic signs as "structures of difference" that are determined by "absent tracts, or traces" and that are to be put under "erasure." [1] But even those successors of structuralism who are more concerned with philosophy and literature than with the social sciences, take structuralist notions for granted. Hence this book, in providing an overview of the basic premises of current French thought, is meant to serve as a guide to further reading for those interested in the theories of one or more of the figures here included, or of their successors. The latter range from such writers as Julia Kristeva and Phillipe Sollers (around *Tel Quel*); to the anti-psychiatrists (Gilles Deleuze and Felix Guattari); and to the "new philosophers" (André Glucksmann, Jean-Marie Benoist, and Bernard-Henri Lévi), who denounce both the structuralists and their opponents as Marxist or establishment mandarins.

As we have seen, definitions of structuralism have gone through many transformations, and structuralist practitioners are no more able to define their discipline than are their observers. Each structuralist has defended his own system of thought; outsiders, however, have perceived them as a group that shares in the search for hidden universal relations—through Claude Lévi-Strauss' anthropology, Roland Barthes' literary theories, Jacques Lacan's psychoanalysis, Michel Foucault's history of knowledge, Louis Althusser's Marxism, or even through Paul Ricoeur's more recent philosophy. In 1964, Barthes stated that "structuralism is neither a school, a movement, nor a vocabulary, but an activity that reaches beyond philosophy, that consists of a succession of mental operations which attempt to reconstruct an object in order to manifest the rules of its functioning." [2] Such a vague definition allowed Derrida to state in turn that "structuralism lives within and on the difference between its promise and its practice"; [3] and it allowed Barthes himself, later on, to refute various aspects of structuralism when his system of semiology no longer promised to become operative.

Still, variations on the Saussurean model of language, which postulates that a linguistic *signifier* has meaning only within a specific system of *significations,* served as the basis for a number of French structuralist theories. We have noted that they all extrapolated from rules and/or relations of grammar and/or speech to explore social phenomena in terms of linguistic oppositions and transformations. This practice was justified on the premise that speech and language are central to every individual within every culture, even before he can formally learn the words and usages of his particular language. The centrality of language to culture, and of culture to language, and their presence in all discourse (including scientific discourse) were taken as proof of a specific underlying human universality. Lévi-Strauss expected this universality to become apparent with the help of his new methodology, so that modern intellectual and social fragmentation would prove to be no more than a "superficial" phenomenon hiding deeply rooted common origins. French structuralists went on to claim that unconscious motivations and underlying sources of language and/or behavior are shared by all of humanity. It is the search for these deep-rooted structures—as part both of the methodology and of the promised results—that has engendered so much confusion.

According to Auzias,

> Structuralism is thought without thinkers. It is the thought of the structures as they reveal themselves by the way of the

human sciences. Structuralism is not Claude Lévi-Strauss' or Michel Foucault's thought. It is the discourse that keeps ethnology in touch with linguistics, medicine in touch with the archeology of knowledge. It is a reading of history and of Freudian analysis. It is a reading of Marx. Each time the author of the discourse is something other than a writer, a thinker, a sociologist. It is the work of the method itself that speaks the actual language of its object. It is the sense that unveils itself, the sense of a myth or a system.[4]

No wonder, then, that expectations of uncovering a closed system of knowledge turned structuralism into a movement with ideologies and slogans, and that when the hidden structures failed to emerge, the methodology itself underwent continual change and "improvement." The ongoing search, however, led to theoretical arguments, which centered on increasingly complex and partial components of linguistic theory. As disagreements among the various structuralists mounted, the search for the structures began to appear as its own end, and distinctions between proponents and opponents, friends and enemies, became blurred. Structuralist and anti-structuralist credos, political and philosophical convictions were increasingly injected into the methodological debates. Alliances and animosities accordingly developed around the implications of methodology. Arguments might center, for instance, on the use of a specific word as a sign or a symbol, or on its meaning within a specific sentence for Barthes or for Foucault.

In great measure, these disputes must be traced to Lévi-Strauss' original theory, to his debatable conception of Saussure, Marx, and Freud; and to his reliance on this conception of them as the major precursors of structuralism. These precursors are generally more important to Parisian intellectuals than they are to their Anglo-Saxon counterparts. Hence all the figures in my book address Saussure, Marx, and Freud as part of their own theories, and in relation to Lévi-Strauss' adaptation of them. Originally, Lévi-Strauss, admiring the unalienated quality of tribal man, had compared this quality to the state of mind of a Freudian-analyzed individual. But he did not realize that he was idealizing both types when he set up a dialectical relationship (of linguistic oppositions, transpositions and transformations) within his linguistic model to account for all the inherent contradictions within this model. Whenever this difficulty was evoked, Lévi-Strauss could refute criticisms by pointing to his own awareness of the problem. The inevitable vagueness and the inclusiveness of this original conception generated both an enthusiastic reception and devastating attacks. The partial and selective use of Freud and Marx, particularly, not only demanded addenda and explanations but opened up alternate interpretations that invited comment upon comment upon comment. The fact that structuralism had constantly to be updated, that it expected to include every aspect of conscious and unconscious thought and reality, itself legitimated and invited more structuralist productions—productions which, again, were to testify to the theory's validity. As a consequence, even when we manage to get out of this quasi-legitimate circularity, we have difficulty in keeping track of the endless transformations and oppositions that purport to stay abreast of social, psychological, and cultural changes.

What then were some of the central theoretical premises? To what extent did Lévi-Strauss' original understanding of Freud and Marx invite criticism from American Freudians and from French Marxists? Or why, for example, did Lévi-Strauss appeal to Lacan and Althusser and upset Ricoeur and Lefebvre? As I have argued, the scholarly application of structural linguistics to social realities had political and philosophical implications which, inadvertently, supported and/or disputed every political and intellectual position. By linking Saussure's dichotomous constructions and Jakobson's phonological observations to extremely partial and "unsophisticated" notions of Marxism and psychoanalysis, Lévi-Strauss not only left enough room for Althusser's and Lacan's major branches of structuralism, but invited many alternate interpretations. Inevitably, the polemics revolved around several central figures and themes.

Saussure

In the introduction and in chapter 1, I indicated the extent of Lévi-Strauss' admiration for Saussure (the first linguist to go beyond the study of grammar, philosophy, and comparative philology) and for Roman Jakobson (the Czech formalist linguist who had postulated binary paths between *phonemes,* the small

units of sound, and *morphemes,* the smallest units of meaning).
Because both Saussure and Jakobson had examined the formation of language in relation to its social base and studied it as a
system of signs, Lévi-Strauss conceptualized language itself as the
production of its society. He went beyond Saussure: from the
laws and rules that underlie spoken language, he tried to get to
the origins of customs, rites, habits, gestures, and to all other cultural phenomena, phenomena which were themselves said to be
intrinsic to the creation of language. This was to lead him to the
hidden structures which he believed existed in some sort of archetypal fashion, in a so-far-undetected universal "programming" of
every human brain.

Like Saussure, Lévi-Strauss focused on *la langue* (language)
rather than on *la parole* (the word). But Saussure had studied the
signs of language both *sychronically,* that is, in their static
interrelations and permutations, and *diachronically,* that is, as
they evolve over time. Lévi-Strauss, however, emphasized the
diachronic dimensions. Saussure, in contrast to previous language
theory, which had for the most part considered language as an
expression of thought, conceived it as a system of signs. Within
this system, he postulated a dialectical relation between *signifiers* (acoustical impressions) and *signifieds* (mental images).
Saussure's primary concern had been the formal analysis of
spoken language within its total language system: for example,
the meaning of the word *hot* cannot be understood without its
opposite *cold* or without the relationship between the two.
Hence, language was perceived as a structure, apart from the
thoughts of a speaker and only in the context of its system of
signs. Binary oppositions allowed Lévi-Strauss to mediate between opposing elements—*hot* and *cold, earth* and *water, old* and
new, male and *female,* etc., etc. And oppositions between
phonemes and *morphemes,* although alleged to be "meaningless"
in terms of the formalization of language, were found to be useful in explaining the evolution of language within its society:
these mediations theoretically "legitimated" structuralism's
"third" dimension, the relational dimension of time which is constantly being brought up to date. This theoretical possibility was Lévi-Strauss' most original—and certainly his most
controversial—contribution.

As we know, he originally constructed this methodology in

order to uncover the universally imprinted structures he believed existed in the minds of all individuals. Because in all natives' tales tribal life and myths move easily from notions of culture to notions of nature, from present to past, etc., Lévi-Strauss thought he could bridge the gap between object and subject not only in the philosophical realm, but in the social sciences—that is, in anthropology, sociology, and politics.

Intellectuals like Touraine did not bother much with structuralist methodology. Binary oppositions of social phenomena, or of social facts, did not interfere with his sociological methods of inquiry, although he inadvertently picked up the sweeping tone. Althusser believed that structuralist methods would help reinstate the "mature" and scientific Marx; Foucault, in his attempt to uncover an unconscious archeology of knowledge, accepted binary oppositions and attempted to go beyond them by confining the oppositions within specific scientific epochs. But others, most intimately concerned with language itself, or with literature, confronted the Saussurean semiology directly.

Binary oppositions between consonants and vowels, for example, allowed the theologian-philosopher Ricoeur to reject Lévi-Strauss' notions of constituent units (the smallest "sense" units in a myth) in favor of the "word." Ricoeur opposed Lévi-Strauss' mediations not only because they move between contradictions in tales, content, feelings, the expressions of the storyteller, explanations of life and death, etc., but also because this very approach interprets the Bible as myth rather than divine message: it "discovers" structures instead of God. The decoding of myths through these structures would automatically destroy the belief in religious symbols, the basis of Ricoeur's own theological enterprise. Thus he attacked Lévi-Strauss for having substituted the *telling* for the *meaning* of myths and proposed a "creative hermeneutics of language" that would reinfuse belief and morals into society. For, if Lévi-Strauss was correct, if the study of myth could explain language and culture, argued Ricoeur, then a change in the language should be able to change the myth and especially the morals it conveys. Since this never happens, Ricoeur focused on *semantics* and *semiotics*. The former, he maintained, are merely signs (phonemes within phonological codes, morphemes, or sememes with lexical codes) and for that reason cannot be related directly to things, events, properties, relations, actions, passions, or states of affairs. The latter, however, are said to contain the creative aspect of language, and the possibility of *metaphor*—as a vehicle for meaning, moral ambivalence, good, and evil.[5] Hence, Ricoeur returned, in part, to examine notions of grammar—notions which Lévi-Strauss had rejected in principle and practice when postulating his constituent units.

Ricoeur objected to Lévi-Strauss on "moral" grounds, even as he elaborately denied that his own critique sprang from his beliefs rather than from the texts. He had an even harder time with Barthes, to whom nothing was ever sacred, and who aimed to "demythologize" all texts, writing, and language. This aim was illustrated when, in *Le système de la mode* (1967), Barthes looked at the hidden sales messages in fashion magazines, or when he "listened to the inner ear" of Balzac's *Sarrasine* in *S/Z* (1970). In reading *Sarrasine,* for instance, Barthes found much androgyny, eroticism, pleasure, and sensuousness—topics that Ricoeur's texts, which tend to deal with morals, good and/or evil, would never embrace. Even before Barthes perfected his semiology, he had tried to find all the hidden messages in written texts, and had stripped them down to "rock bottom"; he had wanted to demythologize writing itself.[6] Both Barthes and Ricoeur by now rely on semiotic methods to uncover social reality through some sort of "interdisciplinary" grammar. Barthes, however, tries to overcome linguistic limitations by inventing new words at the edge of language, whereas Ricoeur looks for hidden meaning in the existing ones; where Ricoeur detects morals, Barthes might locate amorality. And the emphasis on linguistics hides politics for them both.

Barthes' references have always been to literature (fashion writing is *bad* literature), and to such questions as the dissolution of form and content, and writers' creativity in relation to their cultures. Unlike Ricoeur, who "examined" the creative mind, Barthes viewed even himself from his radical perspective—as an expression of his time, or, through his texts, as incidental to his work. Barthes always liked to shock, to experience enjoyment, to push his mind to unexplored limits. This freed him to roam further afield than, for instance, Lefebvre, whose dialectical approach to literature, though wide-ranging, always had the crises of capitalism on its mind. And Lefebvre's brush with structuralism was short.

Foucault's large-scale analyses in his *Archeology of Knowledge,* though bypassing linguistics proper, were based on a methodology that superficially resembled Lévi-Strauss'. His concept of *énoncé* was not too different from Lévi-Strauss' *constituent units;* and his mediations in *The Order of Things,* for instance, which revolved around ideas of *sameness* and *similarities* in the modern world, rely on structuralist assumptions. Like Barthes, Foucault saw writers and artists as products of their society: he found Erasmus, for instance, to have been a precursor of the Enlightment; and perceived in Bosch's painting *The Tree of Knowledge,* the advent of the modern age. Creative individuals, then, were taken to be expressions of their time, although more sensitive to changes in norms than the average person. For Foucault they acted as "agent provocateurs" of impending social upheavals; he saw them in the position of announcing an epistemological break to usher in a new code of knowledge.

This concept of epistemological ruptures in knowledge, which maintains that scientific practices are accompanied by particular beliefs within historical periods, served to define Foucault's scientific epochs and predicted the end of our "era of man." Foucault, however, insisted all along that he did not know what the next era would be like, whereas Althusser, especially during the 1960s, linked it to the coming Marxist revolution. Althusser's Marxism, of course, was very different from Lévi-Strauss' variety.

Marx

Lévi-Strauss' Marxism took off from the premise that life is not determined by consciousness, but consciousness by life.[7] Since men must live before they can think, their thoughts and beliefs necessarily originate from their economic productions. Whereas Marx stressed the economic base of this consciousness (means, mode, and relations of production), which led to the separation of economics from philosophy, morality, and all other thought,

Lévi-Strauss relies primarily on the relation of social life to the ownership of the means of production in pre-industrial societies. He ignored Marx's discussions of surplus value, and of economic polarization as well as questions of political versus civil society, the inevitablity of revolution, the creation of a socialist state, and Lenin's "dictatorship of the proletariat." Instead, he speculated about human relations and the way of life long before capitalism, as he examined production in tribal societies where morality and thought are still closely tied to economic survival. Because he had studied a number of tribes in Brazil (particularly the Bororo) and North America and had found that the myths of very diverse and unrelated tribes are not only tied to survival, but are also similar, Lévi-Strauss assumed that the "savage mind" and the "modern mind" still share underlying structures of thought.

These questions of human existence did, of course, approximate the problems addressed by the idealistic young Marx, problems that both Sartre and Lefebvre (among others) also tried to solve. Lévi-Strauss, however, ignored their work when he began his anthropological exegeses. His ahistorical treatment of myth clashed not only with Sartre and Lefebvre but also with portions of Marx. For all three, the progression of historical/economic epochs was essential, if only because the advent of socialism depends on the collapse of capitalism. In this respect, the acceptance of Lévi-Strauss' ahistorical mediations of myth would preclude a Marxist revolution, a revolution, incidentally, whose seeds Lefebvre continued to find in our "late" capitalism. The well-publicized arguments between Sartre and Lévi-Strauss about history were as unavoidable as Lefebvre's dismissal of structuralism as yet another capitalist mythology, and as eleatism—a philosophical belief in the unity of being and the unreality of motion or change.

Althusser was bound to attack Lévi-Strauss, since for him the young Marx was persona non grata; and only the mature Marx of *Capital,* who focused on political economy, on the labor theory of value, and who had "abandoned his youthful idealism," was valid. So he insisted on rejecting the "anthropological given" that is subsumed in the Sartre/Lévi-Strauss controversy in order to follow up Marx's economic concepts, and separated the social phenomena that "meet the eye" from the underlying laws of class struggle that "operate behind the scenes." This made him a structuralist insofar as he emphasized economic structures, class situations and polarization; but he went beyond structuralism when he bolstered his theory with Bachelard's notions of breaks in knowledge and postulated such breaks not only in technical inventions but in the thought of Marx himself, around 1845. According to Althusser, Marx at that time began to mature, discarding his humanistic and idealistic youth in favor of scientific economics. To bolster this Marxism, Althusser "overlooked" the inherent conservatism of a theory with fixed structures and used structuralism to help establish the scientism of Marxist economics. The break in political structures in some of the Third World countries "located" these countries in the revolutionary vanguard. At the same time, his effort to anticipate the problems of a liberal Marxist state did not put Althusser outside the fold of the Communist party. Eventually, he was attacked by both the socialist left and the Gaullists.

The French, as Raymond Aron so aptly put it, are fed Marxism along with their mothers' milk, so that it is incorporated in their thought. Thus, Althusser, as well as Sartre, Lefebvre, and Lévi-Strauss, all claimed to practice the Marxist dialectic. For Sartre, the dialectic concerns the relations between subject and object; for Lefebvre, it is located between formal logic and humanistic philosophy; for Lévi-Strauss, the dialectic occurs primarily between nature and culture; for Althusser, it is internal to Marx's texts and explicitly rejects every Hegelian influence. To complicate matters further, the anti-Marxist Ricoeur combines Hegelianism with literary structuralism; Foucault's history of knowledge mediates within Bachelardian scientific epochs as he examines the integration of deviants in relation to power, with the help of a neo-Marxism that lacks Marxist formulations. Barthes' Marxism causes fewer problems, insofar as his trenchant social criticism does not pretend to address theory, especially in his most recent works, which appear to avoid politics altogether. Touraine's effort to fuse a systems approach with Marxism is reformist insofar as his theory of revolution tends to encourage cooptation.

Only Lacan seems devoid of Marxism, although his dialectical method has its own Marxist cast. His almost accidental support of the students in 1968, bolstered by Althusser's positive view of Lacanian psychoanalysis, tends to obfuscate the fact that his politics are confined to an individual's language and thus do not really address political action. Hence, among left theorists, Lefebvre is most critical of all structuralism: he categorically rejects Althusser's Marxism, Lacan's psychoanalysis, and Lévi-Strauss' structuralism as subversive of Marx; and he had, as a young philosopher, already rejected Freud.

Freud

Undoubtedly, Lévi-Strauss' success helped French psychoanalysis. Yet Lacan's take-off from Saussurean structural linguistics was very different from Lévi-Strauss'. Because both became fashionable around the same time, it is difficult to say whether French psychoanalysis bolstered structuralism, or whether Lacan's recourse to language popularized Freud. In the late 1950s some disciples of Lévi-Strauss and of Lacan hoped together to uncover unconscious common roots in individuals' dreams and in social myths, myths that had existed since the time of the totemic father of *Totem and Taboo*. Lévi-Strauss, we recall, always looked to Freud's sociology and philosophy rather than to his later clinical theory or data. Lacan, too, stressed social influences and the early Freud who studied hysteria; he focused on Freud's language rather than on symptomatology. Lacan's pronouncements, especially about the unconscious, which is allegedly structured like a language, engendered a specific psychoanalytic ideology. He was aided in part by Barthes and Foucault, whose references to unconscious components in literary texts seemed to reaffirm Lacan's focus on the linguistic aspects of the unconscious. But Lacan had already been in the limelight, in 1936 and in 1949, when he presented his theory of the *mirror-image* as central to the formation of personality, and again in 1953, when he was expelled from the International Psychoanalytic Association.

Essentially, Lacan applied Saussurean linguistic oppositions and transformations to the psychoanalytic relationship as well as to Freud's texts. He argued that by examining Freud's clinical writings from this new perspective, from an emphasis on Freud's use of language, we can find out more about what Freud *really* meant. Lacan, focusing on the *signifier* in Freud's texts, that is, on that word within a sentence which designates the meaning of what follows, constructs *chains of signifiers*.[8] These chains, because rooted in Freud's unconscious, are to lead us to a better understanding of Freud's personality, and also of psychoanalysis itself. Thus this focus on language that was said to open up and enrich the psychoanalytic relationship in Lacan's clinical practice, was to enlighten all of psychoanalysis.

Aware of Lacan's importance to the structuralist enterprise—in literature, in philosophy and in the social sciences—some optimists believed that his apprehension of the unconscious (with its libidinal energy) might lead to the discovery of the knot between our biological and cultural origins. This hope derived from Lacan's emphasis on Freud's early discoveries, which were still rooted in physiology, as well as from his central concept of the *imaginary*, the root of all fantasy, emotions, intellections, future relations, metaphorical thinking, and symbolization—in the *Innenwelt* and the *Umwelt*.[9] Lacan's insistence that every understanding, for example, is fraught with *misunderstanding*, or that *misunderstanding* is the only thing that can approximate understanding, though derived from complicated interpretations of transference and countertransference in psychoanalytical relationships, became quasi-popular subjects (in public seminars and on television). His many discussions of psychic mechanisms, his frequently outrageous plays on words—Lacan's *languisterie*—themselves furthered psychoanalysis, insofar as this approach was less threatening to individual psyches than the peeling away of defense mechanisms and the eventual facing of childhood traumas.

Althusser's attempt to convert the "language of the Oedipus complex," in order to facilitate socialization of infants into a new social order (by changing family ideology), appealed to Marxists. This in turn inspired Lacan to look into the social and/or psychological meaning and origin of religious and political family practices by investigating the meaning of *le nom du père* (the father's name and family heritage) as conservative ideology. In addition, Lacanian thought inspired a spate of books in *le champ freudien*, ranging from clinical studies to structuralist forays into politics and philosophy.[10]

Even Ricoeur became intrigued by Freud—by Freud's epistemology rather than by the clinical aspect of his theory. The Freudian use of unconscious symbols was to infuse meaning into texts, and to broaden Ricoeur's investigation of the symbolism of evil. For Ricoeur, increased self-knowledge, which includes acknowledgement of evil, and the "turning of id into ego," was to tap the best in individuals; the resulting agglomeration of good citizens was to obviate the need for organized communism, for a revolution.

Foucault addressed these issues from a more sociological perspective. He examined madness, psychiatry, and medicine as they are linked to an emerging power structure—through structures of knowledge bound by historical epochs and dominant sciences that subsume the Freudian unconscious and its preoccupations with desire and death. But unlike Lacan's structures, dealing with ideal fathers, with real ones, or with anal fathers, Foucault's structures—of family, medicine, law, etc.—were rooted in society. Madness, for example, dependent upon relations of power, became a social phenomenon, as control of individuals through guilt rather than by physical punishment became the norm. In the modern age, this allegedly "prepared the ground for Freud."

Lefebvre continued to discount psychoanalysis for its adapting of individuals to the status quo and thus retarding the revolution. And Touraine, whose action systems became ever more complex, did not bother with unconscious phenomena; nevertheless, his current research on small groups that simulate social movements will undoubtedly be linked to psychoanalytic notions, since revolutionary theory, ultimately, must grapple with the connections between individuals' consciousness and large-scale movements. The inconclusiveness of the structuralist debates, in part, led to post-structuralism.

Post-Structuralism

By now Lévi-Strauss' original structuralism has been amended almost beyond recognition. It has been incorporated in what might best be called the post-structuralist debate, a debate whose empirical base is no firmer than that of structuralism. Thus, Althusser and Foucault have joined Touraine and Lefebvre in declaring that structuralism is an ideology rather than a science. Lévi-Strauss himself has returned to anthropology and rejects all neostructuralisms; Barthes and Ricoeur have moved into semiotics—the second coming of structuralist linguistics in its more philosophical reincarnation that is said to have rejected its anthropological base.[11] Nevertheless, structuralist premises and thought are pervasive, for, as the Freudians might argue, they have become internalized by every French intellectual; and structuralism has joined the traditions of Plato and Rousseau, of Nietzsche and Kant, of Proust and Flaubert, of Condorcet and Erasmus.

One of the post-structuralist discussions centers around questions of time and space. To Lefebvre, social space is allocated according to class—too much for the rich and too little for the poor, with social planning reproducing the class structure. Foucault, extrapolating from the space allocated to the various types of "deviants," focuses on the powers (mostly medical and legal) that dominate. But whereas he insists that only a change in the power structure and an epistemological break can "save" us, Lefebvre wants to alter social relations with the help of a coalition of architects, sociologists, economists, psychologists, and other left-oriented experts. Touraine mostly addresses the space of consumers, urging that they be sensitized to refuse manipulation; that they reject the domination by the media and subvert the system by furthering their own ends through social organizations in neighborhoods. Consumers are to be de-alienated through participation.

His colleague, Moscovici, goes beyond Touraine's and Lefebvre's denunciation of the technocrats who direct us all for the sake of efficiency in suggesting that we could outsmart them with the help of a new science, political technology.[12] He believes that all sources of energy—social and solar, creative and innovative—could be harnessed with the help of the knowledge elite. But this would not only bolster the installation of Touraine's "system of action" under the aegis of social movements and a super-sociology—perceived as the salvation of modern man (and woman)—but would also parallel Servan-Schreiber's suggestion that modern France meet the challenge presented by American technology.[13] Ultimately, this would support the capitalism Touraine himself hopes to replace with a viable socialism.

Another post-structuralist debate surrounds the "new philosophers" under the unavowed leadership of André Glucksmann, Jean-Marie Benoist, and Bernard-Henri Lévy.[14] According to Lefebvre, the emergence of these figures is a new phenomenon, an indication that the culture industry has gained the upper hand—under the auspices of the French Right. Formerly involved in student activism (much of it neo-Maoist), but disappointed at the lack of support from the Communist Party, these young philosophers now denounce Marx, Freud, and both right and left establishments; they have turned against every theoretical system, and defend personal freedom against Marxist mandarins. Even while they vehemently deny both their own nihilism and intellectual anarchism (in books, on television, and in lectures), they affirm that they must cut every connection to cultural traditions. Yet their verbal agility and their method of discussion are reminiscent of structuralist mediations, and they themselves perpetuate at least the French rhetorical tradition.

Another post-structuralist circle has formed around the magazine *Tel Quel*. Aware that none of the macro-theories—existentialism, Marxism, or structuralism—could deal with the new problems of linguistics, they gradually shifted to micro-theories, to the post-Lacanian psychoanalyst Felix Guattari and to Gilles Deleuze who attack the current uses of psychoanalysis, and to philosophers of language like Derrida, who promise to destructure all aspects of language—in its creation and its use—and thus achieve the original aims of structuralism.[15] Barthes, for a while the group's guru, and Ricoeur, by "emigrating" to American universities, moved to new ways of examining language in literature. They avoid political engagement by concentrating on intricate philosophical and psychoanalytic linguistics. Discussions of "intertextuality," of the "interrogation" of texts by Hegel, Heidegger, Sartre, Plato, Lacan, etc., are said to deconstruct

Western thought. Still, the splitting of psychic factors into ever smaller linguistic units and their rearrangement and generalization into questions of meaning, morals, and politics is a long way from Lévi-Strauss' original search for universal mental structures.

Lévi-Strauss himself is particularly dismissive of the "ministructuralists." In the *Finale* of *L'homme nu* (1971), he accused them of applying structural techniques without "real" structures. True structuralist theory, he stated, does not extrapolate from linguistic distinctions between syntagmatic and paradigmatic aspects of verbal communiation, does not perceive narrative literature as transformation by enlargement of the basic sentence structure, and does not define characters as nouns, their situations or attributes as adjectives, and their actions as verbs. Because their structuralism is not linked to real phenomena, he calls them fiction structuralists of the philosophical literary world who talk only to each other; and he lumps them with the existentialists who ignore science, yet discuss it—regularly—at the Café Commerce (Sartre's hangout). He has no use for this applied literary structuralism, which is "about as related to linguistics and to ethnography as popular entertainment is to physics or biology: both of them are sentimental pastimes which feed on badly-digested summary knowledge"; they both exist only to relieve boredom. Hence he knocks literary structuralism, which "literally" perfects structuralism by applying structural techniques. The student of genuine structuralism, according to Lévi-Strauss, would try to find out why some literary works continue to survive and why only some continue to captivate us.

Lévi-Strauss further criticizes other structuralists for their naive empirical studies of art and music, for infusing meanings and implications that are not there. He reiterates again and again that true structures exist, even if we have not yet found them, and that they do not lend themselves to "artificial constructs." And he attacks the literary critics whose search for intertextuality engages them in what he calls the manufacture of works of art which is neither art nor science but a different—and fraudulent—enterprise. He puts computerized music into this category of non-sense: a computer cannot compose real music but ought instead to be used to find out, for example, how and why after hearing two or three measures, we know who wrote a particular work and/or what it is.[16] Obviously he does not go along with the idea that the *science of semiology* will either help individuals verbalize unconscious desire, or help in their personal liberation.

In any event, semiotics has replaced Lévi-Strauss' version of structuralism as well as semiology. But semiotics seems to be even more difficult to decipher than its predecessors, if only because it superimposes its own complexity on structuralist concepts. Understanding the primary importance of the word over the sentence, for instance, is assumed, as is meaning over symbols in a specific sound image, or in a chain of such images. But the discussion of social facts and phenomena in linguistic terms through the acceptance of structuralist discourse has become the norm among Parisian intellectuals. Whereas in America the trend to individual liberation may be expressed more readily through creating communes, or joining religious sects, or through ideologies of self-fulfillment and near-immediate gratification, the French are more likely to "liberate the unconscious" with the help of linguistics. So even if the Marxist tendencies of both existentialism and structuralism have been replaced by a linguistic Freudianism that acts as an umbrella for scholarly and philosophic inquiries, this is yet another theoretical attempt to radicalize individuals—a radicalization that, eventually, subverts radical politics. Again, this second phase of structuralism (more concerned with implications of language rather than with its social roots), though different from its earlier version by Lévi-Strauss, cannot be understood without a knowledge of its predecessor.

Structuralism could not become popular in America in the way it did in France, although in some select academic circles it promises to become increasingly fashionable. For the pursuit of knowledge, in France and in America, proceeds from different traditions: we are empirical, the French are philosophical; we construct theoretical systems, they build systems of thought; we play down the importance of history, they tend to glorify it; we look to the future, they enshrine the past. These basic differences, intrinsic to intellectual productions, are reproduced in the school system and in the attitude of the public. Without a general knowledge of philosophy by a broad *couche* of intellectuals, the French could not continue to make celebrities of their leading philosophers, psychoanalysts, anthropologists, and literary theorists. Because it is customary for complex ideas to spread from the university to the Parisian salons and coffeehouses, Lévi-Strauss' search for veiled structures could so easily fire political passions, and Althusser's notion of an epistemological break could make news; and the possible existence of underlying structures of thought could become the viable goal of a pursuit that intrigued many readers. Although by now many French intellectuals are critical of the various structuralisms and question the decoding of all human thought by a computer, the attempt itself has had a lasting influence on French thinking. Lévi-Strauss' intent to reunite the separate academic disciplines under a common discipline, of course, did not succeed. But the effort served to open up discussions among the exponents of the various disciplines.

These discussions continue; they are now themselves read as texts, texts that are to open up new avenues of intellectual exploration. Such explorations, in America, have taken different forms. Americans, too, now are trying to broaden interdisciplinary investigations, after years of overspecialization. But both in America and in France, there is a recognition that larger political aims and moral issues—indeed issues that involve survival—cannot be left to the specialists alone. The linguistic-psychoanalytic analyses of *semiology* and of *semiotics* do address some of those issues, however indirectly, although such notions as the author being replaced by his language, or the reader creating his own text, may neither be able to answer questions of ideology, nor to recover all the many meanings in texts. Some readers might consider the discovery of unconscious texts as superfluous or might be bored by the many intricate analyses. Others may deprecate all the structuralisms because they have not answered the questions of human origins and of existence as they originally promised. Perhaps the aims of the structuralists were unattainable: but they did introduce some intriguing and suggestive modes of analysis—demonstrating, once again, the fantastic intellectual virtuosity of French thinkers.

Notes

1. Essentially, the move from semiology to semiotics resulted from the unresolved problems of the former, which appear not be answered by the latter, but to be formulated more precisely. Umberto Eco, for instance, in *A Theory of Semiotics* (Bloomington: Indiana University Press, 1976), p. 3, aims "to explore the theoretical possibility and the social function of a unified approach to every phenomenon of signification and/or communication . . . in the form of a general semiotic theory, considering codes, sign production, the common use of languages, the evolution of codes, aesthetic communication, all types of interactional communicative behavior and use of signs." The difference between *semiologie* and *semiotics* has itself not been resolved and is argued in the literature.

2. Roland Barthes, *Essais critiques* (Paris: Éditions du Seuil, 1964), p. 213.

3. Jacques Derrida, *Writing and Difference* (Chicago: University of Chicago Press, 1978), p. 26.

4. Jean-Marie Auzias, *Cléfs pour le structuralisme* (Paris: Édition Seghers, 1967), p. 7.

5. Paul Ricoeur, "The Task of Hermeneutics," *Philosophy Today* (1973), 17(2–4): 112–128.

6. This was particularly so in *Le degré zéro de l'écriture* (Paris: Éditions du Seuil, 1953), where Barthes addressed Sartre's questions about the meaning and essence of literature, and the place of literature in culture and politics.

7. Karl Marx, *Critique of Political Economy* (1859), Preface.

8. Jacques Lacan, *Écrits* (Paris: Éditions du Seuil, 1966) or *Écrits: A Selection* (New York: W. W. Norton, 1977). Lacan frequently repeats that signifiers exist only in relation to each other and free-associates from signifier to signifier to construct these chains.

9. Lacan's *inner world* and *outer world*. He does not translate these terms of Freud's into French lest he "contaminate" their original meaning; translation, according to Lacan, always distorts.

10. See for example, Serge Leclaire, ed., *Psychanalyse et politique* (Paris: Éditions du Seuil, 1974). This collection features essays by 15 French and Italian intellectuals, with titles such as "The Discussion of the Unconscious and Power," "Micro-politics and Desire," "The Anal Father," etc.; Jean Laplanche, *Hölderlin et la question du père* (Paris: Presses Universitaires de France, 1969); in addition, the works of Barthes and the Tel Quel group subsume Lacan's notions.

11. This was the theme of a conference on linguistics in Milan, Italy, in 1974. At that time, Derrida's work seemed to move into the foreground.

12. Serge Moscovici's best known work is his comprehensive and excellent study of French psychoanalysis from a sociological perspective of the 1950s, *La psychanalyse, son*

image et son public (Paris: Presses Universitaires de France, 1961). The work here referred to is his *Essai sur l'histoire humaine de la nature* (Paris: Presses Universitaires de France, 1968)—a global analysis of culture, nature, politics, economics and society.

13. Jean-Jacques Servan-Schreiber, *The American Challenge* (New York: Pelican, 1969).

14. These new philosophers have declared the death of Marx since the early 1970s.

15. Jacques Derrida's most important book, *Of Grammatology* (Baltimore: Johns Hopkins University Press, 1974) was first published in 1967; Gilles Deleuze and Felix Guattari, *Anti-Oedipus* (New York: Viking, 1977) was first published as *L'Anti-Oedipe* (Paris: Éditions de Minuit, 1972) where it made an immediate splash.

16. Claude Lévi-Strauss, *L'homme nu* (Paris: Plon, 1971), pp. 575–96.

Index